CORRECTIONAL COUNSELING
A Cognitive Growth Perspective

SECOND EDITION

Key Sun, PhD, MSW
Professor
Law and Justice Department
Central Washington University
Ellensburg, Washington

JONES & BARTLETT
LEARNING

World Headquarters
Jones & Bartlett Learning
5 Wall Street
Burlington, MA 01803
978-443-5000
info@jblearning.com
www.jblearning.com

Jones & Bartlett Learning books and products are available through most bookstores and online booksellers. To contact Jones & Bartlett Learning directly, call 800-832-0034, fax 978-443-8000, or visit our website, www.jblearning.com.

Substantial discounts on bulk quantities of Jones & Bartlett Learning publications are available to corporations, professional associations, and other qualified organizations. For details and specific discount information, contact the special sales department at Jones & Bartlett Learning via the above contact information or send an email to specialsales@jblearning.com.

Production Credits
Publisher: Cathleen Sether
Acquisitions Editor: Sean Connelly
Editorial Assistant: Caitlin Murphy
Director of Production: Amy Rose
Production Manager: Tracey McCrea
Production Assistant: Alyssa Lawrence
Marketing Manager: Lindsay White
Project Management Services: DataStream Content Solutions, LLC
Rights and Permissions Manager: Katherine Crighton
Rights and Photo Research Supervisor: Anna Genoese
Cover Design: Scott Moden
Cover Image: © Digital Storm/ShutterStock, Inc.
Manufacturing and Inventory Control Supervisor: Amy Bacus
Printing and Binding: Malloy, Inc.
Cover Printing: Malloy, Inc.

Some images in this book feature models. These models do not necessarily endorse, represent, or participate in the activities represented in the images.

Library of Congress Cataloging-in-Publication Data
Sun, Key.
   Correctional counseling : a cognitive growth perspective / Key Sun.
     p. cm.
   Rev. ed. of: Correctional counseling : a cognitive growth perspective. 2008.
   Includes index.
   ISBN 978-0-7637-9937-3 (pbk.) — ISBN 0-7637-9937-8 (pbk.)
  1. Prisoners--Counseling of--United States.   2. Counseling—United States.   3. Corrections--United States.
  4. Correctional psychology--United States.   I. Title.
   HV9276.S86 2013
   365'.6610973—dc23
                      2011048235

6048
Printed in the United States of America
16 15 14 13 12   10 9 8 7 6 5 4 3 2 1

"The characteristics of a nation's prison system mirror the characteristics of the nation."

—Montesquieu

"Knowing others is wisdom, knowing the self is enlightenment."

—Lao Tzu

TABLE OF CONTENTS

PREFACE

Correctional Counseling: A Cognitive Growth Perspective, Second Edition, is written from an interdisciplinary and integral perspective (psychology, counseling, social work, and criminal justice), as the response to the growing demand of students and practitioners who need a balanced, comprehensive, and updated book about counseling for the correctional population. This updated edition has assimilated many new findings and knowledge in correctional counseling since the publication of the first edition. The major updates and expansions are summarized as follows:

- A new chapter on understanding and treating substance abuse has been added to address the increasing issue of substance abuse for the offender population.

- A new chapter on restorative justice has been added to examine skills and principles of restorative justice, which addresses the needs of the victim, the community, and the offender. Restorative justice has been increasingly used not only in community corrections, but also in prison settings.

- Chapter 1 has updated crime statistics, a further examination of the issue of prisoner reentry, and added information on drug/mental health courts.

- Chapter 3 discusses diverse meanings of evidence-based correctional counseling by integrating viewpoints from both corrections and psychology fields.

- Chapter 5 has expanded the discussion about art therapy for assessment and its techniques and benefits.

- Chapter 7 on counseling processes has included the issue of a gender-sensitive approach in counseling women offenders and assessment and intervention for juvenile offenders.

- Chapter 10 on mentally disordered offenders has expanded the discussion on research about mental illness and violence, and analyzed the debate between the social cognitive explanation and the biomedical explanation for mental disorders.

The correctional population in the United States maintained a record of 7.2 million at the end of 2009. This situation has created diverse and frequent employment opportunities for students and for mental health practitioners with training in correctional counseling. This book provides readers with a knowledgeable background and a balanced and academic coverage of therapeutic models and skills for performing correctional counseling, including: (1) what correctional counselors do; (2) how they do it; (3) the outcomes of their services; and (4) critically analyzing key issues in correctional counseling. This text examines how to understand and assess offenders' issues, and how to perform counseling and interventions for offenders from the interdisciplinary perspective, which integrates treatment models and research in psychology, counseling, social work, and recent advances in social psychology and cross-cultural psychology.

In particular, this book deals with issues of correctional counseling and offender treatment as follows.

First, the text gives a comprehensive, up-to-date, balanced, and concise coverage of correctional counseling issues. The issues include: (a) the purpose of correctional counseling and treatment; (b) offender assessment and classification; (c) interventions; and (d) the theoretical foundations (ranging from relevant criminological theories, behavior interventions, cognitive therapies, social learning models, and positive psychology). In addition, it examines the strengths and limitations of the perspectives in relation to counseling offenders. For example, most counseling models are developed on the basis of research with a non-offender population and they may not address the concerns of correctional counseling.

Second, correctional environments (e.g., prison, jail, and community corrections) are discussed together with the responsibilities of correctional counselors in these settings. The reason for this discussion is so that students of counseling, social work, or psychology (outside criminal justice areas) can obtain the necessary information about the correctional systems.

Third, the discussion goes beyond counseling theories by integrating findings, theories, and research in other areas (e.g., social psychology, cross-cultural psychology) because these issues are relevant to correctional counseling.

Fourth, in addition to examining the main issues of correctional counseling, the purpose of correctional counseling and offender issues is examined from a unique cognitive perspective. In this approach, the purpose of correctional counseling is to help clients understand and overcome conflicts in domains such as law, family, employment, education, relationships, and mental health. A new and more accurate cognition is developed about the self, others, and patterns of social interaction. In other words, correctional counseling reduces recidivism because it gives the clients new cognitive capacities to unlearn past emotional hurts and extricate themselves from fear, anxiety, and depression. It helps them to obtain and maintain good relationships, improve communication, increase cooperation, and live a crime-free life. This cognitive model demonstrates the importance of cognitions in interactions between the self, others, and environments, rather than focusing on the self-schemas alone.

In addition, the author argues that counselors must view correctional clients not only as those who have committed crimes and experienced mental and interpersonal conflict, but also as people who use their cognitions to interpret their crimes, experiences, dysfunctions, need areas, and social stimuli (including other people), and to cope with their problems. In other words, correctional clients have difficulty balancing their lives because they lack cognitive alternatives or an accurate understanding of the interpersonal reality when perceiving and interpreting the self's/others' experiences and actions, and reacting to obstacles and frustrations. Their cognitions reflect their level of awareness of reality, but do not represent reality itself. By the same token, interventions need to focus on changing the clients' cognitions about social reality (including their knowledge structures and processes about the self, others, and the world, and the relationships among them) because people's mental and interpersonal activities (e.g., emotions, motivation, and actions) are regulated and fettered by their cognitions.

It is my sincere hope that this book provides readers not only with the knowledge, skills, and cognitive perspective about correctional counseling, but also with the expanded ability and motivation to help correctional clients, so that all people live in a better and more peaceful society.

ACKNOWLEDGMENTS

I would like to thank my colleagues, students, and staff at Central Washington University. They have supported me with encouragement, comments, assistance, and the time for completing the second edition. In addition, I express my special appreciation to Edward F. Lawlor, Teresa Sarai, and Sylvia Toombs at the Brown School of Social Work, Washington University in St. Louis, and to Tod Sloan and Lisa Pogue at the Graduate School of Education and Counseling at Lewis and Clark College for providing me with the opportunity to do related research in the settings.

Finally and always, I want to thank the correctional staff and numerous correctional clients I worked with at the Washington State Department of Corrections.

We would also like to thank the following people for reviewing the text:
Sandra Barone, Manchester Community College
Elizabeth P. Biebel, University of Kentucky
Joel L. Carr, Angelo State University
Louis F. Garzarelli, Mount Aloysius College
Kelly Gould, Sacramento City College
Michael Holsapple, Ivy Tech Community College
Reverend Professor Kimora, John Jay College of Criminal Justice
Julie McCawley-Self, Grossmont College
Jack S. Monell, Central Piedmont Community College
Barnes K. Peterson, Antioch University New England
Manuel Roman, Jr., Sierra College
Beth A. Wiersma, University of Nebraska at Kearney

ABOUT THE AUTHOR

Key Sun is Professor of Law and Justice at Central Washington University. He previously worked as a correctional mental health counselor at the Washington State Department of Corrections. He received a PhD and MA in psychology from Rutgers University, where he also received a master's degree in criminal justice. In addition, he has a Bachelor of Law degree from Beijing University and a Master of Social Work degree from University of Illinois at Urbana-Champaign. His research interests involve examining mental health and criminal justice issues from a multidisciplinary perspective, integrating psychology, criminal justice, social work, and cross-cultural approaches. His publications have appeared in psychological and criminal justice journals and textbooks.

Chapter 1

Correctional Counselors: Roles, Work Environments, Conflicts, and Challenges

The Need for Correctional Counseling

This chapter gives an overview of the background information related to correctional counseling. The issues examined include the current need for educated counselors in corrections, a history of correctional counseling, basic characteristics that separate correctional counseling from other counseling practices, correctional counselors' responsibilities, as well as the types of competence and challenges for the counselors. Familiarity with the knowledge prepares readers for contents in subsequent chapters.

The criminal justice system consists of a complex and fragmented mixture of many agencies and programs in federal, state, and local jurisdictions that form three interconnected systems: law enforcement, law adjudication, and corrections. Although jails and prisons are the most visible parts of the correctional system, pretrial and posttrial, community-based correctional programs and work release and halfway release programs are inseparable parts of the structure. The goal of the system is both to punish and to rehabilitate (Muraskin, 2005).

Statistics

The correctional population in the United States, which included inmates confined in federal, state prisons and local jails, and offenders in community corrections, was at over 7.2 million at the year-end of 2009, though this number represented less than a 1% decrease from the year-end of 2008 (Bureau of Justice Statistics [BJS], 2010a, 2010b). With only about 5% of the world's population, the United States incarcerates more than 2 million people, or a quarter of the world's 8 million prisoners (Mair & Mair, 2003). In

1

addition, over 5 million adult men and women were under federal, state, or local probation or parole jurisdiction at year-end 2009 (BJS, 2010a, 2010b).

The increasing offender population in corrections in the United States is directly correlated with the reactions of policymakers, politicians, and legislators. They believe that expediting solutions to the crime problem involves building more prisons and passing "get tough" sentencing laws that increased the frequency and length of prison terms. In the late 1980s and early 1990s, 49 states passed or expanded mandatory minimum sentencing laws covering a variety of drug offenses and violent crimes. Most states enacted "truth-in-sentencing" laws that required violent offenders to serve a fixed portion of their prison terms. Many states passed three-strike laws that mandated long prison terms without parole for habitual offenders. These policy changes increased prison populations sharply (Parent & Barnett, 2004).

The rising correctional population is not only produced by the increase in severe punishments. Crime and criminal behavior result from the interaction of many variables, including sociological, psychological, and legal factors. It is certain, however, that building more prisons has not and will not solve the crime problem.

Demand and Supply

The large correctional population creates the need for educated counselors who have the knowledge, skills, values, and motivation to work with correctional clients. Competent counselors should be able to play an effective role in counseling multicultural clients, adhering to social justice, discerning the clients' true problems, selecting and implementing interventions, and reducing recidivism.

There seems to be a mismatch between the demand for correctional counselors and the supply. According to the U.S. Department of Labor (*Occupational Outlook Handbook*, 2010–2011 edition), employment in this field (probation officers and correctional treatment specialists) is projected to grow about 19% between 2008 and 2018, faster than the average for all occupations. In addition to the job openings as a result of growth, many jobs will be created by replacement needs, especially by the expected retirement of large numbers of correctional staff. Probation officers and correctional treatment specialists held about 103,400 jobs in 2008. Most jobs are in state or local government, though some are employed by the U.S. courts and by the U.S. Department of Justice's Bureau of Prisons. In general, correctional counselors may work in federal or state prisons, jails, community corrections (e.g., probation and parole), and facilities for juvenile offenders.

Education Qualifications

The education qualifications for probation officers, correctional treatment specialists, and correctional social workers or counselors vary by state, but most employers require a bachelor's degree (and preferably a master's degree) in social work, criminal justice, psychology, or a related field, or a bachelor's degree with extensive coursework in counseling. Additional requirements by most correctional agencies are that all correctional counselors show a demonstrated interest in working in corrections and a belief that helping to rehabilitate or habilitate offenders is a worthy calling.

Opportunities

A career in correctional counseling provides individuals with a great opportunity to use their knowledge, skills, and values to positively affect individuals as well as their communities and society. The following points elaborate on the opportunities:

1. Counselors can help correctional clients to reach their optimal growth, development, and well-being and to live a crime-free life. They work with individuals in need who are themselves the victims of crime, sexual abuse, family violence, discrimination, and other social problems.

2. Counselors are often required to work both inside and outside the correctional system, interacting and cooperating with family members, social service agencies, groups, community, victims, and other staff in the justice system to enhance the safety and well-being of the community and general public.

3. Counselors are given many opportunities to develop and apply counseling theories and practice.

Correctional counseling thus influences the functioning of society and the smooth operation of the criminal justice system. Through the process of assessment, guidance, and effective intervention and treatment of offenders, correctional counselors help clients to function well in prison or community settings and to balance their mental state and interpersonal relationships. Any individual improvement in social-cognitive capacity, thinking, motivation, emotions, and behavior, regardless of how insignificant it is, will benefit family, community, and society.

A History of Correctional Counseling

According to Schrink and Hamm (1989) and Gendreau, Goggin, French, and Smith (2006), the history of correctional counseling in the United States may be divided into three stages: (1) from the 1870s to 1945, (2) from 1945 to the mid-1970s, and (3) from the mid-1970s to the present.

Stage 1: 1870s to 1945

Well before the turn of the 20th century, correctional counseling in the United States was initiated and sustained by reform-minded people—from probation and parole officers, clergymen, and teachers to a wide variety of other persons working in the corrections system. In addition, advancement in the treatment of offenders had been initiated by concerned citizens from outside the criminal justice system. They had volunteered their time, energy, and personal resources and contributed to this nation's tradition of popular justice. Rather than applying a series of academic research findings or a needs assessment of the criminal justice system, correctional counseling in the early stages was trial and error, struggling to find ways to alleviate the pain of incarcerated individuals rejected by society.

Stage 2: 1945 to the Mid-1970s

After World War II, the rehabilitative ideal became the preeminent corrections philosophy in North America. In 1954, the American Prison Association was renamed the American Correctional Association, and prisons became known as correctional institutions. Prison treatment programs—for example, individual and group counseling, behavior modification, and vocational and educational programming—were widely implemented. Although systematic research to evaluate counseling programs and services was still lacking, counseling became popular, especially in the 1960s. During this period, correctional counseling programs were boosted by the concept of rehabilitation being the penal ideology. Starting in the mid-1970s, however, the idea that offenders can be rehabilitated was seriously questioned in political and academic circles. Martinson's (1974) claim that "nothing works" represented a noticeable attack on rehabilitation as the goal of corrections. Researchers identified many weaknesses in Martinson's work, however. For example, about 40 to 60% of the 231 studies he had reviewed included reports of *positive* effects on at least some types of offenders (Andrews & Bonta, 2003). Martinson's claim did not stop new research on the effect of counseling in reducing recidivism. For example, the report by Kadish, Glaser, Calhoun, and Risler (1999) supported the effectiveness of counseling services. In their study about the effect of the Juvenile Counseling and Assessment Program (JCAP) in Georgia, individual and group counseling services were provided for 55 adjudicated delinquent youths (aged 9–17 years) over a 4- to 6-month period. The recidivism rates of the youths who had received counseling services were compared to the recidivism rates of a control group of 55 adjudicated youths who had not received counseling. A significant difference in the frequency of reoffending was found between the two groups. Of those juvenile delinquents who received counseling, only 25% reoffended, whereas 64% of the youths in the control sample reoffended. A systematic review of the social problem-solving approach with cognitive-behavioral methods indicates that this approach reduces the misconduct of offenders with deficient social problem-solving skills, childhood aggression, personality disorders, substance abuse, self-harm and suicide risk, and criminal activities to a varying degree (McGuire & McGuire, 2005). French and Gendreau's (2006) analysis of 68 studies involving 21,467 offenders showed that cognitive-behavioral and other prison programs reduced institutional misconduct and recidivism.

Stage 3: Mid-1970s to the Present

During this period, the political atmosphere has shifted to devaluating correctional treatment. As a result of the political climate, most correctional counselors are assigned responsibilities that are not strictly counseling and treatment activities, though other mental health professionals (e.g., social workers, psychologists, and psychiatrists) still have some opportunities to engage in counseling-related activities, such as assessment, case management, intervention, and individual and/or group psychotherapy (Gould & Bacharach, 2010).

Opponents of correctional treatment emphasize a "just desert" model, or doing the crime and doing the time. This hard-line approach to correctional programs is well supported in spite of the lack of consensus in research studies concerning the effectiveness of retribution or deterrence as a crime-control strategy. Great disagreement occurs between the proponents and opponents of correctional treatment/counseling, much like the case for capital punishment (Schrink & Hamm, 1989).

The Meaning of Correctional Counseling

Counseling involves the implementation of practices that help individuals, groups, and organizations function optimally by assessing and changing personal and interpersonal dysfunctions that occur in many areas—emotional adjustments, relationship problems, career planning, vocational and educational issues, and/or health problems. Individuals need counseling to improve their well-being, alleviate distress and maladjustment, and resolve conflicts (see Counseling Psychology Division 17 of the American Psychological Association, 2011; Todd & Bohart, 2003). The reorientation of individuals is shared by all helping professionals—from counseling psychologists to social workers.

Although correctional counseling has the same mission as other counseling professions, it includes the following unique characteristics: (1) the characteristics of correctional clients; (2) the training of those who perform correctional counseling; (3) the settings for correctional counseling; and (4) the correctional counselor's responsibilities.

The Characteristics of Correctional Clients

The correctional population is different from other clients because most are **involuntary clients**—offenders who are convicted of one or more crimes (felonies or misdemeanors or both) and are serving mandatory sentences either in incarceration or in the community. Some of them are uncommunicative, hostile, or angry, and they may be physically aggressive. Shearer and Ogan (2002) characterized this type of attitude as clients' "resistance," which includes various beliefs such as the sense of isolation and detachment, counselor distrust, compliance (e.g., offenders do only what they have to do to get through a treatment program), low self-disclosure (e.g., refusing to talk about personal problems to a group), cynicism (e.g., the belief that prison counseling is useless "bull" sessions), and denial (e.g., denying the problem). In addition, clients may have dysfunctions in interpersonal relations, substance abuse, employment issues, mental or physical health problems, and other areas of concern.

In a strict sense, offenders in correctional counseling may not be defined as clients, because the term client generally refers to recipients of a service or treatment who are willing to mutually identify and work on the identified target issues (Ivanoff, Blythe, & Tripodi, 1994). This book uses the terms *offenders/inmates* and *correctional clients* interchangeably to emphasize that both juvenile and mentally disordered offenders and adult offenders need help and counseling. In addition, it is important to recognize that offenders in corrections are not alike. They are far more diverse than the staff in terms of their ethnic, religious, geographical, and work backgrounds (McCullough, 2006). The inmates do not share one voice. People's misconceptions concerning offender motivation for counseling often serve as a psychological obstacle to effective treatment. Although offenders are placed in correctional programs or institutions against their will, and they are required to participate in various types of treatment activities, they often have a range of motivations for counseling (Schrink & Hamm, 1989). Offenders are motivated to understand their experiences and frustrations, just like other human beings (Sun, 2002a).

Who Performs Correctional Counseling?

Correctional counseling is not only the responsibility of officially designated correctional counselors. It may also involve formal or informal tasks carried out by other correctional staff, including social workers, psychologists, psychiatrists, nurses, probation and parole officers, and correctional officers. In addition, prison chaplains play an important role in facilitating inmate adjustment and rehabilitation through counseling. Approximately one in three inmates participate in religious programs (Sundt, Dammer, & Cullen, 2002).

The Settings for Correctional Counseling

Most correctional counselors are employed in state and federal prisons, jails, juvenile residential facilities, and community corrections.

State and Federal Prisons

Prisons are state or federal correctional institutions that typically consist of three security levels: (1) maximum and close-security prisons for the most serious and violent offenders; (2) medium-security prisons for moderately serious offenders; and (3) minimum-security prisons for inmates who demonstrate good behavior by not committing new infractions or by participating in prison programs such as education, prison labor and industry, religious programs, and drug abuse treatment. These programs are funded by either state or federal governments. The professionals who work in prison settings include psychiatrists, nurses, dentists, chaplains, psychologists, psychiatric social workers, and correctional counselors (e.g., classification counselors and correctional mental health counselors).

Jails

Another important element in the American correctional system is the **jail**, a detention facility that differs from a prison as follows:

1. Unlike prisons, which are run by state and federal governments, a jail is a place of confinement typically administered by the county sheriff's department or city police department.

2. Jails house only individuals who are awaiting trial, who are waiting to be transferred to prison, or who are convicted of relatively minor crimes and receive relatively short sentences.

3. Local jails are funded by local administrators (Inciardi, 1999).

Juvenile Residential Facilities

Juvenile residential facilities are places of forced confinement of youths who are deemed to pose a danger to themselves and society. When a youth has been judged guilty of an offense, the juvenile court may impose the most severe sanction by restricting the juvenile's freedom through placement in a **juvenile residential facility**. The facilities may be publicly or privately operated, with either a secure, prisonlike environment or a more open setting. In addition, before the disposition, a youth may be held in detention after arrest or during court proceedings (Carlson, Hess, & Orthmann, 1999). In 2003, more than 92,000 juvenile offenders were held in public or private juvenile residential facilities in the United States. The daily number of committed youths held in these facilities increased 28% between 1991 and 2003, with a greater increase in private rather than in public facilities (Office of Juvenile Justice and Delinquency Prevention, 2006). Because juveniles placed in residential facilities have many needs, including schooling, maintaining family/social relationships, mental health care, and substance abuse treatment, the juvenile counselors may have more diverse responsibilities than counselors in facilities for adult offenders.

Community Corrections

Many correctional counselors work in **community corrections**—community-based correctional settings. Although their official titles may range from juvenile probation counselors to community correctional officers, and from probation and parole officers to correctional social workers, their responsibilities involve supervising, assisting, and counseling offenders serving in the community.

Offenders in community corrections generally come from two sources:

1. *Probationers*, who serve their sentences in the community without being incarcerated in prison or jail.

2. *Ex-prisoners*, who have served their prison/jail terms and reentered the community. **Prisoner reentry** refers to the returning of convicted offenders back to the community after they have served time in federal or state prisons or local jails. Except for those few who die in custody or while serving their life term in prison without the possibility of parole, all prisoners/jail inmates eventually return to society. Therefore, reentry is called the *iron law of imprisonment* (Travis, 2005). Each year, over 700,000 individuals are released from state and federal prisons. In addition, at least 9 million people are cycled through local jails. According to statistics, within 3 years, almost two out of three offenders will have been rearrested and half will be back in prison, either for a new crime or for violating the conditions of their release. In addition, offenders in reentry face more challenges than probationers, including the issues of obtaining housing, education,

employment, family acceptance, health care, and treatment for substance abuse or dependence (The Federal Interagency Reentry Council, 2011). The literature review by Spjeldnes and Goodkind (2009) indicates that although both men and women at the reentry stage face many similar challenges, women also have many unique issues and needs that criminal justice personnel need to understand. Most of the current reentry and reintegration programs have been created to address men's needs because they are overrepresented in incarceration. However, effective reintegration of women offenders depends upon practicing gender-responsive, comprehensive, strengths-based, and culturally competent programs for them. For example, compared with male offenders, female offenders are typically involved in property or drug-related crimes, have low reoffending rates, have experienced trauma and abuse, have stronger parenting needs, and have limited employment and other opportunities. Recognizing and addressing those issues for women offenders in community programs will promote their success in becoming law-abiding community members.

According to Evans (2004), the challenge of supervising these offenders can only be met by an effective approach to community corrections, an effective way to protect the public and reduce reoffending by providing postcustody supervision and support. The goal of community corrections is to assist offenders in breaking the cycle of offending so that they can become productive, contributing members of the community. Community corrections also provide support to victims of crime.

The **setting principle** suggests that services to offenders have been shown to be more effective in a community than in prison (Clear & Dammer, 2003). In addition to being beneficial for the offenders, community corrections have other positive effects, such as helping to reduce institutional crowding, stress, suicides, lawsuits related to crowding, inmate-on-inmate assaults, and inmate-on-staff assaults (Lauren, 1997).

Mental health professionals and correctional counselors generally perform counseling for offenders in three community corrections settings: (1) probation, (2) parole, and (3) intermediate sanctions, as well as for clients in drug and mental health courts.

Probation   Usually considered the least restrictive of the alternatives to incarceration, **probation** is the most frequently used punishment and is a sentence that is served in the community under supervision. Probation is most commonly granted to first-time offenders, drug offenders, property offenders, and low-risk offenders (Clear & Dammer, 2003). About 51% of probationers had been convicted of committing a felony in 2009 (BJS, 2010b).

Although probation is seen as a part of both federal and state corrections, it is managed by the federal or state courts and is supervised and revoked by the courts (Inciardi, 1999).

In some county court systems, there are divisions of labor for probation officers and probation counselors. The former conduct presentencing investigation and arrest, and they hold a probationer for violations; the latter mainly engage in mental health counseling and case management.

Parole   Parole is a distinct form of community corrections related to probation. Unlike probation (a sentence imposed by the court), parole is a common method of reducing a sentence of imprisonment on the basis of federal or state indeterminate sentencing statutes.

Both granting and revoking parole are accomplished by state parole boards, which are separated from the state prison administration, or by the United States Parole Commission, which is separated from the Federal Bureau of Prisons. In other words, the state or federal parole authorities determine the actual length of incarceration to be served in the corrections system. Sentencing laws were changed in about half of the states to remove the discretionary release authority of parole boards. By the end of the year 2000, 16 states had abolished parole-board authority for releasing all offenders, and another four states had put an end to parole-board authority for releasing certain violent offenders (BJS, 2006). According to the U.S. Parole Commission (2007), although offenders for federal crimes committed on or after November 1, 1987, are no longer eligible for parole consideration, the commission still holds substantial responsibilities for granting or denying parole to federal offenders who committed their offenses before that date, offenders convicted of D.C. Code violations, certain Uniform Code of Military Justice offenders, and state probationers and parolees in the Federal Witness Protection Program.

Only a small percentage of prisoners receive parole and go to community corrections. According to Bureau of Justice Statistics (2007), state inmates released from prison as a result of a parole-board decision dropped from 50% of all adults entering parole in 1995 to 31% in 2005, while mandatory releases (based on a statutory requirement) increased from 45 to 51%. Mandatory release occurs when the inmate reaches the end of the prison sentence and has to be released to the community by law.

Intermediate Sanctions   Correctional counselors may also manage offenders in community corrections who have received some type of intermediate sanction. Such sanctions include community services (e.g., public service for nonprofit organizations, cleaning playgrounds, painting houses, or planting gardens), day reporting centers, paying a fine (to the government), restitution (compensating a victim), residence in a halfway house, and house arrest/electronic monitoring (e.g., random phone calls generated by computers to which the offender must respond within a certain time). Offenders may also have received mixed sentencing—serving weekends in jail while undergoing supervision during the week (see Clear & Dammer, 2003).

Drug Courts and Mental Health Courts   As a strategy to respond to a large number of offenders with substance abuse issues, **drug courts** are designed to integrate judicial processes (e.g., involving the judge, prosecution, defense, and offenders) with substance abuse treatment programs for drug-involved participants. At least 1,662 drug court programs were implemented in the United States in 2007. In addition to receiving drug testing, punishments for supervision violations, and rewards for progress, the participants are also given treatment, counseling, and help on issues related to substance abuse, social cognitive skills, parenting, education, and job training (Lindquist, Krebs, Warner, & Lattimore,

2009). The development of mental health courts in the late 1990s in the United States and many other countries represented a creative judicial effort to reduce the number of people with mental disorders in prisons and jails. **Mental health courts** are designated courts with the special responsibility and expertise to handle defendants with mental disorders and other impairments. Mental health providers are involved in the judicial process. The court decisions are based on considering the needs and risks of the mentally ill people, emphasizing mental health treatment, problem solving, diversion, community-based supervision and service, voluntary participation, safety of self and others, monitoring compliance for court-imposed conditions, and expanding other types of support (Linhorst, Dirks-Linhorst, Stiffelman, Gianino, Bernsen, & Kelley, 2010).

Correctional Counselors' General Responsibilities in a Facility of Confinement

Although the facilities of confinement (e.g., prisons, jails, juvenile residential centers) differ in types of offenders, security designations, and the expectations and requirements for counselors, the following general responsibilities for correctional counselors apply across agencies:

1. Assessing the offender's risk factors and needs in such areas as reoffending, anger management, poor impulse control, interpersonal conflicts, prison adjustments, substance abuse, mental health, education, and employment

2. Performing counseling services, case management (matching the offender's needs with available services and treatments and coordinating the services) and other interventions to address offenders' criminogenic needs (factors associated with recidivism) and dysfunctions in those areas

3. Reviewing, preparing, and updating records and reports (either on paper or in a computer file) concerning clients' issues in crime involvement, institutional infraction, institutional program participation, personal relationships, and other areas

4. Initiating recommendations dealing with issues such as offender transfers and custody level reduction/increase based on their new custody scores

5. Serving as a witness at disciplinary hearings for offenders on the counselor's caseload

6. Participating in staff meetings to discuss, develop, and implement rehabilitation plans for a client, as required by rules, policies, and procedures of the correctional system

7. Participating in emergency assignments in which counselors must act as security personnel, perhaps assisting security staff in times of inmate disturbance or conducting a search of an offender's person and cell for contraband

In order to perform counseling tasks, it is important to keep in mind that a facility of confinement does not represent a very salubrious environment. The architectural design of the physical environment (particularly if the prison is fortresslike) is not conducive to counseling and treatment. Counselors should thus be aware that the physical and psychological settings influence the effectiveness of interventions and treatment (Schrink & Hamm, 1989).

The General Responsibilities of a Community Correctional Counselor

The general responsibilities of a community correctional counselor may be more diverse and flexible than those of a counselor working with inmate clients.

First, the priority of community supervision involves making sure offenders (e.g., probationers, parolees, and other reentry offenders) adhere to two types of conditions of supervision: (1) those intended for offender rehabilitation or reform, and (2) those intended for the control of offenders. The rehabilitation-based conditions of community corrections push for offenders to seek a noncriminal way of life by attaining education, employment, substance treatment, and anger management and/or by participating in other programs in the community. The control-based conditions help the correctional agency keep track of those under supervision, including the requirement of reporting to community correctional officers on a regular basis, prohibitions against involvement in certain places (e.g., school), with certain people (e.g., victim, crime partners, potential victims), or in certain behaviors (drugs, alcohol, illegal activities, and hanging out) (State of Washington, Department of Corrections, 2001).

These two types of conditions can be further divided into four categories: (1) *standard conditions*, which may include travel restrictions, no contact with children (for sex offenders), and weekly reports at the local community correctional center; (2) *community placement conditions*, which consist of notice of changing residency and completing treatment and education requirements; (3) *court-ordered conditions*, which specify a particular requirement for the offender on the basis of his or her criminal case, such as no contact with ex-spouse; and (4) *financial conditions*, which are related to offenders' financial responsibility to the government or the victim(s). Probationers and parolees are subject to being returned to jail or prison for violations of the conditions or participating in other offenses.

Second, the counselors' responsibilities include completing intake assessments for offenders initially entering community corrections and performing risk assessments/reassessments, identifying and monitoring the offenders' performance and compliance with conditions and prohibitions during community corrections. The counselor updates supervision plans as needed; conducts presentence investigations (for probation officers) and prepares reports; and investigates and writes reports on alleged correctional violations. A counselor may also conduct searches and arrests, and testify before courts or disciplinary hearings.

Third, counselors have the obligation to meet, observe, and interact with the clients both in the office and in the community (including making home/field visits) and also to maintain contact with a client's family members and employers, other members of the criminal justice system, community agencies, and program-service providers (e.g., providers for mental health, substance abuse treatment, education).

Fourth, community corrections counselors should focus on targeted interventions, which include not only working with high-risk offenders (e.g., working with gang-involved youths, mentally ill offenders, sex offenders, and high-risk violent offenders in the community), but also concentrating on important offender issues such as anger management, employment and job skills training, housing assistance, supportive family relationships, education, treatments for substance abuse and/or mental and physical health issues, counseling, support groups, community support, child care, legal aid, gender-responsive programming, and individualized service plans and reintegration strategies corresponding to the offender's unique risk factors and needs. (Parent & Barnett, 2004; Spjeldnes & Goodkind, 2009).

Fifth, correctional counselors and other staff need to be aware of the societal barriers to reentry and offenders' successful reintegration. Although many of the barriers are built with the intent to increase public safety by excluding ex-offenders from certain opportunities, the staff needs to help offenders understand and deal with the obstacles. For examples, social welfare policies and some statutes restrict the access of ex-offenders to public housing, cash assistance or food stamps, and availability of some employment (e.g., holding professional licenses and certain jobs). These restrictions, coupled with the offender's minimal education, low-level job skills, and experience of discrimination, will undermine the offender's (and his or her parents') efforts to stabilize his or her life and family relationships (including regaining custody or reunifying with children). Reentry offenders (particularly women offenders) also have to deal with the inadequate healthcare system, not only because they have multiple healthcare needs (e.g., treatment for addiction, mental disorders, and other diseases), but also because few of them have private health insurance or are qualified for Medicaid (Spjeldnes & Goodkind, 2009).

According to Visher and Travis (2003), community correctional staff need to view recidivism as being directly affected by four sets of factors:

1. The offender's preprison conditions (e.g., criminal history, substance abuse involvement, demographic profile, work history, job skills, and family types)

2. The offender's in-prison experiences (e.g., the length of the incarceration; longer prison sentences were associated with higher recidivism for both high- and low-risk offenders), the prisoner's involvement in correctional programs, including those focused on individual improvement in education, job skills, cognitive skills, and substance abuse

3. The offender's immediate postprison experiences (e.g., meeting the initial housing needs, transition assistance, and family support)

4. Postrelease integration experiences (e.g., employment experiences, influence of peers, family connections, social service support, criminal justice supervision)

Awareness and Application of Community Resources

Community correctional counselors may be involved in two other tasks: (1) identifying and applying **community resources** (e.g., education, employment, treatment, and social services); and (2) helping clients recognize and use the resources.

Counselors are required to manage offender risk in the community and prevent reoffending through the use of **guardians**—individuals who have the capacity to influence the behavior of offenders. They include victims, citizens, treatment providers, employers, family members, and law enforcement (State of Washington, Department of Corrections, 2001).

In addition to counseling, community correctional counselors or officers may be involved in assisting or facilitating an emerging community program known as **restorative justice**—a process of conflict resolution that brings together all parties affected by harm or wrongdoing (e.g., offenders and their families, victims and their families, other members of the community, and professionals). Although the practice of restorative justice is focused on serving victims whose needs are often overlooked in this country's retributive criminal justice system, it is also meant to heal the wounds of other parties affected by conflict, including offenders. Instead of focusing solely on retribution, restorative justice emphasizes accountability and healing for the victim, offender, and community with a focus on service, social justice, dignity and worth of a person, and value of human relationships (Fred, 2005). It is usually run by nonprofit groups or criminal justice personnel (Morrison & Ahmed, 2006). A comprehensive discussion of the issue appears later in the text.

In short, although the prevention of recidivism is often described as the goal of correctional counseling, its responsibilities are wider (see Hepworth & Larsen, 1993). Correctional counseling helps clients to expand their competence and increase their problem-solving and coping abilities by helping them to understand and deal with their existing problems.

Five Areas of Competence for Correctional Counselors

Competence in knowledge, values, skills, and attitudes are among the essentials in fulfilling the role of the helping professionals (Hepworth & Larsen, 1993). To be effective in performing the professional responsibilities of the correctional counselor, the following five areas of competence are needed:

1. *Knowledge in counseling, psychology, and related social sciences and the ability to apply that knowledge to corrections.* Counselors need to have training and skills in psychology, social work or other social sciences, and adequate knowledge of human behavior in social environments (i.e., understanding how offenders' dysfunctions are created and maintained by the interaction of many systems and factors). Counselors must also be familiar with the operation and structure of the criminal justice system and community corrections as well as with relevant laws, rules, policies, standards, and procedures of correctional operations.

An adequate knowledge of theory and research is only part of the competence needed to evaluate, explain, and understand offenders' mental and interpersonal conflicts. Counselors also need to act as researchers who can test and revise their knowledge of social reality concerning the human mind and behavior in the context of correctional environments. Counseling is an ongoing process of discovery because no current research findings represent a complete understanding of human behavior. The process of developing a new scientific concept or model involves comparing (1) the to-be-rejected model and the to-be-accepted model with reality and (2) the two models with each other. Accepting the new model is based on the discovery that what is anomalous under the old model becomes expected under the new one (see Kuhn, 1970).

2. *Skills in written and verbal communications.* Counseling is about communication. Good communication skills include not only writing and speaking correctly, clearly, objectively, and effectively but also having listening skills and the ability to ask thoughtful questions. These skills have at least three components for correctional counselors:

- Helping offenders to evaluate their personal issues and situations accurately and to adopt an appropriate course of action

- Writing reports, documenting violations, and suggesting improvements for clients, as well as sharing complete and accurate information and professional opinions with other staff members in the justice system, employers, residents, crime victims, and offenders' family members

- Handling various stressors created by a large caseload and excessive paperwork in correctional settings

3. *Developing and maintaining good work relationships with offenders and other correctional personnel.* Correctional counselors must regulate the following two types of human relationships:

- Developing and maintaining a good work relationship with correctional clients by gaining their trust and cooperation and withholding judgment of their offenses. Withholding judgment does not mean that counselors condone or approve of illegal, immoral, abusive, exploitative, manipulative, or irresponsible behavior; neither does it imply that counselors should overlook the offenders' crime (Hepworth & Larsen, 1993). Counselors must assist clients to take responsibility for the part they play in their difficulties. Maintaining a good work relationship suggests that counselors should have the attitude, warmth, open-mindedness, and values to help offenders improve themselves regardless of their crimes. As suggested by the American Correctional Association (ACA) Code of Ethics (1994), "members of the ACA shall respect and protect the civil and legal rights of all individuals," including offenders.

- Developing and maintaining a good work relationship with other correctional personnel, including administrators and supervisory personnel, other treatment personnel (e.g., psychologists, social workers, and psychiatrists) and line staff (correctional officers).

According to the ACA Code of Ethics (1994), good work relationships must be maintained with correctional colleagues to "promote mutual respect within the profession and improve the quality of service" and to "contribute to a work place that is safe, healthy, and free of harassment in any form."

Correctional counselors must understand and deal with ethical and professional conflict. They are required to report to responsible authorities regarding "corrupt or unethical behavior in which there is sufficient evidence to justify a review" (ACA, 1994). The correctional setting is a miniature society that mirrors all the good and bad elements of the larger society. For example, an important source of conflict that occurs in a correctional facility involves coercive power—the situation in which correctional officers may act in unethical ways by abusing power to make life miserable for the inmates they dislike, such as "forgetting" to send an inmate to an appointment, making an inmate stay in lockdown longer than the disciplinary requirement, and writing infractions at their discretion (Pollock, 2004). In addition, correctional officers may cover up for each others' unethical behavior (Pollock, 2004).

Sometimes the psychological environment leads to a debilitating misunderstanding of correctional counseling, particularly when correctional administrators place more emphasis on security than treatment. As a result, counselors may find their best efforts disrupted or thwarted by correctional officers who misunderstand counseling efforts and intentions for the clients (Schrink & Hamm, 1989).

Even worse, African American correctional officers in some institutions say they are subjected to racial slurs and white-supremacist activity, including Nazi salutes in the facility and the distribution of hate literature. Some correctional officers belong to, or have knowledge about, hate groups among correctional personnel (Vogel, 1999).

Some conflict in corrections may result from the different training and background of the various correctional personnel. For example, one type of conflict involves an interpretation of the disruptive behavior of inmates. While the custody staff tends to ignore, dismiss, misidentify, or punish problematic behavior, the mental health staff tends to see such behavior as the product of mental illness or the reflection of a psychotic episode (Mobley, 2006; Sun, 2005; Weinberger & Sreenivasan, 1994).

Deutsch (1993) suggested that when a conflict persists between two sides, facing the conflict rather than avoiding it seems a better solution. Evading conflict (e.g., denial, inhibition, being overly agreeable, postponement, and premature conflict resolution) often produces negative emotional consequences such as irritability, tension, and continuation of the problem. People can avoid the destructive results of conflict by engaging in constructive cooperation between the conflicting parties and using communication that conveys cooperative attitudes, knowledge, and skills contributing to effective fact-finding and problem solving.

Healthy human relationships are based on understanding human behavior. One of the strategies to deal with staff conflicts involves understanding the **power of situation**—a principle suggesting that situations and contexts, especially psychologically controlling environments like prison, have strong influences on social behavior, such as abusive conduct and compliance. This principle argues that social environments shape human social behavior through social interactions in which individuals act and play roles (Haney & Zimbardo, 1998). As shown in the study known as the Stanford Prison Experiment, when a group of psychologically healthy, emotionally stable and normal college students were randomly assigned roles as mock-prisoners and prison guards, they were temporarily but dramatically transformed by 6 days in a prisonlike environment. Those students who were assigned the role of inmate underwent acute mental strain and breakdown. Some of them entreated to be released from the intense pain of the simulated confinement within a couple of days, whereas others became blindly obedient to the abuse of the guards by habituating to the setting. The students who played the guards (many of whom were gentle and caring young college students before the experiment) soon began mistreating the "inmates," sometimes creating viciously inventive ways to harass and degrade them. The attitudes of many mock-guards toward the obvious suffering of the prisoners involved apathy and the failure to intervene and complain about the abuse they witnessed. Interestingly, the worst prisoner treatment occurred when the guards thought they could avoid surveillance and interference (Haney & Zimbardo, 1998).

4. *Computer literacy, including the ability to learn, master, and apply new technologies in correctional settings.* Although many professional counselors and social workers enjoy using computer technology, the complex computer databases related to offender classification, assessments, and data management remain a challenge for some correctional staff, creating an impediment for universal and consistent offender management.

5. *Multicultural competence.* Correctional counselors must have the following skills related to multicultural competence:

   • The ability to deal effectively with persons of varying socioeconomic, racial, and cultural backgrounds

   • An awareness of the interconnections among all people and their contributions to society and civilization

   • An understanding of the psychological cause of prejudice and how to overcome it (Sun, 2002b)

According to Sun (2002b), increasing cultural diversity in criminal justice will eliminate the bad aspects (e.g., discrimination, racial profiling) and promote the good ones (appreciating the cultural achievements of all humanity and increasing cross-cultural understanding). However, three misconceptions concerning the meaning of multiculturalism or cultural diversity may jeopardize the attempt to reach these goals:

- The tendency to treat the concepts of race, ethnicity, and culture as synonymous. In reality, race and ethnicity are two different concepts. Culture, which is associated with ethnicity, is learned (Yee, Fairchild, Weizmann, & Wyatt, 1993). People who are categorized as members of black, white, Hispanic, or Asian racial groups may not know "black," "white," "Hispanic," or "Asian" culture, because their learning experiences do not fit the perceived stereotypic categories (Sun, 2002b).

- The view that culture or ethnicity is the sole determinant of identity and behavior. Actually, culture is just one of the factors that shape personality and behavior. People live not only in a physical world but also in a psychological world. They have opportunities to experience and learn about other cultures through various contacts. Thoughts, feelings, and behavior are thus shaped by interactions among multiple systems—cultural, social, psychological and physical.

- The view that cultures are isolated from one another. In today's world, all cultures are in fact increasingly interacting, forming a global village.

In short, multiculturalism in the criminal justice system emphasizes that culture is knowledge that is learned, not inherited. Correctional counselors must realize that their clients think, feel, and act in certain ways because they have different degrees of learning experience and understanding about social reality (including cultures). Offenders can change and improve as they change their distorted knowledge of social reality concerning themselves, others, and the environment. (A more detailed examination of multiculturalism and elimination of prejudice is discussed later in the text.)

Summary

The recent "get tough" sentencing laws and the new record numbers of the correctional population in the United States have created the need for educated correctional counselors who have the knowledge, skills, values, and motivations to work with correctional clients. Correctional counselors have a great opportunity to use their knowledge, skills, and values to have an impact on individuals as well as the community and society.

Correctional counseling in the United States started during the 1870s and reached its peak in the early 1970s. Although the political atmosphere at present is less favorable to correctional counseling, the progress made in the past has not been entirely abandoned.

Four characteristics separate correctional counseling from other counseling practices: (1) the characteristics of correctional clients, (2) the individuals who perform counseling, (3) the counseling settings, and (4) the counselor's responsibilities. Most correctional counselors are employed in one of the following settings: state or federal prisons, jails, community corrections, or juvenile justice facilities. In addition, correctional counselors may be involved in treatment programs associated with drug or mental health courts.

To be effective in performing their professional responsibilities, correctional counselors need to possess competence in five areas: (1) professional knowledge, (2) written and verbal communication skills, (3) good work relationships with offenders and other correctional personnel, (4) computer literacy, and (5) multicultural competence.

Key Terms

Community corrections

Community resources

Involuntary clients

Jail

Juvenile residential facilities

Parole

Prison

Prisoner reentry

Probation

Restorative justice

Power of situation

Setting principle

Discussion Questions

1. What are the four characteristics of correctional counseling?

2. What are the challenges and opportunities in correctional counseling?

3. How do community correctional counselors working in a community corrections setting and those working in prison or jail differ in their responsibilities?

4. Name the five areas of competence required for correctional counselors.

References

American Correctional Association. (1994). *ACA code of ethics*. Retrieved from http://www.aca.org/pastpresentfuture/ethics.asp.

Andrews, D. A., & Bonta, J. (2003). *The psychology of criminal conduct* (3rd ed.). Cincinnati, OH: Anderson.

Bureau of Justice Statistics, U.S. Department of Justice. (2007). *Probation and parole in the United States, 2006*. Retrieved from http://bjs.ojp.usdoj.gov/index.cfm?ty=pbdetail&iid=1106.

Bureau of Justice Statistics, U.S. Department of Justice. (2010a). *Correctional populations in the United States, 2009*. Retrieved from http://bjs.ojp.usdoj.gov/index.cfm?ty=pbdetail&iid=2316.

Bureau of Justice Statistics, U.S. Department of Justice. (2010b). *Probation and parole in the United States, 2009*. Retrieved from http://bjs.ojp.usdoj.gov/content/glance/corr2.cfm.

Carlson, N. A., Hess, K. M., & Orthmann, C. M. H. (1999). *Corrections in the 21st century: A practical approach*. Belmont, CA: West/Wadsworth.

Clear, T. R., & Dammer, H. R. (2003). *The offender in the community* (2nd ed.). Belmont, CA: Wadsworth/Thomson.

Counseling Psychology Division 17 of the American Psychological Association. (2011). Retrieved from http://www.div17.org/students_defining.html.

Deutsch, M. (1993). Educating for a peaceful world. *American Psychologist, 48,* 510–517.

Evans, D. G. (2004). Why community corrections matters. *Corrections Today, 66,* 6–7.

Fred, S. (2005, February). Restorative justice: A model of healing philosophy consistent with social work values. *NASW News, 50*(2). Retrieved from http://www.socialworkers.org/pubs/news/2005/02/justice.asp.

French, S. A., & Gendreau, P. (2006). Reducing prison misconduct: What works! *Criminal Justice and Behavior, 33,* 185–218.

Gendreau, P., Goggin, C., French, S., & Smith, P. (2006). Practicing psychology in correctional settings. In I. B. Weiner & A. K. Hess (Eds.), *The handbook of forensic psychology* (3rd ed., pp. 722–750). Hoboken, NJ: Wiley.

Gould, J., & Bacharach, A. (2010). Increasing cross-discipline communication. In A. Ruiz, J. A. Dvoskin, C. L. Scott, J. L. Metzner, A. Ruiz, J. A. Dvoskin, & J. L. Metzner (Eds.), *Manual of forms and guidelines for correctional mental health* (pp. 57–81). Arlington, VA: American Psychiatric Publishing, Inc.

Haney, C., & Zimbardo, P. (1998). The past and future of U.S. prison policy: Twenty-five years after the Stanford Prison experiment. *American Psychologist, 53,* 709–727.

Hepworth, D. H., & Larsen, J. A. (1993). *Direct social work practice: Theory and skills* (4th ed.). Pacific Grove, CA: Brooks/Cole.

Inciardi, J. A. (1999). *Criminal justice* (6th ed.). Fort Worth, TX: Harcourt Brace.

Ivanoff, A., Blythe, B. J., & Tripodi, T. (1994). *Involuntary clients in social work practice*. New York, NY: Aldine De Gruyter.

Kadish, T. E., Glaser, B. A., Calhoun, G. B., & Risler, E. A. (1999). Counseling juvenile offenders: A program evaluation. *Journal of Addictions and Offender Counseling, 19,* 88–94.

Kuhn, T. (1970). *The structures of scientific revolutions* (2nd ed.). Chicago, IL: University of Chicago Press.

Lauren, R. J. (1997). *Positive approaches to corrections: Research, policy, and practice*. Lanham, MD: American Correctional Association.

Lindquist, C. H., Krebs, C. P., Warner, T. D., & Lattimore, P. K. (2009). An exploration of treatment and supervision intensity among drug court and non-drug court participants. *Journal of Offender Rehabilitation, 48,* 167–193. doi:10.1080/10509670902766489

Linhorst, D. M., Dirks-Linhorst, P., Stiffelman, S., Gianino, J., Bernsen, H. L., & Kelley, B. (2010). Implementing the essential elements of a mental health court: The experiences of a large multijurisdictional suburban county. *The Journal of Behavioral Health Services & Research, 37,* 427–442. doi:10.1007/s11414-009-9193-z

Mair, J. S., & Mair, M. (2003). Violence prevention and control through environmental modifications. *Annual Review of Public Health, 24*, 209–225.

Martinson, R. (1974). What works: Questions and answers about prison reform. *Public Interest, 35*, 22–84.

McCullough, J. M. (2006). *Managing correctional crises*. Sudbury, MA: Jones and Bartlett.

McGuire, M., & McGuire, J. (Eds.). (2005). *Social problem solving and offending: Evidence, evaluation, and evolution*. New York, NY: Wiley.

Mobley, M. J. (2006). Psychotherapy with criminal offenders. In I. B. Weiner & A. K. Hess (Eds.), *The handbook of forensic psychology* (3rd ed., pp. 751–789). Hoboken, NJ: Wiley.

Morrison, B., & Ahmed, E. (2006). Restorative justice and civil society: Emerging practice, theory, and evidence. *Journal of Social Issues, 62*, 209–215.

Muraskin, R. (2005). Correctional overview. In R. Muraskin (Ed.), *Key Correctional Issues* (pp. 12–18). Upper Saddle River, NJ: Pearson Prentice Hall.

Office of Juvenile Justice and Delinquency Prevention. (2006). *Juvenile offenders and victims: 2006 national report*. Retrieved from http://www.ojjdp.gov/ojstatbb/nr2006/.

Parent, D. G., & Barnett, L. (2004). Improving offender success and public safety through system reform: The transition from prison to community initiative. *Federal Probation, 68*, 25–30.

Pollock, J. M. (2004). *Ethics in crime and justice: Dilemmas and decisions* (4th ed.). Belmont, CA: Thomson & Wadsworth.

Schrink, J., & Hamm, M. S. (1989). Misconceptions concerning correctional counseling. *Journal of Offender Counseling Services and Rehabilitation, 14*, 133–147.

Shearer, R. A., & Ogan, G. D. (2002). Measuring treatment resistance in offender counseling. *Journal of Addictions and Offender Counseling, 22*, 72–82.

Spjeldnes, S., & Goodkind, S. (2009). Gender differences and offender reentry: A review of the literature. *Journal of Offender Rehabilitation, 48*, 314–335. doi:10.1080/10509670902850812

State of Washington, Department of Corrections. (2001). *Strategic plan* (Fiscal years 2001–2007). Olympia, WA: Author.

Sun, K. (2002a, March). *Irrational beliefs v. rational "because" statements: A critique of the cognitive restructuring model*. Paper presented at the annual conference of the Academy of Criminal Justice Sciences, Anaheim, CA.

Sun, K. (2002b, March). *The meanings of cultural diversity and similarity and the implications for criminal justice*. Paper presented at the annual conference of the Academy of Criminal Justice Sciences, Anaheim, CA.

Sun, K. (2005). Mentally disordered offenders in corrections. In R. Muraskin (Ed.), *Key correctional issues* (pp. 120–127). Saddle River, NJ: Pearson Prentice Hall.

Sundt, J. L., Dammer, H. R., & Cullen, F. T. (2002). The role of the prison chaplain in rehabilitation. *Journal of Offender Rehabilitation, 35*, 59–86.

The Federal Interagency Reentry Council. (2011). *Reentry in brief*. National Reentry Resource Center. Retrieved from http://www.nationalreentryresourcecenter.org/documents/0000/1059/Reentry_Brief.pdf.

Todd, J., & Bohart, A. C. (2003). *Foundations of clinical and counseling psychology* (3rd ed.). Long Grove, IL: Waveland.

Travis, J. (2005). Prisoner reentry: The iron law of imprisonment. In R. Muraskin (Ed.), *Key correctional issues* (pp. 65–71). Upper Saddle River, NJ: Pearson Prentice Hall.

U.S. Department of Labor, Bureau of Labor Statistics (2010–2011 ed.). *Occupational outlook handbook*. Retrieved from http://www.bls.gov/oco/ocos265.htm.

U.S. Parole Commission. (2007). *The mission of the parole commission*. Retrieved from http://www.usdoj.gov/uspc.

Visher, C. A., & Travis, J. (2003). Transitions from prison to community: Understanding individual pathways. *Annual Review of Sociology, 29*, 89–113.

Vogel, J. (1999, March 10). White guard black guard. *Seattle Weekly*. Retrieved from http://www.seattleweekly.com/1999-03-10/news/white-guard-black-guard/.

Weinberger, L. E., & Sreenivasan, S. (1994). Ethical and professional conflicts in correctional psychology. *Professional Psychology: Research and Practice, 25*, 161–167.

Yee, A. H., Fairchild, H. H., Weizmann, F., & Wyatt, G. E. (1993). Addressing psychology's problems with race. *American Psychologist, 48*, 1132–1140.

Chapter 2

Offender Classification and Assessment

Offender classification and assessment are two related but distinct processes in the operation of the prison system and community corrections. Both processes permeate the correctional processes from admission to the correctional system and incarceration through sentence completion, release, and postincarceration supervision (Austin, 2003).

Classification and assessment are typically performed by correctional counselors who have three goals in mind: (1) the public's need for protection and community safety; (2) the identification and matching of offender needs for treatment and management with correctional resources; and (3) the improvement of correctional operation and performance while reducing costs and recidivism (Lauren, 1997).

Meanings of Classification and Assessment

Although the terms *classification* and *assessment* are sometimes used interchangeably, they represent two related yet distinctive processes in corrections. **Classification** in the prison system refers to the procedure of placing prisoners into one of several custody levels (e.g., maximum, close, medium, or minimum) to match offender risks and needs with correctional resources (e.g., the type of facility to which they will be assigned and the level of supervision they will receive once they are there). Prison classification systems are intended to differentiate among prisoners who pose different security risks and/or have various management issues (Austin, 2003; Schmalleger & Smykla, 2001). Classification in community corrections consists of identifying and selecting supervision strategies (e.g., levels of supervision, from intensive to minimum) on the basis of assessing the risks and needs of the offenders.

On the other hand, **assessment** in corrections involves gathering information about offenders by employing standardized inventories, interviews, tests, mental health and medical examinations, and/or legal records. The assessment-generated information about an offender may be used for the decision regarding his or her classification or for other purposes, such as case management, treatment, and other interventions for the client.

Five Types of Classification

Subjective and Objective Classifications

Subjective classification, which relies mainly on the experience and judgment of prison administrators, was used by all of the state prison systems in the early period of the nation's corrections system. Prison officials would decide where to house an inmate and under what type of supervision and security (Austin, 2003).

Even today, the subjective classification has not been entirely abandoned. For example, the use of *overrides* allows correctional staff to change the scored classification level according to the policies of the agency. The number of overrides accounts for 5–15% of all classified inmate cases, indicating that it is necessary to combine objective and standard evaluations with the professional judgment of trained classification personnel.

Objective classification has the following core features (Austin, 2003):

1. Reliable and valid criteria that have been examined through empirical research are used to establish a prisoner's custody level.

2. Well-trained and specialized professional personnel perform classification duties, including recommendations that the custody level of an offender be increased, decreased, or maintained. They may also make suggestions about transfers.

3. Each classification decision and the considerations used to make each decision are documented and stored for analysis and examination.

Considerable change in prison classification systems has taken place during the past 3 decades. The California Department of Corrections and the Federal Bureau of Prisons were pioneers in using objective classification systems before 1980. Since then, virtually all 50 states as well as Puerto Rico and the Virgin Islands have fully implemented objective systems.

With the proliferation of the application of objective classification systems in corrections, new research has been conducted that has helped to revise the first generation of prison classification systems by identifying their limitations (Austin, 2003; Andrews & Bonta, 2006).

External and Internal Classifications and Reclassification

All prisoners experience initial (external), internal, and reclassification processes. The initial classification is also called *external prison classification*, which places an offender entering the prison system at a facility classified at the custody level where the prisoner will remain. Most states designate prison facilities by a custody level—such as maximum, close, medium, or minimum—but some states use a system of numbered levels—level 1, 2, 3 or higher—with level 1 facilities used for inmates who pose the least amount of danger to self and others (Gaines & Miller, 2003).

The typical external prison classification system uses a scoring form that evaluates the offender's current offense(s), prior criminal record and history, and other background attributes (e.g., age, medical ailments, mental disorders, and other dysfunctions). Although many factors used for classification (e.g., drug and alcohol use, history of infractions in corrections, sentence length, severity of the offense, and time left to serve) have little predictive capability for inmate risk, they are given primary consideration in the custody designation process (Andrews & Bonta, 2006; Austin, 2003).

Once a prisoner arrives at a facility, she or he will go through *internal classification*—a process that determines the unit and cell assignments and programs to match the prisoner's risk and needs with the security and treatment characteristics of the unit and programs.

After a designated period of time (e.g., annually), offenders may undergo *reclassification*, a review process within a prison system that updates and possibly revises the current classification levels of inmates. However, changes in the conditions of the offender may entail reclassification during other periods. Reclassification places greater emphasis on the prisoner's conduct during incarceration, such as degree of program participation, gang membership, history of violence, and recent disciplinary actions (Austin, 2003).

The Risk-Need-Responsivity Assessment

Currently, the Risk-Need-Responsivity (RNR) model serves as the basis for many assessment tools used for both predicting recidivism and correctional interventions (Andrews & Bonta, 2006, 2010). The instruments typically cover three areas: (1) risk, (2) needs, and (3) responsivity of the offender. The *risk* refers to the danger to self, others, and the community that is presented by the offender. The relevant factors include criminal history, current conviction(s) and violations, and dangerousness of the offense (e.g., violent crimes and sex offenses are considered more dangerous than nonviolent and nonsex offenses). The assessment of the offender's *needs* may include measurements related to education, employment, financial situation, interpersonal relationships, family/marital conditions, accommodation, leisure and recreation, companions, alcohol and drug abuse problems, suitability for treatment, mental health issues and attitudes toward crime, convention, sentence, and the criminal justice system. In addition, the offender's *responsivity* refers to his or her ability, motivation, personality factors, interpersonal competence, and/or learning style that influence how the person responds to correctional interventions (Andrews & Bonta, 2006, 2010).

Assessment is closely associated with correctional classification in that the offender's scores on assessment tools often serve as one of the important bases for decisions in the initial classification and reclassification of the individual. In community corrections, the scores often determine which programs to place the offender in and the intensiveness of the supervision. Assessing the offender's risk, needs, and responsivity (e.g., the offender's ability, learning style, and readiness) for treatment allows correctional staff to use valuable correctional resources much more efficiently according to supervision needs.

Assessment differs from classification, however, because it is frequently performed for offenders for purposes other than classification during the correctional process—the period that begins when entering corrections and concludes with postprison supervision in the community. Scores on the assessment do not always affect offenders' classification levels. For example, assessment scores may be used for identifying clients' mental health or physical health needs.

Four Generations of Risk Assessment

Some scholars believe that the instruments for correctional assessment in North America have gone through four generations:

1. The first-generation risk assessments are subjective clinical assessments based on the professional judgments of correctional authorities.

2. The second-generation risk assessments mainly involve the use of the static factors or items (with few dynamic factors) in appraising the offender's risk—for example, criminal history, age, gender, sentence length, and drug abuse history (Andrews & Bonta, 2006).

3. The third-generation risk assessments integrate substantial dynamic risk factors and allow correctional staff and practitioners to measure and apply them for correctional intervention and treatment and track changes in the offender's risk level (Walsh, 1997).

4. The fourth-generation risk assessments are represented by the current Risk-Need-Responsivity (RNR) model, which emphasizes not only the traditional risk/need assessment but also case management for offenders by appraising their responsivity to correctional interventions. The combined assessment of the three areas provides more valid information for developing strategies to reduce future criminal behavior (Andrews & Bonta, 2006, 2010).

The Level of Service Inventory-Revised (LSI-R)

During the past 20 years, significant developments have occurred in the area of offender assessment. One of these is the **Level of Service Inventory-Revised (LSI-R)**—a theoretically based offender risk-needs assessment that has the most all-embracing research literature among offender assessment instruments (Andrews & Bonta, 2006). In addition, it appears to be the most frequently used instrument for classification and assessment in corrections both in the United States and Canada (Bonta, 2002). LSI-R is an actuarial (predictive) tool that was created and developed in Canadian forensic settings (Andrews & Bonta, 1995; Mihailides, Jude, & Van den Bossche, 2005).

LSI-R has 54 items for consideration. The items are divided into 10 subscales that assess the offender's criminal history: education/employment, finances, family/marital conditions, accommodation, leisure and recreation, companions, alcohol/drug problems, emotional/personal issues, and attitude/orientation (Andrews & Bonta, 2006). Despite its demonstrated use with general offending populations, the LSI-R was not developed for sexual offenders or mentally disordered offenders.

The total number of checked items on the LSI-R provides a total score; the higher the score, the greater the risk of criminal behavior. Correctional authorities may use offenders' scores on the LSI-R to categorize them at three risk levels. Each state may define its own cutoff scores for supervision. For example, some states may use the following cutoff scores:

> 29 or higher = maximum-risk level;
>
> 19–28 = medium risk; and
>
> 0–18 = minimum risk.

Static and Dynamic Risk Factors

The 10 subscales on the LSI-R include some major static and dynamic risk factors in relation to criminal behavior and recidivism (Andrews & Bonta, 2006).

Static risk factors designate variables or conditions that existed in an offender's past or are not responsive to correctional interventions. Examples of static risk factors include the perpetrator's age, number of past offenses committed, intellectual disabilities, favored choice of victim, age at first conviction, gender, race, social class of origin, criminal history, antisocial childhood modeling, and childhood trauma. Some static factors cannot be changed by correctional efforts but they can change naturally, such as age. Because the offender's score on static risk factors cannot be revised by active interventions, correctional staff typically focuses on the conditions, attributes, and attitudes of the offender that can be transformed.

Dynamic risk factors are conditions and attributes related to the offender that can be changed by programs, treatment, counseling, and other interventions. Examples include marital distress, skill deficits, substance abuse, pro-crime attitudes, companions, mental conflicts, low educational attainment, and antisocial supports and peer association. Because these factors are associated with recidivism and criminal behavior, they are referred to as criminogenic needs (Simourd & Malcolm, 1998; Simourd, 2004).

Dynamic risk assessments should be used in conjunction with a static risk measure because it provides a baseline risk appraisal of the stable factor of the client, whereas the dynamic risk assessment can track changes in risk level over time (Walsh, 1997).

LSI-R's Strengths and Limitations

An offender's total LSI-R scores and scores on its 10 subscales (criminal history, education/ employment, financial, family/marital conditions, accommodation, leisure and recreation, companions, alcohol/drug problem, emotional/personal, and attitude/orientation) not only serve as a basis for correctional classifications in many correctional institutes of the United States and Canada but also provide useful information for case management in correctional counseling. For example, counselors can use the clients' scores on education/employment or other subcategories to decide how to connect available services and resources to meet the client's needs. In addition, the scores are a basis for community supervision for the offenders, determining whether the offender needs to receive an intensive level of supervision (e.g., mostly face-to-face contact per week), medium- or minimum-level supervision, and how the contacts should be conducted (e.g., at the client's home, education or workplace, office contacts, contacts with the client's family member or employer).

Since its conception in 1995 (Andrews & Bonta, 1995), considerable research has been conducted on the LSI-R. The studies have shown that this inventory has the power to predict recidivism and to differentiate among different types of criminals. For example, in the study by Simourd (2004), the LSI-R scores of 129 Canadian federally incarcerated offenders serving a mean sentence length of 5 years were compared to various recidivism criteria during a 15-month follow-up period. The results indicated that the instrument had adequate reliability and predictive validity and was successful in distinguishing recidivists from offenders who did not commit new crimes during this period. Lowenkamp, Holsinger, and Latessa (2001) argued that although the LSI-R failed to consider gender or physical and sexual abuse as risk factors by including such items in the inventory, their study indicated that the LSI-R is as valid (predictive) an instrument for their sample of male offenders as for their sample of female offenders. Additionally, their results show that a history of prior childhood abuse fails to enhance the prediction of recidivism for the offenders. Furthermore, the study by Hollin and Palmer (2003) revealed that scores on LSI-R assessments can differentiate between violent and nonviolent offenders. Using 251 male prisoners in 6 English prisons as the research participants who were assessed with the LSI-R, they found that violent offenders, on the basis of either current or previous convictions, scored significantly higher than the nonviolent prisoners on the 4 LSI-R subscales of criminal history, companions, education and employment, and alcohol and drugs. In addition, those prisoners with a record of violent offenses also produced higher total LSI-R scores, indicating an overall higher risk of recidivism. Nee and Ellis (2005) suggested that LSI-R can also be used with juvenile offenders as a measure of the effectiveness of interventions with them.

Mihailides et al. (2005) argued that although the effectiveness of the LSI-R as a risk assessment tool has been accepted in North America, correctional staff should take into consideration the cultural, forensic, and sociopolitical context in different countries when applying the LSI-R. In their comparative study they used LSI-R data from 254 male and

77 female offenders from 5 prison locations in Australia and Canada to compare the Australian samples with the Canadian samples. They found that both male and female Australian offenders scored higher on the LSI-R than Canadian prisoners. In particular, female Australian offenders scored notably higher on the LSI-R than Canadian females.

Furthermore, when using LSI-R to predict inmate aggression in a forensic psychiatric hospital, Daffern, Ogloff, Ferguson, and Thomson (2005) found only a weak association between the total score of the patients and their aggression. This is probably because the context is different from prisons and the LSI-R does not assess the mental disorders and recent hostility of the patients.

Although current assessment models such as the LSI-R are somewhat effective in predicting the risk for offenders, it should be noted that most classification and assessment instruments were developed for the purpose of correctional management, not for correctional counseling.

These instruments have noticeably overlooked (or lack) items that assess the interaction between the mind and the situation. For example, there is no correctional instrument that measures offenders' distorted social cognitions in relation to their dysfunction (e.g., interpersonal and/or emotional conflicts, dysfunctions in legal, family, employment, education areas). Without any knowledge about the deficient social cognition of correctional clients, the information about needs and risk is incomplete, hampering a correctional staff's effort to engage in intervention and therapeutic treatment. This issue is important because a person's mind or cognitive structures of social entities (the self, others, social situations) and their interactions regulate activities (Fiske & Taylor, 1991), including criminal behavior. People suffer dysfunction in legal, interpersonal, educational, employment, and other areas, not only because they encounter adversity and conflict but also because they are unable to overcome invalidation and frustration with their current cognition of the social reality. In other words, correctional counseling and treatment should focus on discerning how offenders perceive themselves and interactions with others and how they explain their conflicts, as well as their criteria for evaluating situations and their experiences (Sun, 2005).

False Positive, False Negative, and Deception

The phrases *false positive* and *false negative* in correctional assessment were derived from early psychological research on visual perception. In the use of the LSI-R as the instrument to predict offenders' risk and recidivism, false positive refers to cases when offenders have a low risk of reoffending but their scores on the LSI-R put them in the high-risk category. In contrast, false negative designates the opposite situation: Offenders have a low score on the measurement when they are actually a high-risk offender. The two types of tendency exist in other assessment instruments for dividing offenders into low- and high-risk categories. For example, Campbell (2003) argued that relevant ethical standards and practice guidelines obligate psychologists to discern the numerous limits and inaccuracies of their data and therefore the conclusions regarding the use of risk assessments with sex offenders. Both dangers exist. On the one hand, selecting low cutoff scores on a recidivism assessment instrument for sex offenders will maximize its sensitivity, thus resulting in a high frequency of false positive classifications. On the other hand, attempts at maximizing specificity (e.g., using too many items or too much specific information to determine recidivism) may create an undesirable frequency of false negative classifications, thus underestimating the client's potential for reoffending.

An additional problem related to the correctional clients' deception when responding to the LSI-R questions has not been given enough attention. Although the accuracy of some of their answers (such as criminal history and instances of prison aggression) can be verified in the official records, for other items of the LSI-R (such as current drug or alcohol use), the offender may not always tell the truth. According to Benedict and Lanyon (1992), deliberate deception in self-presentation is always an issue in psychological assessment, with assessed clients perhaps faking good or faking bad. Their research on the content of such measures involved 305 incarcerated male offenders and 409 college students. The results showed that for both incarcerated offenders and college students, the faking-bad items involved the endorsement of psychiatric symptoms, whereas the faking-good items involved the endorsement of highly desirable characteristics and the denial of normal human frailties.

Other Tools for Classification and Assessment

Correctional counselors and therapists have applied other instruments or inventories to assess clients' issues of substance abuse, risk, and mental health areas. Some of the instruments are described in the following sections.

Correctional Offender Management Profiling for Alternative Sanctions (COMPAS)

COMPAS is an assessment software package designed to evaluate offender risk and needs factors for placement decisions, offender management, and treatment planning in corrections. The software will automatically calculate and analyze the offender's score in comparison to a relevant sample after his or her information from the official record and interview is inputed into the database. The assessed issues include crime involvement, history of violence, history of noncompliance, criminal associates, substance abuse, financial problems and poverty, occupational and educational success, family crime, high crime neighborhood, boredom and lack of constructive leisure activities, residential instability, social isolation versus social support, criminal attitude, and antisocial personality (Brennan, Dieterich, & Ehret, 2009).

Women's Risk/Needs Assessments

Women's Risk/Needs Assessments (WRNAs) were developed jointly by the National Institute of Corrections (NIC) and the University of Cincinnati (UC), and they have been implemented and tested in several state DOC systems. The WRNAs' unique strengths involve assessing both gender-neutral items (including the items in the LSI-R & COMPAS) and gender-responsive factors for women offenders. These gender-responsive factors, which are predictive of recidivism and appropriate treatment programs for women offenders, include trauma and abuse, unhealthy relationships, parental stress, depression, substance abuse, anger/hostility, poverty, safety, and personal strengths (Salisbury, Van Voorhis, & Spiropoulos, 2009; Van Voorhis, Wright, Salisbury, & Bauman, 2010).

Psychopathy Checklist-Revised

Psychopathy Checklist-Revised (PCL-R) is a useful instrument for assessing offenders' psychopathy (Hare, 2006; Hart and Hare, 1997). Hart and Hare argued that psychopathy is a personality disorder for understanding and predicting criminal conduct. Items in the PCL-R include: (1) interpersonal or affective defects (e.g., glibness or superficial charm, grandiose feelings of self-worth, conning or manipulative behavior, lack of remorse or guilt, shallow affects, callousness or lack of empathy, cruel disregard for the rights of others); (2) social deviance (irresponsibility, parasitic lifestyle, impulsivity or disinhibition, a propensity for predatory behavior and violence); and (3) additional items (e.g., unstable relationships, criminal versatility). They found that offenders achieve higher than average scores on the instrument. Psychopathy is synonymous with *antisocial personality disorder* as defined by the American Psychiatric Association (2000).

Static-99

Static-99 is frequently used for conducting sexual violence risk assessment in legal and correctional contexts (Gentry, Dulmus, & Theriot, 2005). The relevant items include the offender's personal characteristics (never married, age 18–24 years) and criminal history (e.g., previous sexual offenses and nonsexual violence, prior convictions and sentencing records, any prior stranger victims, and male victims). In spite of its popularity, this assessment tool has received many criticisms. For example, a review by Sreenivasan, Weinberger, Frances, & Cusworth-Walker (2010) indicates that the offenders who got the same Static-99 score showed varying sexual recidivism rates, from very low to very high. Static-99 appears insufficient for accurate assessment of risk for sexually violent predatory and dangerous offenders when it is used alone. Streenivasan et al. suggest combining the instrument and clinical judgment as a solution.

Chemical Dependency Instruments

For chemical dependency issues, a survey by Juhnke, Vacc, Curtis, Coll, and Paredes (2003) showed that members of the National Board for Certified Counselors had identified the five most frequently used assessment instruments as: (1) the Substance Abuse Subtle Screening Inventory (SASSI); (2) the Beck Depression Inventory; (3) the Minnesota Multiphasic Personality Inventory-2 (MMPI-2); (4) the Addictions Severity Index (ASI); and (5) the Michigan Alcoholism Screening Test (MAST).

Lifestyle Criminality Screening Form

The Lifestyle Criminality Screening Form was constructed to assess career or lifestyle criminality. It includes subscales measuring the client's irresponsibility, self-indulgence, interpersonal intrusiveness, and social-rule breaking. The irresponsibility subscale includes items such as being irresponsible regarding obligations at school, work, and home. The self-indulgent activities include drug and alcohol abuse, sexual promiscuity, repeated gambling, the wearing of tattoos, and regularly encroaching on the rights and personal dignity of others. Such individuals begin at an early age to habitually violate the rules, norms, and customs of society (Walters, Revella, & Baltrusaitis, 1990).

Assessment Instruments for Juvenile Offenders

Consistency is lacking in selecting and implementing assessment instruments for juvenile offenders. Blanc (2002) noted that a survey of 300 juvenile justice agencies in the United States in 1996 revealed that only 20 agencies in 6 states affirmed an assessment program for juvenile delinquents. Although there is no standard assessment instrument for juvenile justice agencies, most agencies apply assessment instruments that evaluate some or most of the following categories for youth offenders: current and previous offending and problem behaviors (aggressive behavior, drug use, and sexual deviance); family relations and conflict; school performance; peer relations; routine activities; attitudes and values toward deviance and justice; social skills and interpersonal maturity; and physical and mental health status. The purpose of the assessments involves several factors: (1) diagnosing "dangerousness" (an investigation of the criminal personality and the social adaptation of the offender); (2) anticipating the offender's potential for recidivism; (3) the possibility of social integration; and (4) developing a treatment plan.

According to Blanc (2002), the Youth Level of Service/Case Management Inventory (YLS/CMI) developed by Hoge and Andrews (1999) appears to be the most promising instrument for conducting assessments in the juvenile justice system today. It has been gradually implemented in the juvenile justice system of Ontario and other places in Canada. It is a revised version of the LSI-R for adult offenders. In the YLS/CMI, 8 categories of risk/needs are subdivided into 42 items to be rated:

1. Offense history (prior and current offense/dispositions)
2. Family circumstances/parenting
3. Education/employment
4. Peer relations
5. Substance abuse
6. Leisure and recreation
7. Personality and behavior
8. Attitudes/orientation

This instrument allows juvenile counselors not only to obtain a summary score for the youth but also to compare the score with a normative sample of adjudicated adolescents. In addition, the instrument includes evaluating the strengths of the youth and additional factors that are relevant for the adolescent for the choice of placement and developing and implementing a case management plan.

DSM-IV-TR

The fourth edition (with text revision) of the *Diagnostic and Statistical Manual of Mental Disorders (DSM-IV-TR)* published by the American Psychiatric Association in 2000, is indispensable for assessing offenders' psychological conditions and mental disorders in correctional settings. Although the newer version, known as DSM-5, is scheduled for release in May 2013 (Kennedy, 2010), the following discussions are still based on the current version of the manual, the DSM-IV-TR, which describes a multiaxial system with five axes:

- *Axis I*—includes cognitive disorders (e.g., amnesia, dementia), substance-related disorders, schizophrenia and other psychotic disorders, mood disorders (e.g., depression, mania), anxiety disorders (e.g., panic disorder, posttraumatic stress disorders), eating disorders, sleep disorders, and adjustment disorders.

- *Axis II*—includes antisocial personality disorder, obsessive-compulsive personality disorder, borderline personality disorder, and mental retardation.

- *Axis III*—assesses a client's general medical condition, such as diseases of the blood system, nervous system, circulatory system, respiratory system, and digestive system.

- *Axis IV*—evaluates a client's problems with primary support group (e.g., family), social environment (lack or absence of social support, discrimination, adjustment to life-cycle such as retirement, education, occupation, housing, economic problems, problems with access to health care services), and interaction with the legal system.

- *Axis V*—assesses the general functioning of a client on a scale from 0 to 100, with a high score indicating better functioning and a low score poor functioning. For example, a client with a score between 71 and 80 may have some temporary problems with no more than slight impairment in some of his or her life. In contrast, a client with a score between 41 and 50 may experience serious impairment in social, occupational, or school functioning (American Psychiatric Association, 2000).

Limits of the DSM System

Clark, Watson, and Reynolds (1995) made a detailed analysis of the DSM system. The major problem with the manual involves its descriptive approach to mental disorders, emphasizing observed or reported clinical features and symptoms but giving no attention to their underlying causal mechanisms. For the most part, the disorders are not grouped in the manual according to their common causal factors or according to other theoretical grounds. The disorders are instead organized into major categories on the basis of shared symptoms. In order to understand the core of the disorder and to explain the observed variation of the symptoms among individuals with the same diagnosis, therapists must uncover causal mechanisms as the defining features of a disorder. For example, some antidepressant drugs have a similar treatment effect on several disorders (e.g., major depression, bulimia, panic disorder, obsessive-compulsive disorder, and attention-deficit disorder), suggesting that these disorders share a common pathophysiologic underlying cause and that grouping them together under the label of *affective disorder* in the manual is more appropriate. In addition, PTSD (posttraumatic stress disorder) and the adjustment disorders should be put together under a category of stress disorders or *trauma disorders* because stressful events may play a causal role in the development of these conditions.

The second problem is that most of the DSM diagnoses are based on satisfying a certain number of equally important criteria. Because a diagnosis depends upon passing several but not necessarily all of the required criteria, clients with the same diagnosis are likely to be different from one another even in their symptoms.

The third problem is that research shows that nearly all of the Axis I DSM disorders have high concurrent and/or lifetime rates of comorbidity—the simultaneous occurrence of more than one disorder in the same individual. For example, anxiety and eating disorders, antisocial personality disorder and substance abuse, anxiety and depressive disorders tend to co-occur. Polcin (2000) observed that substance-abuse disorder is one of the mental disorders that occurs frequently with other mental dysfunctions. Counseling professionals will inevitably work with clients who have comorbidity in substance-use disorders and other diagnoses. Statistics show that approximately 29% of clients with a current mental health problem also have a history of a substance-use disorder. Clients with a diagnosis of schizophrenia have a 47% lifetime history of substance abuse or dependence.

In short, it is common in clinical settings to find clients who are diagnosed to have both a mental disorder and other types of psychopathology.

Summary

Offender classification and assessment are two related but distinct processes in correctional operations. Classification intends to match offender risk and needs with correctional resources by placing offenders at one of several custody or supervision levels. Subjective classification is based on the subjective judgment of prison officials, whereas objective classification employs standard evaluation instruments that have been proven through research. Although assessment serves as a basis for classification decisions, it is frequently performed for offenders for purposes other than classification.

The Level of Service Inventory-Revised (LSI-R), one of the most frequently used correctional assessment instruments, measures both static and dynamic risk factors. Static factors designate conditions of the offender that have happened in the past and cannot be modified with correctional interventions. Dynamic risk factors are those conditions and attributes of the offender that can be changed by programs, treatment, and other interventions.

When the LSI-R is used as an instrument to predict offenders' risk and recidivism, false positives and negatives may occur. The false positive refers to those cases when offenders actually have a low risk for reoffending but their scores on the LSI-R put them in the high-risk category. The false negative may involve offenders who have a low score on the measurement when they actually are high-risk offenders.

The *Diagnostic and Statistical Manual of Mental Disorders (DSM-IV-TR)*, a reference published by the American Psychiatric Association, is used by correctional counselors to assess offenders' psychological conditions and mental disorders in correctional settings.

Key Terms

Assessment

Classification

Diagnostic and Statistical Manual of Mental Disorders (DSM-IV-TR)

Dynamic risk factors

False positive and false negative

Level of Service Inventory-Revised (LSI-R)

Objective classification

Psychopathy Checklist-Revised (PCL-R)

Static risk factors

Subjective classification

Discussion Questions

1. Describe the five types of classification.
2. In addition to the items listed in the LSI-R, what other items do you think correctional assessment needs to include? Why?
3. When you use the LSI-R to assess an offender, how do you reduce the errors resulting from false positives and false negatives?

References

American Psychiatric Association. (2000). *Diagnostic and statistical manual of mental disorders* (4th ed., text revision). Washington, DC: Author.

Andrews, D. A., & Bonta, J. (1995). *The Level of Service Inventory-Revised*. Toronto, Canada: Multi-Health Systems.

Andrews, D. A., & Bonta, J. (2006). *The psychology of criminal conduct* (4th ed.). Newark, NJ: LexisNexis/ Matthew Bender.

Andrews, D. A., & Bonta, J. (2010). Rehabilitating criminal justice policy and practice. *Psychology, Public Policy, and Law, 16*, 39–55. doi:10.1037/a0018362

Austin, J. (2003). *Findings in prison classification and risk assessment.* Washington, DC: National Institute of Corrections.

Benedict, L. W., & Lanyon, R. I. (1992). An analysis of deceptiveness: Incarcerated prisoners. *Journal of Addictions and Offender Counseling, 13*, 23–31.

Blanc, M. L. (2002). Review of clinical assessment strategies and instruments for adolescent offenders. In R. R. Corrado, R. H. Roesch, D. Stephen, & J. K. Gierowski (Eds.), *Multi-problem violent youth: A foundation for comparative research on needs, interventions and outcomes* (pp. 171–190). Amsterdam, Netherlands: IOS Press.

Bonta, J. (2002). Offender risk assessment: Guidelines for selection and use. *Criminal Justice and Behavior, 29*, 355–379.

Brennan, T., Dieterich, W., & Ehret, B. (2009). Evaluating the predictive validity of the COMPAS risk and needs assessment system. *Criminal Justice and Behavior, 36*, 21–40. doi:10.1177/0093854808326545.

Campbell, T. W. (2003). Sex offenders and actuarial risk assessments: Ethical considerations. *Behavioral Sciences and the Law, 21*, 269–279.

Clark, L. A., Watson, D., & Reynolds, S. (1995). DSM-IV. *Annual Review of Psychology, 46*, 121–153.

Daffern, M., Ogloff, J. R. P., Ferguson, M., & Thomson, L. (2005). Assessing risk for aggression in a forensic psychiatric hospital using the Level of Service Inventory-Revised: Screening Version. *International Journal of Forensic Mental Health, 4*, 201–206.

Fiske, S. T., & Taylor, S. (1991). *Social cognition* (2nd ed.). New York, NY: McGraw-Hill.

Gaines, L. K., & Miller, R. L. (2003). *Criminal justice in action* (2nd ed.). Scarborough, Ontario: Wadsworth.

Gentry, A. L., Dulmus, C. N., & Theriot, M. T. (2005). Comparing sex offender risk classification using the Static-99 and LSI-R assessment instruments. *Research on Social Work Practice, 15*, 557–563. doi:10.1177/1049731505275869

Hare, R. D. (2006). Psychopathy: A clinical and forensic overview. *Psychiatric Clinics of North America, 29*, 709–724.

Hart, S. D., & Hare, R. D. (1997). Psychopathy: Assessment and association with criminal conduct. In D. M. Stoff, J. Breiling, & J. D. Maser (Eds.), *Handbook of antisocial behavior* (pp. 22–35). Hoboken, NJ: Wiley.

Hoge, R. D., & Andrews, D. A. (1999). *The youth level of service/case management inventory and manual* (revised). Ottawa, Ontario: Carleton University, Department of Psychology.

Hollin, C. R., & Palmer, E. J. (2003). Level of Service Inventory—Revised profiles of violent and non-violent prisoners. *Journal of Interpersonal Violence, 18*, 1075–1086.

Juhnke, G. A., Vacc, N. A., Curtis, R. C., Coll, K. M., & Paredes, D. M. (2003). Assessment instruments used by addictions counselors. *Journal of Addictions and Offender Counseling, 23*, 66–72.

Kennedy, G. J. (2010). Proposed revisions for the diagnostic categories of dementia in the DSM-5. *Primary Psychiatry, 17*, 26–28.

Lauren, R. J. (1997). *Positive approaches to corrections: Research, policy, and practice.* Lanham, MD: American Correctional Association.

Lowenkamp, C. T., Holsinger, A. M., & Latessa, E. J. (2001). Risk/need assessment, offender classification, and the role of childhood abuse. *Criminal Justice and Behavior, 28*, 543–563.

Mihailides, S., Jude, B., & Van den Bossche, E. (2005). The LSI-R in an Australian setting: Implications for risk/needs decision-making in forensic contexts. *Psychiatry, Psychology, and Law, 12*, 207–217.

Nee, C., & Ellis, T. (2005). Treating offending children: What works? *Legal and Criminological Psychology, 10*, 133–148.

Polcin, D. L. (2000). Professional counseling versus specialized programs for alcohol and drug abuse treatment. *Journal of Addictions and Offender Counseling, 21*, 2–11.

Salisbury, E. J., Van Voorhis, P., & Spiropoulos, G. V. (2009). The predictive validity of a gender-responsive needs assessment: An exploratory study. *Crime & Delinquency, 55*, 550–585.

Schmalleger, F., & Smykla, J. O. (2001). *Corrections in the 21st century*. New York, NY: McGraw-Hill.

Simourd, D. J. (2004). Use of dynamic risk/need assessment instruments among long-term incarcerated offenders. *Criminal Justice and Behavior, 31*, 306–323.

Simourd, D. J., & Malcolm, P. B. (1998). Reliability and validity of the Level of Service Inventory—Revised among federally incarcerated sex offenders. *Journal of Interpersonal Violence, 3*, 261–274.

Sreenivasan, S., Weinberger, L. E., Frances, A., & Cusworth-Walker, S. (2010). Alice in actuarial-land: Through the looking glass of changing Static-99 norms. *Journal of the American Academy of Psychiatry and the Law, 38*, 400–406.

Sun, K. (2005, March). *The importance of understanding offender cognitive distortions in correctional assessments*. Paper presented at the annual meeting of the Academy of Criminal Justice Sciences, Chicago, IL.

Van Voorhis, P., Wright, E. M., Salisbury, E., & Bauman, A. (2010). Women's risk factors and their contributions to existing risk/needs assessment: The current status of a gender-responsive supplement. *Criminal Justice and Behavior, 37*, 261–288.

Walsh, A. (1997). *Correctional assessment, casework, and counseling* (2nd ed.). Lanham, MD: American Correctional Association.

Walters, G. D., Revella, L., & Baltrusaitis, W. J. (1990). Predicting parole/probation outcome with the aid of the lifestyle criminality screening form. *Psychological Assessment, 2*, 313–316.

Chapter 3

Meanings of the Evidence in Evidence-Based Correctional Counseling

In the last decade, evidence-based practice (EBP) has been adopted as a guideline for administering services in the criminal justice and mental health fields (Crime and Justice Institute and Guevara, Loeffler-Cobia, Rhyne, & Sachwald, 2010; "Evidence-Based Practice in Psychology," 2006). However, the meaning of the evidence or "what works" varies with different agencies and professions that have diverse roles, missions, trainings, and focuses in the society. Although correctional counselors, social workers, or psychologists who work with criminal justice clients are guided by policies in the criminal justice systems, they are also affiliated with the mental health professions. Therefore, they may need to understand and implement EBP in correctional counseling by considering one or several perspectives. This chapter examines four different yet related positions regarding the meaning of *evidence* in evidence-based correctional counseling.

Reducing Recidivism

The first position argues that correctional counseling aims to reduce **recidivism**. There seems to be considerable agreement among the general public and a substantial number of criminal-justice policymakers about the goal of correctional counseling, which is public protection. Every correctional counseling activity is designed to have a desirable impact on recidivism, either eliminating or at least reducing it, by targeting malleable criminogenic offender characteristics. Therefore, the success of correctional counseling or treatment is defined by reducing reoffending; failure is defined by the client's recidivism, as measured by the criteria of the official record (Gendreau, Goggin, French, & Smith, 2006; Latessa, Cullen, & Gendreau, 2002).

Although successful correctional counseling will eventually enable offenders to improve their many relationships (including conflicts with the legal system) and to eradicate their chances of reoffending, the proposition of using recidivism as the measurement of effective correctional counseling is problematic. This is because crime prevention and control are the mission and responsibility of the *whole* correctional system and the whole criminal justice system, or more broadly, the *whole* society. Many factors influence criminal behavior—ranging from the operation of the criminal justice system to family, school, and childhood experiences; from employment, education, media violence, and subculture issues to cognitive structures and processes, values, and belief systems. Given that correctional counselors are typically assigned a heavy caseload (it is not unusual for correctional counselors to have 100 or more clients; see Schrink & Hamm, 1989), it is unfair and inaccurate to evaluate the success or failure of correctional counseling on offenders' recidivism.

Reducing Reoffending by Following Evidence-Based Principles

The second position also emphasizes reducing offender risk and consequently preventing new crime and improving public safety, but it suggests achieving these goals by implementing eight core principles regarding risk reduction (Crime and Justice Institute & Guevara et al., 2010):

1. Apply empirically valid and reliable instruments to assess an offender's risk (likelihood of reoffense) and needs and use the information as the basis for treatment and intervention for risk reduction.

2. Activate an offender's intrinsic motivation and individual reasons for change by helping him or her identify the discrepancy between his or her personal goals and current dysfunctional conditions.

3. Target high-risk offenders and individual criminogenic needs by allocating resources, prioritizing supervision, and integrating treatment into the sanction requirements.

4. Employ cognitive behavioral therapies to both deter criminal thinking/behavior and reinforce new cognitive skills and prosocial behaviors.

5. Emphasize rewarding positive and compliant behavior over punishing non-compliant or negative behavior.

6. Use prosocial forces, such as family, friends, and the community to help the offender follow supervision requirements and practice self-regulation.

7. Collect relevant data on correctional practices.

8. Use data-based feedback to guide the operation of correctional systems.

These recommendations, however, are intended to create and maintain an evidence-based community correctional organization or system. They are not developed for the practice of correctional counseling. In addition, the above principles have not included another evidence-based practice in the counseling profession: the therapeutic alliance or relationship, which has been found to strongly increase better outcomes for the client. The therapeutic alliance is defined as a collaborative relationship characterized by three primary components: (1) agreement between the counselor and the client on the goals of intervention; (2) a joint effort in developing and completing the goals; and (3) therapeutic values (e.g., trust, respect, acceptance, empathy, and support) (see Matthews & Hubbard, 2007).

Evidence-Based Practice in Psychology

According to the American Psychological Association (see "Evidence-Based Practice in Psychology," 2006), the evidence-based practice in psychology consists of integrating three aspects of treatment: (1) the best available research, (2) clinical expertise, and (3) patient (client)-related variables.

The best available research includes multiple types of empirically-supported principles and research evidence in assessment, case formulation, therapeutic relationship, treatment, and other interventions that benefit valid psychological practice. For a specific type of intervention, its effectiveness is based on satisfying two requirements: treatment efficacy (i.e., the systematic and scientific appraisal of whether a treatment produces the desired result) and clinical utility of the intervention (i.e., its applicability and suitability in the specific setting, as well as its generalizability in other environments). For example, cognitive behavioral therapy may be effective in decreasing depressive symptoms both in community and in prison, thus it has the applicability and suitability in specific and generalized settings. However, not all treatment models work well with all clients in all environments.

Clinical expertise, which comprises several areas of competency, increases the therapist's ability to integrate and apply scientific research, training, interpersonal expertise, self-reflection, resources, and knowledge of individual and cultural differences in assessment, diagnostic judgment, treatment planning, referrals, clinical decision making, and selecting interventions, thus creating the highest probability of achieving the goals of therapy. Clinical expertise is important in evidence-based practice because experts and novices differ in their cognitive capacity to recognize and understand meaningful patterns of complex tasks in relation to available research and in how to adapt to new situations and challenges.

Patient-related variables, which strongly influence the effectiveness of clinical interventions, include mental health or counseling issues (e.g. symptoms, disorders, or dysfunctional behavior), developmental stage (e.g., age, disability, and life stage), sociocultural factors (e.g., gender, ethnicity, culture, social class, religion, sexual orientation), environmental stressors (e.g., unemployment, family conflict, life events), and personal beliefs, preferences, and experiences about a specific treatment and its outcomes.

Developing More Accurate Social Cognition

The fourth position maintains that correctional counseling is intended to help offenders balance their important relationships, and understand and overcome their internal and external conflicts through developing more accurate social cognitions and understanding about themselves and others as well as the patterns governing their interactions (Schrink & Hamm, 1989; Sun, 2005). This argument is supported by two premises.

The first premise is the correctional client's need for new cognitive abilities to understand and handle conflicts and dysfunctions in interpersonal, employment, educational, mental health and other areas that keep them from functioning more effectively in the present environment, including living a crime-free life. Like other people, correctional clients have **two basic psychological needs**: mental peace and interpersonal harmony. It is important to see offenders as individuals who seek to understand and solve their problems and to balance their mental and interpersonal relationships. The issue of mental peace includes such topics as how to create and maintain inner tranquility, how to experience healing and joy, and how to unlearn past emotional hurts and extricate oneself from fear, anxiety, and depression. The issue of interpersonal harmony covers such issues as how to obtain and maintain love and good relationships, improve communication, increase cooperation, create a better future and achieve success, and avoid or overcome human discord, tribulation, and calamity.

Offenders are most likely to seek and accept counseling for difficulties relating to crises that arise in their daily lives in the correctional section (Schrink & Hamm, 1989). Offenders have many immediate conflicts to deal with, including a number of crises and issues that are unique to the prison environment. They include anger management, interpersonal conflict resolution, admission to an educational program, obtaining a prison job or transferring to a more suitable living unit, mental health concerns, homosexual panic and temptation, adjustment disorders and depression as a result of losing freedom of movement and being thrust into a threatening environment. In addition, inmates may suffer anxiety if their family members experience severe illness or other types of crises. Because clients' goals, expectations, and beliefs regarding their problems, the available services, and the results of counseling are likely to influence the helping process (Gambrill, 1997), the focus of correctional counseling is to assist the clients in dealing with their issues.

The second premise is that offenders' crimes and criminal behavior are just symptoms of dysfunctions that are rooted in their distorted cognitions about themselves, others, the environment, and the patterns that regulate their conflict-ridden interactions. Although their criminal conviction is the official reason that they enter the correctional system, counseling efforts that focus only on their crimes miss the causal factors that led to their violation of the law. The most important causal factor among those variables that can be addressed by correctional counseling involves the client's distorted social cognition for evaluating, explaining, and adjusting personal experiences and actions. It is offenders' cognitions and interpretations that mediate how they understand and explain conflicts and whether they react in a prosocial or criminal way (Sun, 2005). Offenders' antisocial behavior is regulated by their antisocial personality, which can be defined as a set of stable cognitive or knowledge structures that individuals use to interpret events in their social world and guide their behavior (Anderson & Bushman, 2002). There are three relevant subtypes of cognitive structures: (1) **perceptual schemas**, which are used to identify everyday objects (chair, person) or social events (positive or negative interpersonal communications); (2) **person schemas**, which include cognitions about a particular person or groups of people; and (3) **event scripts**, which hold information about how people act in varying situations.

The process of how the offenders' distorted cognitions regulate their antisocial activities is the central concern of correctional counseling. Their cognition of social reality includes mental representations of thoughts, feelings, and actions as well as the consequences of those actions for self and others. It also includes higher-order cognitive processes (or perceived patterns and standards) that govern their internal and external relations (relations with others and with various systems, such as the justice apparatus, and social, educational, employment, and community agencies). Offenders use their knowledge structures to guide perception, interpretation, appraisals, attributions, decision making, action, and responses to the social (and physical) environment.

Offenders commit violent acts and other illegal activities because their perceived standards are based on a distorted reality that allows them to rationalize and justify their thinking and actions so that they are not in conflict with normal moral standards (Sun, 2006; Ward, 2000). For example, common justifications for violence include the excuse that the aggression is for the good of the self, others, or society. These justifications can be seen at work in various situations, from a parent's child abuse to war violence that kills innocent people. Dehumanizing the victim is another form of distorted cognition that emphasizes that a potential victim is a member of an out-group or is an enemy that has no human qualities and that the normal moral standard is inapplicable to him or her (Anderson & Bushman, 2002). Other justifications include denials of injury to the victim or responsibility for the act. Although the justification methods of offenders were first examined in criminological research (Minor, 1981) as the offender's techniques of neutralization, these concepts have become a focus of social cognition research known as *attribution theories.*

Research in social cognition has shown that **self-serving bias** tends to characterize offenders' explanations for their actions (Bodenhausen, Macrae, & Hugenberg, 2003; Fiske & Taylor, 1991). This includes rationalizing their actions and making them desirable and reasonable from the agent's viewpoint (Davidson, 1990).

A good counseling model must explain two factors: (1) how conflicts influence offenders' actions and behavior; and (2) how the mind and conflict interact to cause criminal behavior. Therefore, understanding offenders' cognitions (including how they evaluate and interpret social stimuli and react to them, and how they explain and understand their own experience, dysfunction, and need areas) is vital for assessing, evaluating, and performing interventions for the clients. In short, counselors should see offenders not only as criminals or patients who need to be corrected or treated but also as individuals who use their cognitions to understand and explain their crimes, mental disorders, and/or need areas. Their dysfunction shapes the limited or distorted social cognition that they use to make sense of their experience. Any counseling efforts that fail to help them understand their experiences cannot have lasting benefits on their functioning.

Summary

Evidence-based practice (EBP) has become a guideline for administering services in the criminal justice and mental health fields. However, the meaning of the evidence varies with different agencies and professions. This chapter examined four different yet related positions regarding the meaning of the evidence in evidence-based correctional counseling, including: (1) reducing recidivism, (2) reducing reoffending by following evidence-based core principles, (3) evidence-based practice in psychology (integrating the best available research, clinical expertise, and patient-related variables), and (4) developing more accurate social cognition for the client.

Key Terms

Recidivism

Self-serving bias

Two basic psychological needs

Discussion Questions

1. This chapter describes four positions regarding the meaning of the evidence in correctional counseling. Which is your position? Why?

2. What are the two basic psychological needs for correctional clients?

References

Anderson, C. A., & Bushman, B. J. (2002). Human aggression? *Annual Review of Psychology, 53,* 27–51.

Bodenhausen, G. V., Macrae, C. N., & Hugenberg, K. (2003). Social cognition. In T. Millon & M. J. Lerner (Eds.), *Handbook of psychology* (Vol. 5, pp. 257–282). Hoboken, NJ: Wiley.

Crime and Justice Institute and Guevara, M., Loeffler-Cobia, J., Rhyne, C., & Sachwald, J. (2010). *Putting the pieces together: Practical strategies for implementing evidence based practices.* Washington, DC: National Institute of Corrections.

Davidson, D. (1990). Paradoxes of irrationality. In P. K. Moser (Ed.), *Rationality in action: Contemporary approaches* (pp. 449–464). New York, NY: Cambridge University Press.

Evidence-based practice in psychology. (2006). *American Psychologist, 61,* 271–285. doi:10.1037/0003-066X.61.4.271

Fiske, S. T., & Taylor, S. (1991). *Social cognition* (2nd ed.). New York, NY: McGraw-Hill.

Gambrill, E. (1997). *Social work practice: A critical thinker's guide.* New York, NY: Oxford University Press.

Gendreau, P., Goggin, C., French, S., & Smith, P. (2006). Practicing psychology in correctional settings. In I. B. Weiner & A. K. Hess (Eds.), *The handbook of forensic psychology* (3rd ed., pp. 722–750). Hoboken, NJ: Wiley.

Latessa, E. J., Cullen, F. T., & Gendreau, P. (2002). Beyond correctional quackery—Professionalism and the possibility of effective treatment. *Federal Probation, 66,* 3–49.

Matthews, B., & Hubbard, D. (2007). The helping alliance in juvenile probation: The missing element in the "what works" literature. *Journal of Offender Rehabilitation, 45,* 105–122. doi:10.1300/J076v45n01_09

Minor, W. W. (1981). The neutralization of criminal offense. *Criminology, 18,* 103–120.

Schrink, J., & Hamm, M. S. (1989). Misconceptions concerning correctional counseling. *Journal of Offender Counseling Services and Rehabilitation, 14,* 133–147.

Sun, K. (2005, May). *Anxiety reduction, interaction schemas, and negative cognitions about the self.* Poster session presented at the annual meeting of the American Psychological Society, Los Angeles, CA.

Sun, K. (2006). The legal definition of hate crime and the hate offender's distorted cognition. *Issues in Mental Health Nursing, 27,* 597–604.

Ward, T. (2000). Sexual offenders' cognitive distortions as implicit theories. *Aggression and Violent Behavior, 5,* 491–507.

Chapter 4

Criminological Theories and Their Relevance to Correctional Counseling

All theories and models of correctional counseling attempt to identify the basic components of mental structures and processes. They also help to explain how such mental mechanisms instigate dysfunction or sustain healthy functions. The research that has influenced correctional assessment and interventions as well as the counseling and management of correctional clients includes not only the conventional psychological models in counseling but also some sociological and criminological theories about criminal behavior. These models can help counselors understand not only how some dysfunctional environmental and learning factors are responsible for initiating criminal behavior, but also how correctional interventions may help reduce recidivism by minimizing crime-prone social conditions. This chapter will examine some of the most relevant criminological theories for correctional counseling and management.

Cultural Deviance Theories

Cultural deviance theories in criminology consist of three models: Social disorganization theory, differential association theory, and culture conflict theory. All the theories dwell on the postulate that individuals learn to become criminals through cultural or group environments where they are socialized (Adler, Mueller, & Laufer, 2007). Only the first two theories are introduced here because culture conflict theory has little influence on correctional counseling.

Social Disorganization Theory

Social disorganization theory was proposed by Shaw and McKay (1942), who rejected the idea that criminal conduct is genetically inherited or can be traced to universal antisocial impulses. They also postulated that criminal acts are learned beliefs that view crime as an appropriate response to social conditions. Criminals are nothing more than social individuals who are behaving in accordance with the values of their particular group, neighborhood, or community. Their research findings in Chicago's dysfunctional neighborhoods supported the social disorganization model. In addition, this theory also pioneered another criminological theory—subculture theory. *Subculture* is defined as a segment of society that holds norms, values, and beliefs contradictory to or deviating from those of the dominant culture (Adler, Mueller, & Laufer, 2007).

Differential Association Theory

This model was formulated by Edwin H. Sutherland (1947). It represents one of the earliest efforts in criminology to explain criminal behavior in a cultural context from the perspective of a learning theory.

The basic postulates of the theory can be condensed into five points:

1. Criminal behavior is learned, as is any noncriminal behavior. Criminal behavior is not explained by general human needs and values (e.g., the need for more money or for social recognition), because noncriminal behavior is an expression of the same needs and values.

2. Criminal behavior is learned in the process of communicating and interacting with others. This learning occurs particularly in intimate personal groups.

3. Learned criminal behavior involves not only the methods of committing crime but also crime-related motives, rationalization, and attitudes.

4. Learned criminal behavior may not become actualized until a particular mental process takes place. The process that makes a person commit delinquent or criminal acts involves an excess of attitudes favorable to the violation of law over attitudes or beliefs unfavorable to the violation of law. In other words, a person not only learns criminal behavior but also learns to see law violation as favorable.

5. The process that results in criminal behavior can be quantified. There are varying degrees of differential association for different people. Namely, those with more frequent learning opportunities, longer duration, priority (earlier exposure to the methods of committing crime as well as crime-related attitudes and rationalization), and more intensive learning are more likely than others to become criminals or delinquents.

The limitations of social disorganization theory and differential association theory include the abstruseness of both models in explaining why the majority of people who grow up in subcultural environments do not become criminals. In addition, they have difficulty elucidating what makes some individuals adopt favorable attitudes to violation of the law and have difficulties unlearning criminal behavior, motives, and methods.

Life-Course-Persistent Versus Adolescence-Limited Juvenile Offenders

Terrie E. Moffitt (1997) developed a unique explanation for juvenile delinquency. According to this model, there are two types of juvenile delinquents: (1) life-course-persistent offenders, and (2) adolescence-limited offenders. The theory suggests that life-course-persistent antisocial individuals are persistent and pathological but there are relatively few of them, whereas adolescence-limited individuals are widespread and relatively transient.

Life-course-persistent juvenile offenders have the following characteristics:

1. They engage in antisocial behavior at every stage of life. They may bite and hit others at age 4 years and steal at age 10. When they reach adulthood, they may have accumulated a long criminal record, including robbery, rape, aggravated assault, and other violent crimes. From early on, they already show impulsiveness, poor social skills, antipathy for others, aggressiveness, below-average interpersonal skills, poor academic performance, and resentment toward school rules and regulations. Other characteristics of life-course-persistent persons include relative detachment from their family of origin and the desire to make their own rules.

2. Although they may suffer from neuropsychological deficits (such as brain injuries and poor prenatal nutrition), it is the dysfunctional social interaction between problem children and problem parents that sustains their antisocial behavior. They carry one of the following two types of interaction with environments: (1) *reactive interaction*, which includes misconstruing nonaggressive interactions of others as actions with aggressive intention; and (2) *proactive interaction*, which refers to selecting or creating environments that support their deviant or criminal lifestyles.

3. Examining the sequence of their delinquent or criminal behavior from childhood to adulthood may show either of two characteristics: (1) *cumulative continuity*, which suggests that the offender's early delinquent behavior facilitates and aggravates later deviant behavior and makes it more serious; and (2) *contemporary continuity*, which indicates that the offender continues to carry into adulthood the same underlying traits (e.g., poor impulse control or violent temper) that got him or her into trouble as a child.

Adolescence-limited juvenile offenders show different behavioral patterns:

1. They are involved in crime temporarily in adolescence, and they do not maintain their delinquent behavior into adulthood.

2. They have many alternatives to criminal activities. They already have adequate social skills, a record of average or better academic achievement, adaptable capacities, and positive family environments.

3. Unlike the life-course-persistent juvenile offenders who have delinquent peers, do not have a law-abiding parent, and lack attachment to prosocial institutions (school, church, or community organizations), adolescence-limited persons have the ability to desist from crime because they have cognitive skills and capacities, positive social environments, and conflict-free, supportive family settings. This model reminds correctional counselors that they need to differentiate between the two types of juvenile offenders when performing assessments and interventions.

Social Control Theory

Social control theory was proposed by Hirschi (1969) and focuses on what keeps people from committing crimes rather than concentrating on the factors or conditions that produce crime. Like early control theories that assume that everyone pursues self-interest and has the tendency to engage in deviant or criminal behavior (see Miller, Schreck, & Tewksbury, 2006), it contends that most people live a law-abiding life not because of their immunity from deviant motivation but because they operate in strong socially controled environments. This theory asks such questions as "Why don't most people commit crimes?" and "What are the characteristics of nonoffenders?" The answer to such questions is that people do not commit crime because they are influenced by four strong social bonds: (1) *attachment*, which refers to affective or emotional ties to other people; (2) *commitment*, which refers to conventional goals and actions (e.g., having a conventional job, family, and lifestyle) that support and enhance conformity; (3) *involvement*, which refers to time spent on engaging in normal and crime-free activities (e.g., watching TV, playing sports); and (4) *belief*, which is related to having a law-abiding attitude—the extent to which an individual believes that he or she should obey the norms and rules of society.

Social control theory assists correctional intervention and management in at least three ways:

1. It serves as a theoretical source for routine activity theory. According to this theory, three situational elements are necessary for committing a criminal act: (1) a potential criminal, (2) a suitable target, and (3) the absence of a capable guardian against crime—for example, a person, protection device, or specific situation (Cohen, Felson, & Land, 1979). Routine activity theory helps guide correctional management by suggesting how to monitor offenders in community corrections.

2. It influences the formulation of correctional assessment instruments. For example, some items of the LSI-R (Level of Service Inventory-Revised), such as offenders' leisure-time activities, attitude toward conventions, and relationships with noncriminal family members and friends or acquaintances are based on, at least in part, the central ideas of the four types of social bond specified by social control theory.

3. It can be used to develop specific interventions for reducing recidivism. For example, the study by Berg and Huebner (2011) shows that positive family ties

not only help procure and maintain stable employment for ex-prisoners but also serve as a buffer against reoffending by offering emotional support and acceptance and monitoring behavior. Family ties are also found to mediate how reentering offenders' drug addictions influence their chance of recidivism. Specifically, drug addiction increases their involvement with new offenses by jeopardizing their family relationships and stable employment (Huebner & Berg, 2011).

Labeling Theory

Becker's (1963**) labeling theory** is concerned more with the stigmatizing effects of the reactions of criminal justice officials to offenders than the process of interaction. This model assumes that delinquents and criminals are basically "normal people" who are initially involved in illegal or deviant acts by chance or as a part of the developmental process. However, they become real criminals after they are labeled as offenders by police, judges, and other criminal justice personnel, and they internalize the stigma. In summary, deviance is not a quality of the act the person commits but rather a consequence of the reactions of criminal justice authorities to an "offender."

Although today's political atmosphere has shifted, the influence of the labeling theory on correctional management can still be felt in areas involving *diversion*—a process that tries to rehabilitate offenders, to avoid criminal records for them, to save tax dollars, and to provide service to the community. It is a form of pretrial release program. Offenders can be diverted away from the criminal justice system at the stage of arrest, prosecution (pretrial diversion), or jail incarceration before trial. Diversion programs are often created for special groups of offenders, but never for sex offenders (Clear & Dammer, 2003).

Strain Theory

Two strain theories have been described by researchers.

The **original strain theory** was proposed by Merton (1938). He argued that both lower- and middle-class people share in the American dream and value consensus. However, lower-class people do not have a legal way to achieve their goal, or their goal of monetary success does not match the legitimate opportunities available to them. Criminal behavior is generated from the lower classes out of frustration with their legitimate aspirations combined with limited channels.

The **revised strain theory** was developed by Agnew (1999). He maintained that there are three major sources of strain:

1. The failure to achieve positively valued goals as a result of one of the three disjunctions between what one wants and the actual outcomes. They involve the disparity between aspirations and achievement, between expectations and achievement, and between the perception of just/fair outcomes and actual outcomes.

2. The loss of something good or the removal of positively valued stimuli (e.g., job loss).

3. The presentation of negative stimuli such as bad or abusive relationships.

According to Agnew (1999), strain is a necessary condition for an individual to engage in delinquent or criminal behavior. The likelihood of a person's responding to strain by engaging in criminal activities is mediated by individual factors such as his or her coping strategies. Although some individuals may resort to criminal activities to alleviate their strain, others may adopt coping strategies for strain that do not lead to criminal behavior. These strategies include cognitively minimizing the importance of adversity and maximizing positive outcomes, or accepting the responsibility for adversity. The relevant adaptive emotional coping strategies may include meditation and using biofeedback.

The Relevance of Strain Theories for Correctional Counseling

Strain theories have influenced correctional assessment items such as employment and education. Correctional staff must evaluate a client's needs in these areas because a lack of employment and education increases the tendency to engage in criminal activities by blocking the person from reaching socially valuable goals.

However, strain theories may explain some property crimes (burglary, robbery, larceny, motor vehicle theft, etc.) but they have difficulty accounting for violent crimes and other offenses (e.g., white collar crime) that are not directly related to frustrations in reaching the American dream. In addition, as a sociologically based model, strain theories are rudimentary in dealing with cognitive and emotional coping strategies instigated by mental strain and conflict.

Situational Factors and Criminal Behavior

Some research has examined how situational factors and contexts trigger aggression, violence, or other criminal activities. *Human aggression* can be defined as any behavior directed toward another individual that is carried out with the mental state (intent, negligence, or recklessness) to cause harm (Anderson & Bushman, 2002). Situational factors include any important features of the situation, such as provocation or an aggressive cue. Like personal factors, situational factors influence aggression by influencing the offender's cognition, affect, and arousal.

Understanding situational factors helps correctional counselors understand why clients are involved in crime and how to assist them in recognizing dangerous cues so that they can actively avoid these triggering conditions.

Deindividuation is a focus of social psychological research that refers to the crime-prone mental state created by the belief that a person's illegal or deviant behavior cannot be identified in a situation either because others are doing the same thing or because the self cannot be recognized in a setting that generates anonymity (Zimbardo, 1970). This phenomenon is associated with antisocial or violent behavior because individuals who experience deindividuation tend to lose personal responsibility for their actions and are less concerned about the consequences. This phenomenon may explain why normally nonviolent and law-abiding individuals are capable of violence, intolerance, and cruelty in mob situations. One of the reasons that youth offenders are more violent in a gang than as individuals is because juvenile or criminal gangs create a sense of deindividuation by alleviating potential offenders' self-control over their behavior, making them believe that it is group membership rather than individual characteristics that is responsible for the offense (Sun, 1993).

Anderson and Bushman (2002) have identified other significant crime-triggering situational factors:

1. **Aggressive cues:** Objects such as tools that can activate aggression-related thoughts are categorized as aggressive cues. For instance, it was found that the mere presence of guns (versus sports items) enhanced the aggressive behavior of angered research participants. Additionally, pictures of weapons and words related to weapons, as well as exposure to violence through television, movies, or video games, also appear to automatically generate aggressive thoughts.

2. **Provocation:** Interpersonal provocation is regarded as the most important single source of interpersonal violence. The three typical interpersonal provocations include (1) insult, rudeness, and other forms of verbal aggression or nonverbal hostility; (2) physical aggression; and (3) interference with attempts to reach an important goal. Workplace violence, aggression, and bullying either involve or are produced by these provocations.

3. **Frustration:** The blocking of a goal results in frustration. In correctional settings, offenders may either experience *internal blockage* (they have limited or inadequate skills or capacities to reach such goals as obtaining GED certificate or employment) or *external obstructions*, which may be caused by others' interference or the unavailability of positive support or resources. Individuals who experience frustration tend to engage in aggression against a person who did not cause the initial frustration and who was not responsible for the failure to reach the goals. This phenomenon is known as *displaced aggression*.

4. **Physical aversive conditions:** The experiencing of physical aversive conditions such as hot temperatures, loud noises, smoke, and unpleasant odors increase aggression by producing pain and discomfort and leading to feelings of repulsion.

5. **Drugs:** The direct correlation between various drugs such as alcohol and caffeine and violent crime has been well documented. However, this effect appears to be indirect rather than direct, interacting with other situational cues (e.g., provocation) and psychological mechanisms.

Summary

Several criminological and sociological models have influenced correctional counseling. According to social disorganization theory, criminals are nothing more than social individuals who are behaving in accordance with the values and norms of their particular group or subculture. Subculture is defined as a segment of the society that holds norms, values, and beliefs contradictory to the dominant culture of the society.

Differential association theory suggests that criminal behavior is learned in the process of communication and interacting with others, particularly within intimate personal groups.

Another model has identified two types of juvenile delinquents. Life-course-persistent juvenile offenders are chronic and persistent delinquents whereas adolescence-limited juvenile offenders are relatively transient youth offenders who already have adequate social skills and academic achievement as well as positive family environments.

Social control theory maintains that individuals do not commit crime because of four strong social bonds: (1) attachment, (2) commitment, (3) involvement, and (4) belief.

Labeling theory assumes that individuals become criminals due to the negative effects of labeling by police, judges, and the criminal justice process.

The original strain theory suggests that criminal behavior results from the combination of legitimate goals and limited means for lower-class individuals. The revised strain theory argues that strain is generated by the failure to achieve positively valued goals, the loss of something good, or the presentation of negative stimuli such as bad or abusive relationships.

Various situational factors can trigger aggression, violence, or other criminal activities. They include deindividuation, aggressive cues, provocation, frustration, physical aversive conditions, and drugs.

Key Terms

Adolescence-limited juvenile offenders

Aggressive cues

Cultural deviance theories

Deindividuation

Differential association theory

Diversion

Labeling theory

Life-course-persistent juvenile offenders

Original strain theory

Revised strain theory

Routine activity theory

Social control theory

Social disorganization theory

Strain theory

Discussion Questions

1. What are the differences between social disorganization theory and social control theory? Do they also share similar assumptions?

2. What are the advantages and limitations of diversion?

References

Adler, F., Mueller, G. O. W., & Laufer, W. S. (2007). *Criminology* (6th ed.). New York, NY: McGraw-Hill.

Agnew, R. (1999). Foundation for a general strain theory of crime and delinquency. In F. R. Scarpitti & A. L. Nielsen (Eds.), *Crime and criminals: Contemporary and classic readings in criminology* (pp. 258–273). Los Angeles, CA: Roxbury.

Anderson, C. A., & Bushman, B. J. (2002). Human aggression? *Annual Review of Psychology, 53,* 27–51.

Becker, H. S. (1963). *Outsiders: Studies in the sociology of deviance.* New York, NY: Free Press.

Berg, M. T., & Huebner, B. M. (2011). Reentry and the ties that bind: An examination of social ties, employment, and recidivism. *Justice Quarterly, 28,* 382–410. doi:10.1080/07418825.2010.498383

Clear, T. R., & Dammer, H. R. (2003). *The offender in the community* (2nd ed.). Belmont, CA: Wadsworth/Thomson.

Cohen, L. E., Felson, M., & Land, K. C. (1979). Property crime rates in the United States: A macrodynamic analysis, 1947–1977, with ex ante forecasts for the mid-1980s. *American Journal of Sociology, 86,* 90–118.

Hirschi, T. (1969). *Causes of delinquency.* Berkeley, CA: University of California Press.

Huebner, B. M., & Berg, M. T. (2011). Examining the sources of variation in risk for recidivism. *Justice Quarterly, 28,* 146–173.

Merton, R. K. (1938). Social structure and anomie. *American Sociological Review, 3,* 672–682.

Miller, J. M., Schreck, C. J., & Tewksbury, R. (2006). *Criminological theory: A brief introduction.* Boston, MA: Pearson.

Moffitt, T. E. (1997). Adolescence-limited and life-course-persistent offending: A complementary pair of developmental theories. In T. P. Thornberry (Ed.), *Developmental theories of crime and delinquency* (pp. 11–54). New Brunswick, NJ: Transaction Publishers.

Shaw, C. R., & McKay, H. D. (1942). *Juvenile delinquency and urban areas.* Chicago, IL: University of Chicago Press.

Sun, K. (1993). The implications of social psychological theories of group dynamics for gang research. *Journal of Gang Research: An Interdisciplinary Research Quarterly, 1,* 39–44.

Sutherland, E. H. (1947). *Principles of criminology* (4th ed.). Philadelphia, PA: Lippincott.

Zimbardo, P. G. (1970). The human choice: Individuation, reason, and order versus deindividuation, impulse, and chaos. In W. J. Arnold & D. Levine (Eds.), *Nebraska symposium on motivation, 1969.* Lincoln, NE: University of Nebraska Press.

Chapter 5

Psychological Models in Correctional Counseling

This chapter explains the major psychological models for correctional counseling (e.g., behavioral therapy, cognitive therapy, social learning theory, self-efficacy theory, positive psychology, and art therapy), discusses the techniques that apply to them, and critically analyzes their strengths and limitations.

Behavioral Therapy

Behavioral therapy is also known as *behavior modification,* which is often combined with cognitive therapies (to be examined later in this chapter) to treat offenders in a correctional setting. This joint approach is termed *cognitive-behavioral therapy* (CBT). Rather than discussing the theories as one model, we will examine them in separate sections to clarify the characteristics of each approach. Behavioral therapy is based on two types of learning theories: (1) classical (respondent) conditioning; and (2) instrumental (operant) conditioning. Both theories have been used to explain how learning experiences shape or promote deviant, antisocial, or undesirable behavior and how to use the learning mechanisms to help control, treat, or minimize harmful and dysfunctional behaviors.

Classical Conditioning Theory

The theory of **classical conditioning** was developed by the Russian physiologist I. P. Pavlov (1849–1936), whose experiments on digestion won him the Nobel Prize in Medicine in 1904 (Martin & Pear, 1996; Pervin & John, 1997). While doing research on the digestive process of dogs, he discovered that stimuli (e.g., the sound of a bell) other than food could elicit the dog's salivation if the stimuli had been paired with food. He discovered that before the conditioning or learning process, the dog salivated at the sight of food. This process is innate and automatic without any previous experience of learning. At this stage, the sound of the bell had no effect on the dog's response. However, after repeatedly pairing an originally neutral stimulus (e.g., the sound of a bell) with the significant stimulus (e.g., sausage, food) the dog would in time learn to associate the sound of the bell with the food, causing it to salivate at the mere sound of a bell, a response it usually reserved for food. The essential characteristics of such a learning process are that a previously neutral stimulus becomes capable of eliciting a response because of its association with a stimulus that automatically produces the same response.

This learning process consists of four basic components:

1. **Unconditioned stimulus (US):** A stimulus, object, or event induces the subject's response without previous learning experience of the stimulus. In the above example, food is considered to be such a stimulus.

2. **Unconditioned response (UR):** The response by the subject is automatic, innate, and unrelated to previous learning experiences. The dog's salivation at the sight of food is an example of an unconditioned response.

3. **Conditioned stimulus (CS):** A neutral stimulus is associated with the unconditioned stimulus many times and elicits the subject's response by itself (e.g., the sound of the bell elicits the dog's salivation without food). The sound of a bell is conditioned or learned by the subject after its repeated association with the US.

4. **Conditioned response (CR):** The salivation is a conditioned response to the sound of a bell because it is not caused by the food, but by the bell, which is a conditioned or learned stimulus.

This procedure for studying behavior is a principle of learning that had a profound effect on the fields of psychology and social science (Pervin & John, 1997).

How Does Classical Conditioning Explain Dysfunctional Behavior?

According to classical conditioning theory, some deviant or criminal behavior results from inappropriate classical conditioning processes (Eysenck, 1983). For example, impulsiveness is a predictor of juvenile delinquency (Daderman, 1999). Delinquents, as a whole, seek immediate gratification instead of waiting for larger but delayed rewards. In addition, research shows that most offenders who are convicted of crimes against a person (e.g., assault, homicide) have habitual response patterns of reacting violently in particular situations (Toch, 1992). They act violently and on impulse to minor provocations in their interpersonal relationships with surprising consistency.

Eysenck (1983) contended that impulsive violence becomes a habit for offenders, not because individuals fail to use their thinking to control their anger and dysfunctional behavior but because they lack (or have not learned) the sense of guilt or conscience to regulate their antisocial activities. Youths who grow up with parents who display little self-control and apply inconsistent and unjust discipline are unlikely to learn the appropriate way to interact with others. People learn a sense of guilt not by a complicated mental-cognitive process, but by the process of classical conditioning, particularly during childhood. This process involves the association of anxiety generated by morality violation (conscience) with an unconditioned stimulus (e.g., an impulsive act). Most law-abiding people do not act on impulse or engage in antisocial behavior because they experience anxiety generated by their conscience to monitor their actions. In addition, Eysenck (1983) noted that criminal behavior is the result of an interaction between certain environmental conditions and features of the nervous system such as "conditionability." People with different personalities have a varying degree of conditioning potential, which interacts with the types of social environment (i.e., prosocial versus pro-criminal environments) to influence their tendency to engage in antisocial activities. For example, in a prosocial milieu, youths with low conditionability (e.g., a low ability to learn from a positive environment) are more likely to engage in behavior contrary to society's laws than people with high conditionability. However, in a pro-criminal setting, the reverse is true. People with high conditionability learn techniques and attitudes to commit crimes more readily than those with low conditionability.

Implications for Correctional Counseling

Aversive therapy, also called *counterconditioning*, was developed largely by the repeated association of an undesirable yet tempting stimulus (e.g., drug or sex addiction) with an aversive event such as pain or nausea (Martin & Pear, 1996). For example, when aversive therapy is used to treat alcohol addiction, Antabuse (a drug that inhibits the enzyme system's capacity to metabolize alcohol) serves as the unconditioned stimulus that elicits unconditioned responses (e.g., flushing, throbbing in the head and neck, respiratory difficulty, nausea, vomiting, sweating, thirst, chest pain, and blurred vision) when combined with small amounts of alcohol. The alcohol is the original undesirable reinforcer or neutral stimulus. However, after it is paired with Antabuse enough times, it becomes the conditioned stimulus that can cause the negative reaction without the presence of Antabuse.

Systematic Desensitization

Systematic desensitization is a treatment technique used in behavioral therapy in which a competing response (relaxation) is conditioned or associated with stimuli that previously aroused anxiety (Pervin & John, 1997). This method is often used to treat a variety of phobias, but it is used less frequently in correctional settings than in the community.

The theory of classical conditioning can thus better account for responses associated with emotions (e.g., anxiety, avoidance) and for the development of psychopathology than cognitive models. The reason is that classical conditioning and emotions are both regulated by the autonomic nervous system, the system that also regulates key activities related to survival of the organism—from the heartbeat and digestion to the glandular system. This system operates separately from the neocortex of the brain, which controls cognitive activities (Eysenck, 1983). It can be divided into two parts: (1) the sympathetic nervous system, which activates the body for emergencies (including fight or flight response) by increasing heart rate, respiration flow, blood flow, and perspiration, and (2) the parasympathetic nervous system, which brings the body back to its normal state of arousal.

The Theory of Operant Conditioning

The theory of **operant conditioning**, also called *instrumental conditioning*, was formulated by psychologist B. F. Skinner (1904–1990). He defined *operant behavior* as behavior controlled by its consequences. Although operant conditioning was not entirely new, Skinner's theory and method of automated training with intermittent reinforcement schedules led to discoveries, studies, and applications of the learning mechanism in a variety of social and clinical fields in the following decades. Although his theory is called behaviorism, Skinner did not deny the existence and sometimes the usefulness of private mental events or internal stimuli (Staddon & Cerutti, 2003).

The Basic Postulates of Operant Conditioning

The operant conditioning model maintains that a response (for example, a prosocial act such as volunteering to help needy persons, or an undesirable act such as stealing a car) is determined by the consequence that follows the response. If an event following a response (e.g., food, money, verbal praise, and other rewards) increases the probability of future responding, the event is called the *reinforcer* (Martin & Pear, 1996), which can be further divided into positive and negative reinforcers.

A *positive reinforcer* is an event that, when presented immediately following a behavior, causes the behavior to increase in frequency (Martin & Pear, 1996). In prison, for example, positive reinforcers for offenders include early release from incarceration, transferring from a close-custody facility to a medium- or minimum-custody facility, having opportunities to participate in more programs or enjoyable activities (e.g., sports, education, and employment), verbal praise, or certificates that show achievements.

A *negative reinforcer* is synonymous with escape conditioning, which refers to an event that strengthens the response by removing an aversive stimulus for the individual. In prison, for example, if an early completion of lockdown for an inmate who has committed some infractions increases his or her future rule-abiding behavior, the removal of the aversive condition (lockdown) can be considered a negative reinforcer.

According to Martin and Pear (1996), negative reinforcement should be separated from punishment, which refers to noxious or painful stimuli that, when presented immediately following a behavior, causes the behavior to decrease in frequency (e.g., physical restriction of freedom, reprimands).

Partial or *intermittent reinforcement schedules* are more powerful in producing and maintaining reinforced responses than *continuous reinforcement schedules* because they are more resistant to *extinction,* which refers to the weakening of a learned response when the response is no longer followed by reinforcement (Pervin & John, 1997).

A partial or intermittent reinforcement schedule is a procedure that delivers a reinforcer according to some well-defined rule by reinforcing responses intermittently rather than constantly. There are two types of schedule: (1) the *ratio-based schedule,* which involves a fixed or variable number of responses before a reinforcer is delivered, and (2) the *time-based schedule,* in which the reinforcer is delivered after a fixed or variable time period. In total, there are four typical partial reinforcement schedules (Pervin & John, 1997; Staddon & Cerutti, 2003):

1. **Fixed-ratio schedule:** Reinforcement occurs each time a fixed number of responses of a particular type is emitted. In other words, reinforcement is given after a fixed number of correct responses according to a ratio of nonreinforced-to-reinforced responses. For example, awards may be given to offenders after they participate in adult basic education every five times, and the awards will help them continue their educational efforts.

2. **Variable-ratio schedule:** The number of responses required to produce reinforcement changes unpredictably. Reinforcement is given after a varying number of nonreinforced correct responses. Research has shown that a variable-ratio schedule of reinforcement yields the highest rates of response. In correctional settings, for example, staff may praise an offender who participates in an adult basic education class according to the variable-ratio schedule. The praise is delivered according to the varying amount of the client's participation. This procedure has more positive effects on the offender's behavior than a constant reinforcement.

3. **Fixed-interval schedule:** Reinforcement is given for the first correct response after a fixed interval of time has elapsed. For example, in most correctional institutions or workplaces, employees receive a biweekly check or direct deposit. This type of reinforcement is carried out according to the fixed-interval schedule.

4. **Variable-interval schedule:** The period that precedes reinforcement varies. For example, some agencies often give their employees financial or other benefits after every unpredictable period. Giving these benefits is not based on individuals' performance during this period. If the rewards encourage the workers to continue what they have been doing in their agencies, this is considered to be a variable-interval schedule of reinforcement.

How Operant Conditioning Theory Explains Deviant or Criminal Behavior

According to the operant conditioning model, dysfunctional behaviors are learned by the same process as prosocial or functional behaviors, but they represent responses that have been reinforced inappropriately.

Conger and Simons (1997) presented the **matching law approach** based on the operant theory to show how the relative, rather than absolute, value of reinforcements and punishments generated by multiple environmental contingencies shape youths' antisocial behavior. This law suggests that both the conventional and antisocial behaviors of children are largely a function of the immediate and continuing rewards available in the closest environments. However, unlike middle-class children, lower-class children's antisocial behavior is more likely to get reinforced than their conventional behavior because of their environment. This is because youths who live in a high-crime neighborhood and have families with severe financial disadvantages, low parent education, and a use of violence and physical punishment for disciplinary control, are unlikely to be rewarded for their academic skills. However, their deviant behavior can get frequent reinforcement from their delinquent peers. According to the model, adolescents become delinquents because the three settings (family, school, and community) all tend to give low rewards for their conventional behavior whereas their antisocial behavior is reinforced by delinquent peers—the only stable association they have. This model explains two research findings:

1. The reinforcement process explains why adolescent crime involves a developmental progression from relatively minor to more serious antisocial behavior.

2. The lack of reinforcement for delinquents in the family plays a major role in the origin and perpetuation of delinquent careers, because dysfunctional family interactions (lack of reinforcement for appropriate behavior) involve both parent and child behaviors that mutually aggravate the probability of child misconduct and disrupt successful child caring.

Operant Conditioning and Correctional Counseling

Research has demonstrated that reinforcement based on operant conditioning and related principles can be used to improve treatment outcomes for a wide range of different substance use disorders and populations (Higgins, Heil, & Lussier, 2004).

In addition, most correctional institutions have a system of reinforcement that encourages offenders to participate in programs approved by the correctional staff and discourages them from perpetrating serious infractions. For example, offenders may earn a portion of a sentence reduction by their active program participation (e.g., educational, vocational programs). They may also receive a good conduct time (e.g., a few days per 30-day period served, varying with correctional institutions) for not committing infractions during this period. This system, which involves the application of the principles of operant conditioning, is commonly referred to as a *token economy program*—a reinforcement procedure that enables clients to earn tokens (e.g., sentence reduction or good-conduct time) in exchange for engaging in designated, socially appropriate behaviors. In some cases, clients will also lose tokens because of their inappropriate behaviors (Stuve & Salinas, 2002).

How to Implement Behavioral Therapy

In addition to identifying the available and appropriate reinforcers, counselors should consider two issues when trying to implement behavioral therapy with a client: The first is to define the client's problems to be modified in terms of behavioral deficits (too little behavior of a particular type) or behavioral excesses (too much behavior of a particular type). The second issue involves observing and establishing a behavioral baseline, which is a measure of behavior before any behavioral intervention (Martin & Pear, 1996).

Limits of Behavioral Therapy

The main weakness of the behavioral approach is its indifference to how offenders use their cognition to interpret, explain, and adjust to their experiences and environment. We cannot understand offenders' criminal behavior without understanding their mental process (thoughts and motivations). Neither can we appreciate the effects of behavioral therapy without knowing how clients perceive, evaluate, interpret, rationalize, and validate or invalidate environmental stimuli and their mental experiences. For example, the clients may not evaluate counselors' reinforcements as having reinforcing properties based on their standards. In addition, punishment or deprivation of reinforcement that is perceived to be unfair will cause anger and aggression rather than reducing undesirable behavior. These limitations can be addressed only by cognitive approaches to correctional counseling.

Dialectical Behavioral Therapy

The behavioral modification approaches examined above need to be separated from **dialectical behavioral therapy (DBT)**, which uses different theoretical assumptions and techniques. Dialectical behavioral therapy was formulated in 1993 (Heard & Linehan, 1993) and is an evidence-based therapeutic model. Although DBT was initially developed to treat clients with borderline personality disorder, who exhibited severe difficulties in regulating and controlling emotions and behavior (e.g., impulsivity, aggressiveness, self-harm, feelings of shame and hopelessness, fear of abandonment) as a result of early experience of invalidation, this approach has been successfully applied with correctional clients. They include offenders with intellectual disability (Sakdalan, Shaw, & Collier, 2010) and female juvenile offenders who have childhood trauma, substance abuse, misconduct, risk taking and other behavioral problems (Trupin, Stewart, Beach, & Boesky, 2002).

The "dialectical" aspect of DBT emphasizes that the self is viewed as a dialectical process, defined by the interaction of culture/environment and the individual (Heard & Linehan, 1993). Therapists help clients recognize that they can adopt both *change* and *acceptance* strategies simultaneously in dealing with their issues. Change what they can change but accept things that they cannot modify (Sweezy, 2011). In addition, DBT teaches clients four cognitive behavioral skills, including: (1) distress tolerance, which involves shifting attention away from disturbing thoughts or situations and integrating a Zen Buddhist idea of acceptance, (2) emotional regulation, and focusing on understanding emotion, (3) assertiveness, including how to achieve their interpersonal goals by making effective requests and saying no to unreasonable demands, and (4) mindfulness, which involves nonjudgmental observation (see Sweezy, 2011).

Cognitive Therapies

It is through cognitive capacity that each person is able to transcend the present and think about the future as well as the past. People with many sophisticated cognitive structures can evaluate and react to behavior and events in more complex ways than those with few cognitive structures.

Although cognitive therapy involves a diverse set of terms and procedures, it shares the basic postulate that cognition or thinking largely determines feelings and behavior (Beck, 1991; Ellis, 1993). Three frequently used cognitive models in correctional counseling are examined in this chapter: (1) cognitive therapy, which focuses on revising a person's negative self-concept; (2) the cognitive approach, which targets the development of offenders' social and problem-solving skills; and (3) the cognitive model, which helps offenders discern how their deviant thinking leads to their criminal acts. Before elaborating on the three cognitive models, we need to review the meanings of cognitive (knowledge) structures and processes regarding social entities (the self, others, situations).

Cognitive Structures (Schemas)

Cognitive structures (schemas) are defined as organized mental representations of the social and physical entities (the self and others, events, situations), their interactions, and perceived patterns that govern mental and interpersonal experiences. Because all human experiences involve the interaction between the self and others, cognitive structures include perceived regularities in patterns of interpersonal relatedness (Baldwin, 1992; Fiske & Taylor, 1991). The term *schemas,* often used as a synonym for the phrase *cognitive structures,* is used to describe organized and abstract cognitive or knowledge structures representing individuals, facts (or presumed facts), real and imagined objects, events, categories, behavioral sequences, rules, skills, beliefs, attitudes, theories, and associations among the entities. Schemas facilitate the encoding, evaluating, explaining, storing, and retrieving of information, and they constitute a framework for individuals to experience the world (Cantor & Kihlstrom, 1989).

Cognitive Processes

Cognitive processes refer to the application of cognitive structures or schemas to make sense of social experience and the living environment by administering such mental processes as encoding, evaluating, recalling, reasoning, explaining, and decision making (Cantor & Kihlstrom, 1989; Fiske & Taylor, 1991).

It should be noted that cognition is different from *motivation,* which refers to internal factors that arouse, maintain, and direct behavior toward a goal. Motivation can be further divided into *physiological* and *social motivations.* Physiological motivations are biologically based, including hunger and sex. However, social motivations (which are learned rather than inherited) arouse, maintain, and guide behavior toward culturally or socially approved goals. Examples include the need for achievement, self-esteem, or the justification of actions (Sun, 1993).

The following sections examine three types of cognitive therapy typically used in correctional environments.

Cognitive Therapy That Focuses on Altering Negative Self-Concepts

Self-concepts or self-schemas represent the sum of a person's beliefs about his or her own attributes (e.g., athletic, smart, short, shy). These cognitive components influence cognitive processes (evaluations, perceptions, interpretations, recall, for example). On matters relevant to self-schemas, people make rapid judgments about themselves and are quick to recall past actions or predict future ones (Brown, 1998).

A cognitive approach related to self-concepts and self-schemas assumes that it is irrational or negative *beliefs* about the self, rather than negative *experiences,* that lead to negative emotional states (e.g., depression or anxiety) and dysfunctional behavior. The behavior includes a sense of defeat and the withdrawal of investment in people and in conventional goals as well as an intensified sense of vulnerability (Beck, 1970, 1991; Ellis, 1987, 1993).

Clients may often find themselves thinking negatively about themselves, their world, and their future. Examples of negative cognition (irrational beliefs) include low self-esteem, self-blame and self-criticism, negative predictions, unpleasant memories, erroneous interpretations of experiences, all-or-nothing thinking (dichotomous thinking), jumping to conclusions, selective abstraction, overgeneralization or exaggeration of negative experiences, the presence of a negative cognitive shift (i.e., positive information relevant to the individual is filtered or blocked out, whereas negative self-relevant information is readily admitted). In short, for these individuals, negative cognitions permeate internal conversations about self-evaluation, attributions, expectancies, inferences, and recall.

The purpose of cognitive therapy is to restructure a client's irrational or negative beliefs into rational or positive ones (Beck, 1991; Ellis, 1987, 1993).

Ellis and Beck's Models

Although both Ellis's and Beck's models can be categorized as representative of self-focused cognitive therapies, they do differ from each other. Ellis's (1987, 1993) cognitive model is known as **rational-emotive therapy** or the *A-B-C theory of personality. A* is the experience of an objective fact (the so-called "activating event"); *B* is subjective interpretation (belief about the fact); and *C* represents the consequence. According to Ellis, negative experiences do not cause mental conflicts. It is the faulty belief system or cognition, which is structured around an individual's tendency to exacerbate his or her discomfort, that contributes to emotional pain and poor behavior.

According to Beck (1991), the relation between negative cognition and mood disorders, such as depression, is more complicated. Three factors are involved:

1. Most mental conflicts such as depression have motivational, affective, and behavioral symptoms, and negative automatic thoughts constitute an integral part of the mental picture. However, negative beliefs predispose individuals to develop depression. Intervention at the cognitive level may reduce the emotional, motivational, and/or behavioral symptoms, whereas persistence or exacerbation of the cognitive processes may sustain the other symptoms.

2. Depression and other mental disorders may be caused by any combination of biological, genetic, stress, or personality factors. Personality factors play a significant role in developing depression. For example, individuals who are heavily invested in autonomy (e.g., inclinations for independent achievement, mobility, and solitary pleasures) are prone to become depressed after failure, immobilization, or enforced conformity. People who deeply value closeness, dependency, and sharing are vulnerable and prone to become depressed after experiencing social deprivation or rejection (Beck, 1991).

3. Depression has its source in stressful environments. The most frequent environmental stressors have to do with relations with other people. Dysfunctional interpersonal relationships shape the development of depression and other mental pathological outcomes when bad relationships interact with partners' distorted cognitions—misunderstanding a partner's behavior, misreading motives, and acting on this misconstruction (Beck, 1991).

The Techniques

To perform assessments and interventions for clients by using this type of cognitive approach, therapists first assess the clients' difficulties and formulate plans of action. Clients are then taught how to identify automatic thoughts (such as "If I don't succeed, I am helpless") and the link between thoughts and negative feelings through education. Next, they learn to monitor their automatic thoughts (e.g., using a daily record of upsetting events, automatic and dysfunctional thoughts, and emotional responses). Once clients learn how to identify automatic thoughts, therapists begin to help them test the validity of their beliefs by asking them to provide evidence that supports and refutes their thoughts and to perform role playing (what they would say to someone else who had their problem). They also challenge and change a client's fundamental beliefs by generating alternative adaptive beliefs (Steiman & Dobson, 2002; Todd & Bohart, 2003).

Cognitive Therapy That Focuses on Social (Cognitive) Skill Training

The second type of cognitive therapy teaches **social (cognitive) skill training** in the interpersonal domain, helping offenders learn interpersonal cognitive problem-solving skills that will contribute to their rehabilitation process. Clients are taught how to identify, appraise, and resolve interpersonal problems, and how to overcome their cognitive skill deficits, such as poor self-regulation skills and an inability to think consequentially or to take another person's perspective (Foster & Crain, 2002; Platt & Husband, 1993; Smith & Faubert, 1990). This cognitive skill training covers four areas:

1. Values education or social perspective training (how to recognize and understand other people's views and feelings as well as to teach values and concern for others)

2. Assertiveness training (nonaggressive, socially appropriate ways to meet their needs)

3. Interpersonal cognitive problem solving (the thinking skills required to creatively deal with interpersonal problems and conflicts)

4. Teaching logical and rational thinking about the cause-effect relationships in interpersonal interactions

The General Techniques of Social Skill Training

This type of training includes five skills necessary for effective interpersonal problem solving:

1. Helping offenders recognize that interpersonal problems exist and are often unavoidable in human interactions

2. Learning about how to go beyond the immediate reaction by mentally generating alternative solutions to a problem; for example, counselors can teach violence-prone clients about the awareness of the causes and consequences of violence and knowledge of the alternatives (such as using fact-supported communications) to violence

3. Evaluating the likely consequences of different actions; for example, weapons or anger can lead to violence (homicides are frequently precipitated by arguments, uncontrolled anger, and the abuse of alcohol and drugs)

4. Using a logical, sequential process to reach a goal (understanding there are multiple methods to reach the same goal) and obtaining awareness of various cause–effect relations in interpersonal interactions; clients can be taught to discern the true causes of their anger and to use healthy, realistic ways of expressing anger, including actively channeling anger in nonviolent ways that are unlikely to provoke violence from the other

5. Understanding the perspective of other people in a given situation through group activities, role-playing, feedback, and modeling (demonstrating and practicing socially acceptable and efficacious interpersonal behaviors) (Deutsch, 1993; Foster & Crain, 2002; Platt & Husband, 1993; Smith & Faubert, 1990)

In short, cognitive skill training involves instructing offenders to identify problem situations, stop and think about them, define the nature of the problem, generate solutions for the problem, evaluate and pick the idea most likely to produce a positive outcome and minimize negative outcomes, and plan and implement the idea behaviorally.

Why Should Correctional Counseling Include Problem-Solving Training for Clients?

The limited ability of many offenders to adjust to social–interpersonal problems encountered in daily life is often associated with their involvement in illegal activities. For many persistent offenders, a central reason for their offending behavior involves their lack of, or failure to apply, a number of problem-solving skills (Wexler, 1999). According to social information processing theory, interpersonal responses (e.g., criminal behavior or substance abuse) are the outcome of a series of cognitive processes, including encoding and perceiving external and internal cues or stimuli, interpreting and mentally representing those stimuli, clarifying or selecting a goal to address the stimuli, constructing potential responses, and behaviorally implementing the responses. For example, individuals with poor problem-solving and social skills tend to experience frustration or unsatisfactory outcomes in interpersonal situations and tasks. The result generates negative emotional states that may precipitate substance abuse or criminal behavior (Platt & Husband, 1993).

Two Characteristics That Lead to Conflict

According to Deutsch (1993), counselors who perform social skill and conflict resolution training should recognize that individuals (including offenders) may have one of two opposite dysfunctional psychological traits (including attitudes, behavior, perceptions, and emotions) that tend to initiate and sustain interpersonal conflicts:

1. Individuals may have attitudes that provoke interpersonal conflict and a preoccupation with conflict—obsessive thoughts about fights, dominance, control, disputes, and quarrels, a "macho" attitude, excessive irritability, and a propensity to seek out conflict. Their behavioral characteristics involve the inclination to take a tough, aggressive, dominating, unyielding response to conflict. They tend to aggravate any conflict by generalizing it as including themselves, family, ethnic group, the nature and number of the immediate issues, or the motives of participants. The specifics of the conflict get lost and such escalation of the conflict makes it more difficult to resolve constructively. Some inappropriate emotional communications may generate or sustain conflict—for example, a compulsion to reveal whatever they think and feel about the other person in an irrational or distorted manner, including their suspicions, hostilities, and fears, attaching intense emotions to all communications and confusing the significant with the insignificant or trivial.

2. Avoiding assertiveness may also sustain conflict. Some individuals may fail to recognize that the opposite tendency (including attitudes, thoughts, behavior) that is intended to avoid conflict may actually sustain or induce it. Such dysfunctional attitudes may include denial, repression, suppression, avoidance, and continuing postponement of facing conflict. People are afraid that others see their assertiveness as being mean, hostile, or presumptuous. They are often excessively gentle and expect the other person to read their mind and know their needs.

A related dysfunction in emotional expression involves people who have a fear of revealing any feelings or thoughts and the belief that in expressing their emotions they will do something destructive, foolish, or humiliating. Emotion is subdued or isolated during communication.

Cognitive Therapy That Focuses on Offenders' Deviant Thoughts

The third type of cognitive therapy is the most widely used treatment model for sexual offenders. The basic premise of this cognitive method suggests that the offenders' deviant or maladaptive thoughts (e.g., denial, justification of sexual offenses, minimization of consequences, blaming the victim, and violent sexual fantasies that precede offending) are the psychological cause of their sex crimes.

Cognitive factors are also involved in controlling deviant sexual behavior. Therapists or counselors can apply cognitive strategies to increase offenders' ability to rectify the belief systems that have led to their deviant, faulty sexual behavior (Moseley, Briggs, & Magnus, 2005). The following techniques are used:

1. Offenders are made aware of the relationship between thoughts and behavior. They are taught to see the link between their criminal behavior and their maladaptive thoughts, understanding how their sexual fantasies, victim blaming, denial, and justification of sexual offenses and other types of deviant thinking promote and facilitate their involvement in crimes.

2. Offenders are taught to replace maladaptive thoughts with more adaptive and functional cognitions (e.g., empathy, self-confidence in social interactions) in order to increase offender self-control, reduce impulsivity, and prevent relapse.

3. Offenders learn to identify and avoid high-risk situations where they are likely to commit new offenses (e.g., situations with the availability of potential victims and low levels of monitoring) and to control and minimize deviant thoughts when in high-risk situations.

These relapse-prevention methods are central to many current correctional programs. For example, the Cognitive Self-Change program in Vermont institutions requires offenders to develop their individual relapse-prevention plans by using these principles. The contents of the plan include the offender's observations of his or her own thinking, and reporting on the content of that thinking. In addition, the offender must (1) identify the patterns of thinking that have led him or her to perform criminal acts and violence in the past and that posed a risk of recidivism, recognizing the consequences of that thinking; (2) learn specific skills for intervening in and controlling these patterns of thinking; and (3) summarize these patterns and interventions in the plan for controlling each offender's high-risk thinking in the community (Wexler, 1999).

A Critique of Self-Focused Cognitive Therapy

Self-focused cognitive therapy has been shown to be superior to medication for the symptoms of depression and anxiety (Hollon, Stewart, & Strunk, 2006). It has also been successful when applied to populations recovering from addictive disease (Beck, 1991; Ellis, McInerney, DiGiuseppe, & Yeager, 1988). However, self-focused cognitive therapy does not solve the main cognitive deficiencies of the offender population. The reason is that such therapy was formulated for nonoffender clients, unlike the cognitive models that emphasize social skill training and the discernment of the relations between deviant thoughts and criminal behavior. This model thus has the following limitations when applied to correctional counseling.

First, although there are some mentally disordered offenders in the correctional population (Sun, 2005a) and some of them suffer from depression or anxiety, negative self-concept does not represent the main issue in offenders' dysfunction in their mental and interpersonal relationships. One of the issues for correctional clients is that offenders are supposed to feel guilty about their criminal acts. This type of negative self-concept is accurate rather than irrational or distorted. In this sense, self-blame may be conducive to rehabilitation, which is the purpose of correction.

Second, this cognitive therapy uses such terminology as negative self-concepts, irrational belief about the self, dysfunctional self-concept, and biased cognitions about the self (see Ellis, 1993; Beck, 1991), as if they are synonymous and interchangeable. In fact, they have diverse meanings. Research has shown that the valence of evaluations (e.g., being positive or negative) is independent and separate from the accuracy of evaluations. In many cases, clients' appraisals and reports of their negative or distressful experiences are quite rational, realistic, and accurate. For example, their experiences of sexual or physical abuse at the hands of another or the tragedies of their loved ones have left enormous scars in their lives. In such circumstances, cognitive restructuring exercises, with an emphasis on reframing reality and not on changing it, do not deal with the true problem (Bergner, 2003).

On the other hand, positive self-evaluations may be dysfunctional and maladaptive. Dunning, Heath, and Suls (2004) show that it is the positive rather than the negative self-assessment that is characterized by inaccuracy and bias in the fields of health and education and in the workplace. For instance, guided by mistaken but seemingly plausible expert opinions or medical theories of health and disease, people are unrealistically optimistic about their own health risks compared with those of other people. They also tend to misdiagnose themselves. Students' assessments of their performance in education tend to be inaccurate and to agree only moderately with those of their teachers and mentors. They are unable to evaluate how well or how poorly they have understood recently learned material. In the workplace, employees are inclined to overestimate their skills; CEOs also display overconfidence in their own judgments. All self-assessment may thus be flawed. The correlation between self-ratings of skill and actual performance in many domains (e.g., health, education, and the workplace) is moderate to small. Often other people's prediction of a person's outcomes proves more accurate than that person's self-prediction. In addition, people tend to overrate themselves, overestimate the likelihood that they will engage in desirable behaviors and achieve favorable outcomes, and reach judgments with too much confidence (Dunning, Heath, & Suls, 2004). These flawed self-assessments hold true in correctional settings, where offenders may exaggerate their symptoms to get special attention or favorable treatment (Benedict & Lanyon, 1992).

Third, the self-focused cognitive model puts a strong emphasis on examining the association between negative thoughts and mental dysfunction, but it has not answered the question of why individuals choose to focus on their negative attributes when the positive evaluation of the self is more accurate. Research in social psychology has shown that people have two types of self-evaluation:

1. They are motivated to see themselves positively and to avoid a negative self-concept, exhibiting a self-serving bias (including blaming failures on the situation while taking credit for success) (Campbell & Sedikides, 1999).

2. They have a tendency to blame themselves and to evaluate themselves negatively, particularly when depressed. Beck's suggestion that adversity in childhood leads to negative self-schemas (the activation of which later in life generates and fortifies negative cognitions about the self) appears insufficient to explain negative self-cognitions (Abela & Sullivan, 2003).

An alternative explanation of negative self-concepts derives from the model of **interaction schemas** (Sun, 2005b). According to this perspective, interaction schemas refer to cognitions about the self and others and to the principles or patterns that govern social interactions and environmental factors. Such schemas serve as criteria for evaluating, explaining, and adjusting experiences and the actions of social entities (e.g., the self and others) and for determining mental and interpersonal experiences, including positive and negative self-evaluations and explanations. For individual offenders, such interaction schemas may include their knowledge of human actions and value systems (e.g., various beliefs, morality, love, social desirability, aggression, and/or being right, beautiful, positive, or desirable), and other standards that the perceiver regards as controlling the reality of interaction. For example, positive self-evaluations arise from a perceived consistency between attributes and interaction schemas (e.g., beauty, power, social desirability). In contrast, negative self-evaluations and related emotional pains (e.g., low self-esteem, diffidence, guilt, unworthiness, fear, depression/anxiety, self-blame, and anger) are decided by the person's perceived aberrations from the criteria.

Sun's (2005b) study indicated that self-blame and negative self-concepts may be promoted and maintained by the interaction of three factors: (1) prolonged and failed attempts in dealing with interpersonal anxiety; (2) motivation for anxiety reduction; and (3) distorted interaction schemas that serve as the criteria for self-evaluation and explanation. A case analysis of individuals who had a relatively stress-free childhood yet all experienced recent mental conflicts (depression and anxiety) showed that they had developed self-blame and negative self-cognitions after going through a recent process of failed attempts to reduce prolonged anxiety in interpersonal situations. The experience of anxiety motivated them to reduce anxiety and restore certainty. Their adoption of negative self-cognitions appeared to help them reduce interpersonal anxiety and served as a maladaptive coping strategy to make sense of, predict, and control their interpersonal experiences. The motivation for anxiety reduction seems to take precedence over the motivation to have a positive self-image.

This motivation alone, however, cannot explain why the perceivers attributed frustrations to their own internal and individual deficiencies rather than to external, unstable, and situational factors. Their experiences of anxiety and frustration were transformed into negative self-evaluations and self-blame because they adopted distorted interaction schemas that served as the criteria for self-evaluation. For example, a woman in the case analysis (Sun, 2005b) who suffered severe depression and self-blame believed the apathetic and lukewarm attitude of her boyfriend toward her was caused by her violation of some moral values—he dated her before he was legally divorced (which she was unaware of at the time). In other words, offenders' negative self-concepts result from seeing their attributes or behavior as deviating from some criteria (interaction schemas) that are often inconsistent with the true patterns governing human interaction. Therefore, it is only appropriate to view the motivational factor as interacting with interaction schemas, which mediate and regulate the impact of experienced adversities on the perceiver's self-cognitions. These findings are consistent with previous research (Sun, 2002), which demonstrated that it is not the clients' obsession with their negative experiences that caused their emotional problems. Their self-related effects and attribution (such as low self-esteem, feelings of guilt and unworthiness, depression, anxiety, and self-blame) come from the inability of their cognition to understand and deal with frustration in their attempt to balance internal and external relationships.

Evaluation of the Other Two Cognitive Approaches

Cognitive therapies that focus on social skill training and the discernment of the relations between deviant thoughts and criminal behavior have an advantage over self-focused cognitive therapy in correctional counseling in that they intend to change offenders' distorted social cognition of their interpersonal relations. This interpersonal approach is consistent with the research finding that most dysfunctional beliefs are inherently interpersonal, having been learned in interpersonal contexts and having interpersonal consequences (Safran & Segal, 1990).

However, both interpersonally based approaches appear to have overlooked another important part of offenders' cognition. This involves their mental representation of childhood sexual or emotional trauma, which still influences their current criminal activities. Burn and Brown (2003) noted that adolescents who have been abused as children show less empathy than nonabused children, have trouble recognizing appropriate emotions in others, and have difficulty taking another person's perspective. The main premise is that children who are sexually victimized are at an increased risk of becoming sex perpetrators. Although it has been recognized that not all offenders who have been abused go on to abuse, negative early childhood experiences are consistently seen as an important precursor. Hunter and Becker (1994) have observed that when young offenders are compared to appropriate control groups, a history of sexual victimization is one of the few distinguishing factors between the groups. Renshaw (1994) found that among convicted child sexual offenders, those who had been sexually abused as children reported almost three times as many victims as the offenders who had not been sexually abused. In addition, Davis and Leitenberg (1987) found that adolescent sex offenders had witnessed greater family violence and had experienced more physical and sexual abuse than nonsexual adolescent offenders. They suggested that due to such early experiences, offenders do not learn to inhibit their aggression, and their sexual deviancy may be a response to unresolved psychological needs, misplaced anger, or a replication of their own abuse. Therefore, assessment, treatment, and resolution of the client's cognition about childhood trauma should be an important component of cognitive therapy.

The cognitive skill training approach seems to mix the idea of cognitive skills with the notion of cognitive understanding. Individuals may have the ability to take another's perspective, but they may lack the capacity to understand their experiences. For example, clinical observations show that the clients or the victims of abuse can take the abusers' perspective and know what they want and their feelings, but the victims are unable to make the abusers understand their viewpoint and experience without eliciting retaliation in a situation of power disparity. One type of correctional clients' cognitive struggles and emotional anguish involves their inability to make sense of their experiences of sexual, emotional, or physical abuse inflicted on them when they were too young to defend themselves (Sun, 2001a, 2001b, 2002). Cognitive–social skill training has not, apparently, addressed this type of cognitive deficiency.

Another limitation of the social skill training model is that it ignores the complexity of distorted social or interpersonal cognition. For example, offenders may be taught to take another's perspective, and this training may provide them with the motivation to do so, but the motivation to take another's viewpoint does not exemplify a new and accurate understanding of interpersonal reality. Cognition cannot execute assessments, perceptions, decisions, and actions that are beyond the mental gamut, just as imbuing elementary school children with the motivation for doing calculus does not give them an understanding of the topic.

The cognitive approach that has been devised to increase offenders' awareness of the link between maladaptive thoughts and criminal behavior has missed some important components of offenders' cognition. These mental schemas include offenders' cognitive distortions about their victims' mental state and context and how the victims validate or invalidate their communication. For example, the offender may perceive a victim's greeting and goodwill as signs of hostility and rejection or may view disdain for the self as a mark of admiration.

In short, effective cognitive treatments require identifying and altering offenders' distorted and limited cognitions that misguide their mental and interpersonal activities, expanding beyond revising their cognition about negative self-concepts or about their crime issues.

Social Learning Theory and Self-Efficacy Theory

Albert Bandura is credited with developing two influential social-psychological models: **social learning theory** (1983) and **self-efficacy theory** (1997). Social learning theory expands the concepts of reinforcement and punishment examined in the behavioral model of operant conditioning (see discussion earlier in this chapter). The theory includes the idea of how a person's behavior is influenced by observing another's conditioning (reward/punishment) and internal or self-administered rewards and punishments. This model maintains that direct and observational learning and the internal reward or punishment determines how people acquire and execute antisocial responses, just as they acquire and implement other forms of social behavior. Self-efficacy theory investigates how the belief about one's ability to behave influences success and failure in life, including how to execute the response necessary to stop maladaptive behavior.

Social Learning and Human Aggression

Bandura (1983) contended that the social learning perspective views the mechanisms that regulate human aggression via three components: (1) the origins of aggression; (2) the instigators of aggression; and (3) the regulators of aggression.

The **origins of aggression** include factors that prepare a person for the capacity for aggressive behavior. These factors include human biological conditions (human neurophysiological mechanisms), direct learning experience about aggression, observational learning (e.g., learning violence by observing others' experiences of reward and punishment), and related mental processes (e.g., attentional processes, memory representation, desensitization, and habituation to violence). It should be noted that Bandura argued that vicarious reinforcement (observing the actions of others that are rewarded or reinforced) strongly influences a person's aggression by conveying useful aggression-related information.

In addition, people may not perform learned aggression unless there are two other mechanisms: (1) the **instigators of aggression** (e.g., aversive treatment, physical assaults, and frustrations of goal-directed behavior, and modeling instigators); and (2) the **regulators of aggression**, which refer to the maintaining mechanisms or external and internal (mental or self-regulated) reinforcement and punishment that sustain or control aggression.

Self-Efficacy Theory

Bandura's (1997, 2006) **self-efficacy theory** focuses on the belief that self-efficacy and human agency are a cognitive and motivational mechanism. *Self-efficacy* is defined as individuals' confidence in their ability to organize and execute a given course of action to solve a problem or accomplish a task by mobilizing motivation and cognitive resources. Put simply, self-efficacy is defined as the core belief that the individual has the power to bring about change or exercise control over a variety of tasks through his or her actions. Self-efficacy is a multidimensional construct that varies in strength (e.g., some people have a strong sense of self-efficacy and others do not), generality (e.g., some have efficacy beliefs that cover many situations, whereas others have narrow efficacy beliefs), and level (e.g., some believe they are efficacious even in the most difficult tasks, whereas others believe they are efficacious only in easier tasks).

Bandura (1997, 2006) noted that among the mechanisms of human agency, none is more central or pervasive than the belief in personal efficacy. If people do not believe they can produce desired effects by their actions, they have little incentive to act or to persevere in the face of difficulty. They may perform poorly, adequately, or extremely well depending on individual variations in perceived self-efficacy. Belief in efficacy is a key resource in personal development and change.

According to Bandura (1997, 2006), individuals' self-efficacy influences their psychological activities (including cognitive, motivational, affective, and decisional processes) in at least two ways:

1. Efficacy expectations are the major determinant of goal setting, activity choice, willingness to expend effort, and persistence. Such beliefs affect people's choice of goals and desires, how well they motivate themselves, and their perseverance in the face of difficulty and adversity.

2. Efficacy beliefs influence whether individuals think optimistically or pessimistically, in self-enhancing or self-debilitating ways. Efficacy beliefs also shape expectations as to whether their efforts will produce favorable outcomes or adverse ones. In addition, efficacy beliefs determine how people view opportunities and impediments.

How to Develop Self-Efficacy

Several sources of self-efficacy have been identified (Bandura, 1997, 2006; Whittinghill, Whittinghill, Rudenga, & Loesch, 2000): (1) mastery or successful experiences, which provide tangible evidence of personal ability; (2) vicarious experiences, which establish personal beliefs derived from comparing oneself to others; (3) verbal persuasion, which shapes personal beliefs in self-efficacy from comments made by significant others whose opinions are cherished; and (4) good affective and physiological states, which give the perception of personal well-being and competence.

Bandura (2006) viewed human interaction as an important factor that either enhances or undermines self-efficacy because most human functioning is socially situated. In an interpersonal interaction, people are each other's environments. For example, a given action can be a source of influence, a response, or an environmental outcome, depending on the sequence of the exchange between the people involved. In human transactions, the "environment," "behavior," and "outcomes" are not fundamentally different events.

Because individuals also function as environments, self-efficacy theory sees collective efficacy or group affiliation as either strengthening or diminishing self-efficacy, depending on the individual's perception of the support group's competence (Bandura, 1997).

Self-Efficacy and Juvenile Delinquency

A recent survey by Caprara, Regalia, and Bandura (2002) on self-efficacy and juvenile delinquency indicated that efficacy beliefs affected personal development and functioning through their impact on cognitive, motivational, affective, and choice processes, including youths' resistance to peer pressure to engage in antisocial activities. In their survey, 350 adolescents completed questionnaires measuring perceived self-regulatory efficacy and scales measuring their violent conduct and parent–adolescent communication patterns. The results showed that the participants' beliefs of efficacy to resist peer pressure had a wide impact on engagement in violence both directly and through the mediation of communication with parents. Namely, those who have high self-efficacy or possess both high self-efficacy and open communication with their parents are less likely to prove their identity through involvement in antisocial activities or through joining deviant peers than adolescents who have low efficacy. The results demonstrated that supportive parental communication counteracts substance abuse and delinquency by encouraging youths to develop their sense of efficacy by providing social modeling and evaluative feedback.

Self-Efficacy and Substance-Abuse Treatment

According to Whittinghill et al. (2000), the concept of self-efficacy can be used at different stages of substance-abuse treatment. When it is applied to clients with the problem, self-efficacy is germane to an individual's perception of his or her ability to mobilize the necessary motivation, knowledge, and behavior to control or abstain from the use of alcohol or other drugs. In dealing with substance-abuse problems, counselors can imbue clients with several types of efficacy depending upon the phase of treatment:

1. **Resistance self-efficacy** refers to an individual's perceived ability to resist attempts and persuasion to use alleged experimental substances for the first time. This type of self-efficacy is similar to what counselors have traditionally referred to as a prevention approach. For example, research shows that children and adolescents who successfully complete refusal skill training, and thus increase their resistance self-efficacy, are much better able to overcome the temptation of first-time use of tobacco, alcohol, or other drugs.

2. **Harm-reduction self-efficacy** denotes the ability to regulate the frequency and quantity of substance abuse and alcohol drinking after initial use. This type of efficacy is for individuals who have begun to experiment with psychoactive substances. Although the majority are not addicted, they experience serious physical, psychological, and social problems as the result of excessive alcohol and drug use and need help to minimize problematic drug use. Research indicates that a harm reduction approach, although it does not prevent substance abuse, helps these individuals to minimize the consequences and dysfunction by improving their perceived capacity to restrict the personal use of alcohol and drugs.

3. **Action self-efficacy** is closely related to harm reduction. It is defined as a person's ability to implement the behavior necessary to stop (or at least reduce) the use of a psychoactive drug. This type of self-efficacy is ideal for people who have become

addicted to alcohol or other drugs but lack the capacity to perceive themselves as capable of reducing or quitting.

4. **Coping self-efficacy** refers to a person's competence to handle tempting and high-risk situations after successfully negotiating the action stage and achieving abstinence. Individuals who have reached initial self-control over substance abuse are often faced with high-risk situations (e.g., family discord, peer pressure, financial problems, or temptation) that threaten their newly established self-efficacy. If relapse-prevention counseling teaches clients about effective coping self-efficacy, they are more likely to deal successfully with crises or tempting situations.

5. **Recovery self-efficacy** refers to the ability to maintain long-term recovery when experiencing setbacks or relapses after achieving sobriety. Many offenders lack personal belief in their ability to recover from a setback and often view themselves as powerless and vulnerable to cravings, pressures, and temptations, thus failing to take further action to return to abstinent behaviors. This efficacy guides clients' future drug-related behavior by helping them to view the relapse as a learning experience and to intensify their efforts to return to and maintain sober behavior.

In addition, because group affiliation may either enhance or diminish self-efficacy, counselors can improve treatment success and help clients to increase their efficacy by using resources from a variety of external support groups, while discouraging association with those groups the clients regard as ineffective or harmful.

Self-Efficacy and the Strengths Perspective

The self-efficacy theory has been used to treat clients with substance-abuse problems (Whittinghill et al., 2000). In addition, it has been integrated into a counseling model known as the *strengths* or *empowerment perspective* (Petrovich, 2004).

The **strengths perspective** in counseling and social work practice can be defined as a belief in the basic goodness of humankind, a faith that individuals, however unfortunate, can discover strengths or potentials in themselves that are not commonly realized. Counselors' and social workers' primary responsibility is to promote the well-being of clients by tapping into possibilities rather than focusing on their current negative conditions (Van Wormer, 1999).

Some research has shown that the strengths perspective helps recovering mothers and their children shift from problem-oriented to possibility-oriented thinking in dealing with their family conflicts and the alcohol addiction of the mothers (Juhnke & Coker, 1997). In this study, the intervention focused on creating solutions and identifying successful behaviors that establish functional family dynamics and healthy hierarchical structures. The results indicated increased parenting confidence and satisfaction, and maternal alcohol abstinence. Children also reported a noticeable increase in family harmony and greater family order.

To apply the strengths perspective in correctional counseling, counselors and social workers can do the following (Van Wormer, 1999):

1. Therapists should avoid labeling clients by using such negative metaphors as *deficit* and *disease,* which have pervaded treatment at every stage of the process, from intake to termination.

2. Because correctional clients often find their very identity defined by their crimes, counselors need to see the source of the crime problem not as internal but as the result of the interaction between the individual and society.

3. Social workers and other helping professionals must listen to the client's personal and family history. These stories are an excellent source of information for discovering latent strengths.

4. When experiencing ethical and professional conflict in correctional settings, the helping staff should advocate on behalf of clients by refusing to engage in practices inconsistent with professional values and ethics. They should do their best to promote change within the system.

Solution-focused therapy is another type of therapy based on the strengths perspective. It focuses on solutions rather than problems, on client strengths rather than their deficiencies, and on the future instead of the past. The solution-focused model makes the following core assumptions (Cepeda & Davenport, 2006):

1. Correctional staff should do what works. If a method does not work, they should change to a different approach and, if it is effective, do more of it.

2. Clients have the capacity to change.

3. Clients' problems result from limited awareness or ignorance about alternatives concerning their issues.

4. A solution to a problem can be initiated by a small step.

Limits of Self-Efficacy Theory for Correctional Counseling
Although the self-efficacy theory has affected both practice and research, as examined previously, it suffers from some limitations. One of the flaws involves its views on how to increase self-efficacy. For both research and counseling practice, this issue appears more important than the benefits of self-efficacy after it has been achieved. Bandura (1997, 2006) listed several factors that may develop self-efficacy, such as mastery or successful experiences, comparing oneself to others, encouraging comments from others, good affective and physiological states, and supportive interpersonal environments. However, many of the conditions are generally unavailable to correctional clients except for the supportive interpersonal milieus. Counselors can at least do their best to give support during the counseling sessions but cannot guarantee all positive interactions for the clients in prison or in the community. For those correctional clients who have many unsuccessful experi-

ences, have received overwhelming negative and abusive comments from others, and suffer from poor emotional and physical health, the question of how to develop self-efficacy remains to be answered by self-efficacy theory.

Bandura (1997) distinguished between two kinds of expectancy beliefs: (1) the belief that certain behaviors will lead to certain outcomes (e.g., the belief that practicing will improve performance); and (2) the belief that the behaviors necessary to produce the outcome can be performed. These two kinds of expectancy belief are different because individuals can believe that a certain behavior will produce a certain outcome but may not believe they can perform the behavior (see Eccles & Wigfield, 2002). To apply the distinction to correctional counseling, we need to recognize that clients' knowledge that self-efficacy is beneficial for them does not increase their self-efficacy. Clients cannot obtain the competence to understand and overcome their mental and interpersonal conflicts simply because they have the willingness, belief, or determination to do so. In fact all people, including correctional clients, are willing to obtain a higher level of self-efficacy. The self-efficacy theory does not explain how the cognitive structures and processes influence dysfunction in encoding, evaluation, perception, interpretation, memory, and adjustment. Therefore, it lacks some fundamental solutions for correctional counseling.

Positive Psychology

Emerging in the late 1990s, **positive psychology** suggests that psychology should look beyond human weakness, damage, and remediation to regain one of its fundamental missions: *the understanding and facilitation of human strength and virtue,* rather than examining pathology and dysfunction (Kelley, 2004; Seligman & Csikszentmihalyi, 2000; Seligman, Rashid, & Parks, 2006). Although it is a new model, positive psychology has integrated many findings and principles from earlier research, including such issues as subjective well-being, optimism, happiness, and self-determination (e.g., competence, belonging, and autonomy). Some conceptual overlaps occur between positive psychology and the self-efficacy model.

The Purpose of Positive Psychology

Positive psychology and the related positive psychotherapy intend to create and maintain happiness by developing the pleasant life, the engaged life, and the meaningful life (Seligman & Csikszentmihalyi, 2000; Seligman, Rashid, & Parks, 2006).

Developing the pleasant life consists of generating a lot of positive emotion about the present, past, and future and obtaining the skills to magnify the intensity and duration of these emotions. The positive emotions related to the past include satisfaction, gratification, fulfillment, honor, serenity, and forgiveness. Positive emotions about the future contain hope and optimism, faith, trust, and confidence. To live an engaged life entails involvement and absorption in work, intimate relations, and leisure. Pursuing a meaningful life consists of using key strengths and talents to belong to and serve something regarded as bigger than oneself.

The Techniques of Positive Psychotherapy

According to Seligman (see Seligman, Rashid, & Parks, 2006), positive therapeutic methods for treating depression typically involve six exercises conducted in group sessions or during spare time. Participants are given the following instructions:

1. Identify five strengths and think of ways to use them more often in your daily life.

2. Think of three good things/blessings that happened and explain why you think they came about.

3. Write a positive obituary/biography for yourself. Imagine that you have lived a fruitful and satisfying life and describe some details.

4. Think of some individuals to whom you are very grateful but have never properly thanked. Imagine that you are speaking directly to each person about your appreciation.

5. Practice some active-constructive responding (i.e., responding in a visibly positive and enthusiastic way) at least once a day, to someone you know.

6. Once a day, take the time to enjoy savoring something that you usually hurry through (e.g., eating a meal, taking a shower, or walking to class). Document the event and contrast it with an experience that involves an absence of enjoyment.

Positive Psychotherapy for Sex Offenders

Ward and Mann (2004) maintained that the good lives model of offender rehabilitation (derived from the principles of positive psychology) has the necessary conceptual resources to provide therapists with some guidelines for treating sex offenders. This new model examines the limitations of current treatments that focus only on the deficits of the offenders.

The conventional rehabilitation model has been called the **risk–need approach**. Its weaknesses include an inability to deal with the relation between etiology (causation) and treatment of criminal behavior. This approach views offenders only as owners of risks (e.g., criminogenic needs or dynamic risk factors). The purpose of treatment is that of recidivism prevention with a focus on reducing the psychological and social deficits associated with each individual's offending, as if a period of containing his or her activity is the only way to avoid offending. Consequently, this model fails to see offenders as a human agents with basic human needs or to understand their influence in determining offending. Furthermore, this perspective often produces a mechanistic approach to treatment without considering the clients' unique characteristics and contexts.

On the other hand, the **good lives model** of offender rehabilitation suggests that therapists need to view offenders from the perspective that human beings are active goal-pursuing individuals who are constantly seeking meaning in their social and mental experiences. All intentional and important human actions manifest attempts to accomplish the main human goods—life (healthy living and functioning), mental peace, knowledge, excellence in performance, a sense of control (autonomy and self-directedness), friendship (including intimate, romantic, and family relationships), spirituality, happiness, and creativity. From this perspective, sexual offending embodies an offender's attempt to achieve valued human goods without possessing the necessary skills to achieve them. Alternatively, sexual offending may result from a sense of incompetence, frustration, or dissatisfaction caused by the inability to achieve valued human goods.

The good lives model indicates that correctional assessment instruments should include not only scales measuring the offender's risk, needs, and suitability for treatment, but also interview questions that evaluate the client's own goals, life priorities, and aims for the intervention. Such questions need to examine a number of different issues with respect to each human good. For example, the counselor can ask the client the meaning and importance of an intimate relationship and how the client has taken steps to achieve that goal. The counselor can ask about the obstacles that prevent the client from achieving the goal—in particular, whether the client has the capacity or capabilities to implement his or her plan.

Treatment and intervention based on the model of positive psychology are intended to increase the offender's range of personal functioning rather than to simply manage or remove a problem. In other words, the aims of treatment are described as what clients will achieve rather than what they will cease to think or do. The core idea of this holistic approach rests on the principle that the best way to reduce risk is to help offenders live more fulfilling lives by equipping them with the necessary understanding and methods. The essential procedure involves two facets:

1. Offenders learn to construe themselves as people who can use socially acceptable and personally rewarding ways to achieve all the important human goods.

2. The treatment programs should focus on helping offenders to develop the scope of goals, capacities, coherence among the goods being sought, and methods necessary for reaching healthy good-life plans.

Like the rest of humanity, most offenders need to be loved and appreciated, to operate competently, and to share a community with others.

Criticism of Positive Psychology

Sweeny, Carroll, and Shepperd (2006) have contended that although optimism is beneficial, a person's shift from optimism can also produce benefits:

1. By making an attempt to prepare for possible disappointment, clients can diminish the negative affect generated by unrealized expectations.

2. Clients may shift from optimism so that they can either cease pursuing undesired goals or minimize their consequences.

3. Making optimistic predictions (a type of magical thinking) may actually diminish the likelihood that a desired result will occur.

The three ways of shifting from optimism can be illustrated with an example: A woman finds a lump in her body; she may shift from optimism by adopting negative expectations (i.e., believing that the lump indicates cancer) to avoid negative feelings associated with optimistic expectations if her suspicions are correct. In addition, embracing negative expectations may also prompt her to take action by seeking medical treatment. Finally, she may believe that she could unconsciously make a negative outcome more likely by assuming the best.

In short, a less optimistic outlook can make people feel better about the outcomes they experience. A pessimistic outlook may prompt a person to take preventive or recuperative actions that diminish or eliminate the negative consequences.

Kelley (2004) argued that the principles of positive psychology have not elaborated on causal principles that explain optimal adolescent psychological functioning. For example, learned optimism is memory-based, deliberately generated, and artificial. The **health realization (HR) model**, which serves as a unifying conceptual framework to fulfill the task, consists of three key concepts: (1) mind, (2) consciousness, and (3) thought. This model defines the mind as the source or energy of life itself, the universal, creative intelligence within and behind life, humans, and the natural world. Consciousness allows people to be aware, to be cognizant of the moment in a knowing way by transforming thought or mental activity into subjective experience. Accordingly, thought is seen as the mental-imaging ability of human beings. In sum, according to the HR model, mental health is the result of natural feelings of exhilaration and well-being produced effortlessly by free-flowing thinking. Although a person may make the occasional implementation of analysis when appropriate, he or she never gets stuck in the analytical processing mode. In other words, the model asserts that the potential for healthy psychological functioning is innate.

Art Therapy in Corrections

Art therapy uses visual art media (two- and three-dimensional materials, such as drawings, paintings, sculptures, and images) and the creative process as an assessment and intervention tool to understand and overcome mental and interpersonal conflicts. Counselors can use the process of creating the arts to help clients enhance their healing and well-being and increase awareness of self and others (Cohen-Liebman, 2002).

Benefits of Art Therapy

Although most correctional counselors are not art therapists by training, research has shown that using arts in the processes of correctional counseling can help both counselors and clients understand a client's mental conflict, traumatic experience, hope, creativity, and potential. For example, Gussak (2004) conducted a study to test the effect of art therapy on improving inmates' mental condition and behavior. Forty-eight incarcerated offenders in a medium- to maximum-security male adult correctional institution participated in art therapy group sessions during a 4-week period. This involved a quasi-experimental, single group pretest/posttest design. The results showed that prison inmates who received art therapy services exhibited a marked change in their behavior and attitude, experienced an improvement in their mood, socialization, and problem-solving abilities, and cooperated more readily with the staff and other inmates. These improvements were verified by the statements and observations of the correctional staff.

In addition, two studies by Gussak (2007, 2009) with men and women incarcerated in the Florida prison system demonstrated that art therapy programs effectively reduced their depressive symptoms and improved their self-evaluations. Studying 46 incarcerated boys in Virginia juvenile justice system enrolled in an art therapy program, Persons (2009) found that the program benefited the youths in several ways, including:

1. Enhancing emotional well-being by relieving stress, reducing anger, depression, and anxiety, shifting attention away from upsetting things, and serving as an emotional outlet

2. Developing positive interpersonal relationships, receiving support and appreciative recognition from others

3. Increasing self-confidence, creativity and pride

4. Improving the ability to concentrate, focus, and persevere in spite of occasional frustrations and challenges

Assessment in Art Therapy

The most typical way of assessing the client's mental health in art therapy involves the employment of two standard procedures. First, the participants are requested to draw a picture of a person picking an apple from a tree (PPAT) with standardized art materials. Second, the therapist evaluates the art works by using the Formal Elements Art Therapy Scale (FEATS). The FEATS consists of 14 scales, each of which assesses 14 different aspects of the art piece, including (1) prominence of color (amount of color used), (2) color fit (how colors match the drawn targets), (3) implied energy, (4) space (arrangement of the drawn objects on the page), (5) integration (relationships among the objects), (6) logic (consistency with the requirement), (7) realism, (8) problem solving (e.g., use of a ladder to reach the apple), (9) developmental level, (10) details of the objects and setting, (11) line quality (the amount of control), (12) person (accurate drawing of the person), (13) rotation (object and person in relation to imaginary vertical axis), and (14) perseveration. The results of the assessment are used to give four major diagnoses: including (1) major depression, (2) bipolar disorder, (3) schizophrenia; and (4) other cognitive disorders (see Gussak, 2007, 2009).

However, freely chosen artistic expressions can also be used for assessment. Person's (2009) study with male juvenile offenders with severe mental disorders and behavioral problems show that the boys' art works (based on what they imagined or their adaptations from art books and magazines) revealed their nine psychological needs, including:

1. Identity issues
2. Need for security and tranquility
3. Need for freedom, adventure, and fun
4. Need for ideal parental relationships
5. Need for affiliation and affection
6. Erotic and sexual needs
7. Expression of depression
8. Expression of childhood trauma and other serious psychological problems
9. Spiritual or religious needs (p. 439)

Understanding those needs helps therapists address those issues by making focused treatments or interventions.

Why Art Therapy Is Uniquely Helpful

Research has shown that art therapy is uniquely helpful for correctional clients for the following reasons (see Gussak, 2007, 2009; Persons, 2009):

First, most offenders are involuntary clients who have suspicion and defense about treatment programs. In addition, they also have difficulty in articulating their mental and emotional problems because of a low level of education or other intellectual challenges. However, art therapy does not rely on the client's verbal skills for assessment and intervention, and it also stimulates strong participation and intrinsic motivation of the clients.

Second, most art therapy programs combine both individual and interactive group activities. When correctional clients engage in producing art works with others in a relaxed, joyful, and expressive environment, they (particularly youths) feel safe to share about their past experiences of abuse, emotional anguishes, and about their hopes for the future. This process creates spontaneous human connections, mental concentration, and reflection.

Third, art therapy not only helps the participants learn about themselves and one another, and develop their creativity and ability for cooperation, it may also help with cognitive development and generate new and healthy changes in the brain (particularly for juveniles) by creating more neural connections in the cerebral cortex.

Summary

Behavioral therapy is based on the theories of classical (respondent) conditioning and instrumental (operant) conditioning. Classical conditioning theory can explain both how people learn a sense of guilt and how to apply the mechanisms of aversive therapy and systematic desensitization. Operant conditioning theory postulates that a response is determined by the consequence that follows the response. If an event following a response increases the probability of future responding, the event is called reinforcement. A partial or intermittent reinforcement schedule is defined as a procedure that delivers reinforcement to an organism according to either ratio-based schedules or interval (time)-based schedules.

Cognitive therapy is based on the postulate that cognition or thinking largely determines how a person feels and behaves. There are three frequently used cognitive models in correctional counseling: (1) cognitive therapy, which focuses on revising negative self-concepts, (2) the cognitive approach, which targets the development of offenders' social and problem-solving skills, and (3) the cognitive model, which helps offenders discern how their deviant thinking leads to criminal acts.

Social learning theory maintains that antisocial behavior is regulated by vicarious reinforcement and punishment and by self-administered reward and punishment. Self-efficacy is defined as an individual's confidence in his or her ability to organize and execute a given course of action to solve a problem or accomplish a task. This model is used at different stages of substance-abuse treatment.

Positive psychology emphasizes understanding and facilitation of human strength and virtue, instead of examining pathology and dysfunction. Offenders are seen as active goal-pursuing individuals who are constantly seeking to understand meanings of their social and mental experiences and to accomplish main human goods—healthy living and functioning, mental peace, knowledge, excellence in what one does, the sense of control, friendship, spirituality, happiness, and creativity. Therefore, treatment and interventions based on the positive psychology model are intended to increase the offender's range of personal functioning, rather than to simply manage or remove a problem.

Art therapies in correctional counseling can help counselors and clients better understand the clients' mental conflicts, traumatic experiences, hope, creativity, and potential, and produce emotional healing, positive conduct, and interpersonal relationships.

Key Terms

Art therapy

Aversive therapy

Behavioral therapy

Classical conditioning

Cognitive structures (schemas)

Depression, as defined from the cognitive perspective

Fixed-ratio schedule of reinforcement

Good lives model

Intermittent reinforcement schedule

Irrational belief

Operant conditioning

Overgeneralization

Positive psychology

Rational-emotive therapy

Self-efficacy theory

Social (cognitive) skills training

Social learning theory

Solution-focused therapy

Strengths perspective

Token economy program

Variable-interval schedule of reinforcement

Variable-ratio schedule of reinforcement

Discussion Questions

1. Are negative self-concepts the same as irrational beliefs about the self?
2. What is the principle shared by the cognitive therapies?
3. How does the classical conditioning theory explain criminal behavior?
4. Describe some examples of defining a client's problems in terms of behavioral deficits and behavioral excesses.
5. What are the differences between cognitive skills and cognitive understanding?
6. Why should offenders learn social and cognitive skills?
7. What are the benefits of shifting from optimism?

References

Abela, J. R. Z., & Sullivan, C. (2003). A test of Beck's cognitive diathesis-stress theory of depression in early adolescents. *Journal of Early Adolescence, 23,* 384–404.

Baldwin, M. W. (1992). Relational schemas and the processing of social information. *Psychological Bulletin, 112,* 461–484.

Bandura, A. (1983). Psychological mechanisms of aggression. In R. G. Geen & E. I. Donnerstein (Eds.), *Aggression: Theoretical and empirical reviews* (Vol. 1, pp. 11–40). New York, NY: Academic Press.

Bandura, A. (1997). *Self-efficacy: The exercise of control.* New York, NY: Freeman.

Bandura, A. (2006). Toward a psychology of human agency. *Perspectives on Psychological Science, 1,* 164–180.

Beck, A. T. (1970). The core problem in depression: The cognitive triad. In J. H. Masserman (Ed.), *Depression: Theories and therapies* (pp. 47–55). New York, NY: Grune and Stratton.

Beck, A. T. (1991). Cognitive therapy: A 30-year retrospective. *American Psychologist, 46,* 368–375.

Benedict, L. W., & Lanyon, R. I. (1992). An analysis of deceptiveness: Incarcerated prisoners. *Journal of Addictions and Offender Counseling, 13,* 23–31.

Bergner, R. M. (2003). Emotions: A relational view and its clinical applications. *American Journal of Psychotherapy, 57,* 471–490.

Brown, J. D. (1998). *The self.* Boston, MA: McGraw-Hill.

Burn, M. F., & Brown, S. (2003). A review of the cognitive distortions in child sex offenders: An examination of the motivations and mechanisms that underlie the justification for abuse. *Aggression and Violent Behavior, 11,* 225–236.

Campbell, W. K., & Sedikides, C. (1999). Self-threat magnifies the self-serving bias: A meta-analytic integration. *Review of General Psychology, 3,* 23–43.

Cantor, N., & Kihlstrom, J. F. (1989). Social intelligence and cognitive assessments of personality. In R. S. Wyer Jr. & T. K. Srull, *Social intelligence and cognitive assessments of personality* (pp. 1–59). Hillsdale, NJ: Lawrence Erlbaum.

Caprara, G. V., Regalia, C., & Bandura, A. (2002). Longitudinal impact of perceived self-regulatory efficacy on violent conduct. *European Psychologist, 7,* 63–69.

Cepeda, L. M., & Davenport, D. S. (2006). Person-centered therapy and solution-focused brief therapy: An integration of present and future awareness. *Psychotherapy: Theory, Research, Practice, Training, 43,* 1–12.

Cohen-Liebman, M. S. (2002). Art therapy. In M. Hersen & W. Sledge (Eds.), *Encyclopedia of psychotherapy* (Vol. 1, pp. 113–116). Amsterdam, The Netherlands: Academic Press.

Conger, R. D., & Simons, R. L. (1997). Life-course contingencies in the development of adolescent antisocial behavior: A Matching Law approach. In T. P. Thornberry (Ed.), *Developmental theories of crime and delinquency* (pp. 55–99). New Brunswick, NJ: Transaction Publishers.

Daderman, A. M. (1999). Differences between severely conduct-disordered juvenile males and normal juvenile males: The study of personality traits. *Personality and Individual Differences, 26,* 827–845.

Davis, G. E., & Leitenberg, H. (1987). Adolescent sex offenders. *Psychological Bulletin, 101,* 417–427.

Deutsch, M. (1993). Educating for a peaceful world. *American Psychologist, 48,* 510–517.

Dunning, D., Heath, D., & Suls, J. M. (2004). Flawed self-assessment: Implications for health, education, and the workplace. *Psychological Science in the Public Interest, 5,* 69–106.

Eccles, J. S., & Wigfield, A. (2002). Motivational beliefs, values, and goals. *Annual Review of Psychology, 53,* 109–132.

Ellis, A. (1987). Rational-emotive therapy: Current appraisal and future directions. *Journal of Cognitive Psychotherapy, 1,* 73–86.

Ellis, A. (1993). Reflections on rational-emotive therapy. *Journal of Consulting and Clinical Psychology, 61,* 199–201.

Ellis, A., McInerney, J. F., DiGiuseppe, R., & Yeager, R. J. (1988). *Rational-emotive therapy with alcoholics and substance abusers.* New York, NY: Pergamon Press.

Eysenck, H. J. (1983). Personality, conditioning, and antisocial behavior. In W. S. Laufer & J. M. Day (Eds.), *Personality theory, moral development, and criminal behavior* (pp. 51–80). Lexington, MA: Lexington Books.

Fiske, S. T., & Taylor, S. (1991). *Social cognition* (2nd ed.). New York: McGraw-Hill.

Foster, S. L., & Crain, M. M. (2002). Social skills and problem-solving training. In F. W. Kaslow & T. Patterson (Eds.), *Comprehensive handbook of psychotherapy: Cognitive-behavioral approaches* (Vol. 2, pp. 31–50). Hoboken, NJ: Wiley.

Gussak, D. (2004). Art therapy with prison inmates: A pilot study. *The Arts in Psychotherapy, 31,* 245–259.

Gussak, D. (2007). The effectiveness of art therapy in reducing depression in prison populations. *International Journal of Offender Therapy and Comparative Criminology, 51,* 444–460. doi:10.1177/0306624X06294137

Gussak, D. (2009). The effects of art therapy on male and female inmates: Advancing the research base. *The Arts in Psychotherapy, 36,* 5–12. doi:10.1016/j.aip.2008.10.002

Heard, H. L., & Linehan, M. M. (1993). Problems of self and borderline personality disorder: A dialectical behavioral analysis. In Z. V. Segal, S. Blatt, Z. V. Segal, S. Blatt (Eds.), *The self in emotional distress: Cognitive and psychodynamic perspectives* (pp. 301–333). New York, NY: Guilford Press.

Higgins, S. T., Heil, S. H., & Lussier, J. P. (2004). Clinical implications of reinforcement as a determinant of substance use disorders. *Annual Review of Psychology, 55,* 431–461.

Hollon, S. D., Stewart, M. O., & Strunk, D. (2006). Enduring effects for cognitive behavior therapy in the treatment of depression and anxiety. *Annual Review of Psychology, 57,* 285–315.

Hunter, J. A., & Becker, J. V. (1994). The role of deviant sexual arousal in juvenile sexual offending: Etiology, evaluation, and treatment. *Criminal Justice and Behavior, 21,* 132–149.

Juhnke, G. A., & Coker, J. K. (1997). A solution-focused intervention with recovering, alcohol-dependent, single parent mothers and their children. *Journal of Addictions and Offender Counseling, 17,* 77–87.

Kelley, T. M. (2004). Positive psychology and adolescent mental health: False promise or true breakthrough? *Adolescence, 39,* 257–278.

Martin, G., & Pear, J. (1996). *Behavior modification* (5th ed.). Upper Saddle River, NJ: Prentice Hall.

Moseley, S., Briggs, W. P., & Magnus, V. (2005). Hypnotic psychotherapy with sex offenders. *Journal of Addictions and Offender Counseling, 26,* 38–51.

Persons, R. W. (2009). Art therapy with serious juvenile offenders: A phenomenological analysis. *International Journal of Offender Therapy and Comparative Criminology, 53,* 433–453. doi:10.1177/0306624X08320208

Pervin, L. A., & John, O. P. (1997). *Personality: Theory and research* (7th ed.). New York, NY: Wiley.

Petrovich, A. (2004). Using self-efficacy theory in social work teaching. *Journal of Social Work Education, 40,* 429–443.

Platt, J. J., & Husband, S. D. (1993). An overview of problem-solving and social skills approaches in substance abuse treatment. *Psychotherapy: Theory, Research, Practice, Training, 30,* 276–283.

Renshaw, K. L. (1994). Child molesters: Do those molested as children report larger numbers of victims than those who deny childhood sexual abuse? *Journal of Addictions and Offender Counseling, 15,* 24–32.

Safran, J. D., & Segal, Z. V. (1990). *Interpersonal process in cognitive therapy.* New York, NY: Basic Books.

Sakdalan, J. A., Shaw, J. J., & Collier, V. V. (2010). Staying in the here-and-now: A pilot study on the use of dialectical behaviour therapy group skills training for forensic clients with intellectual disability. *Journal of Intellectual Disability Research, 54,* 568–572. doi:10.1111/j.1365-2788.2010.01274.x

Seligman, M. E. P., & Csikszentmihalyi, M. (2000). Positive psychology: An introduction. *American Psychologist, 55,* 5–14.

Seligman, M. E. P., Rashid, T., & Parks, A. C. (2006). Positive psychotherapy. *American Psychologist, 61,* 774–788.

Smith, J. A. III, & Faubert, M. (1990). Programming and process in prisoner rehabilitation: A prison mental health center. *Journal of Offender Counseling Services, 15,* 131–153.

Staddon, J. E. R., & Cerutti, D. T. (2003). Operant conditioning. *Annual Review of Psychology, 54,* 115–144.

Steiman, M., & Dobson, K. S. (2002). Cognitive behavioral approaches to depression. In F. W. Kaslow & T. Patterson (Eds.), *Comprehensive handbook of psychotherapy: Cognitive-behavioral approaches* (Vol. 2, pp. 295–317). Hoboken, NJ: Wiley.

Stuve, P., & Salinas, J. A. (2002). Token economy. In M. Hersen & W. Sledge (Eds.), *Encyclopedia of psychotherapy* (Vol. 2, pp. 821–827). Amsterdam, The Netherlands: Academic Press.

Sun, K. (1993). The implications of social psychological theories of group dynamics for gang research. *Journal of Gang Research: An Interdisciplinary Research Quarterly, 1*, 39–44.

Sun, K. (2001a, March). *Knowing your clients and correctional counseling education.* Paper presented at the annual conference of the Academy of Criminal Justice Sciences, Washington, DC.

Sun, K. (2001b, March). *The implications of understanding the interpersonal and mental disconnections for correctional counseling.* Paper presented at the annual conference of the Academy of Criminal Justice Sciences, Washington, DC.

Sun, K. (2002, March). *Irrational beliefs v. rational "because" statements: A critique of the cognitive restructuring model.* Paper presented at the annual conference of the Academy of Criminal Justice Sciences, Anaheim, CA.

Sun, K. (2005a). Mentally disordered offenders in corrections. In R. Muraskin (Ed.), *Key correctional issues* (pp. 120–127). Upper Saddle River, NJ: Pearson Prentice Hall.

Sun, K. (2005b, May). *Anxiety reduction, interaction schemas, and negative cognitions about the self.* Poster presented at the annual convention of the American Psychological Society, Los Angeles, CA.

Sweeny, K., Carroll, P. J., & Shepperd, J. A. (2006). Is optimism always best? Future outlooks and preparedness. *Current Directions in Psychological Science, 15*, 302–306.

Sweezy, M. (2011). Treating trauma after dialectical behavioral therapy. *Journal of Psychotherapy Integration, 21*, 90–102. doi:10.1037/a0023011

Toch, H. (1992). *Violent men: An inquiry into the psychology of violence* (Rev. ed.). Washington, DC: American Psychological Association.

Todd, J., & Bohart, A. C. (2003). *Foundations of clinical and counseling psychology* (3rd ed.). Long Grove, IL: Waveland.

Trupin, E. W., Stewart, D. G., Beach, B., & Boesky, L. (2002). Effectiveness of dialectical behaviour therapy program for incarcerated female juvenile offenders. *Child and Adolescent Mental Health, 7*, 121–127. doi:10.1111/1475-3588.00022

Van Wormer, K. (1999). The strengths perspective: A paradigm for correctional counseling. *Federal Probation, 63*, 51–58.

Ward, T., & Mann, R. (2004). Good lives and the rehabilitation of offenders: A positive approach to sex offender treatment. In P. A. Linley & S. Joseph (Eds.), *Positive psychology in practice* (pp. 598–616). Hoboken, NJ: Wiley.

Wexler, D. B. (1999). Relapse prevention planning principles for criminal law practice. *Psychology, Public Policy, and Law, 5*, 1028–1033.

Whittinghill, D., Whittinghill, L., Rudenga, L., & Loesch, L. C. (2000). The benefits of a self-efficacy approach to substance abuse counseling in the era of managed care. *Journal of Addictions and Offender Counseling, 20*, 64–74.

Chapter 6

Advances in Interpersonal Cognitive Research and the Implications for Correctional Counseling

We previously examined offenders' issues and frequently used psychological models to explain them. The discussions have generated several questions that now need to be examined:

- What is the purpose of (offenders') cognition? To make themselves feel better or to balance their interactions with others and the environment?

- Do offenders have a separate cognition for administering their criminal activities or does the same cognitive system regulate all their internal and external social relations?

- If cognitive systems represent the self, others, and environments, how are the interactions among the entities organized and performed?

- How do environmental factors and human interactions (including counselors' interventions) influence (confirm, revise, or develop) individuals' cognitions that regulate their psychological activities?

This chapter will explore these issues of cognition by reviewing and analyzing recent advances in a broad psychological area (social cognitive research, criminal psychology, and humanistic psychology). The discussion will focus on the following aspects of social cognition:

1. Social cognition includes mental representations of the self and of the interrelationships with others and the environment (including how the self and others validate and invalidate each other's communications), rather than perceptions of the self and other entities in isolation.

2. Cognitive representations of social reality recognize the perceived patterns, rules, and norms that govern human interaction, rather than simply focusing on how people interact.

3. Perceived relations (which include consistency and inconsistency) are studied with perceived patterns and criteria to regulate and balance a person's internal and external relations. Cognitive schemas identify three related aspects of cognition: (1) mental representations of the self, others, and situations; (2) patterns and rules governing their interactions; and (3) perceived relations between the self and others and the patterns or criteria involved. These are described as *interaction schemas* or interaction-based cognition.

4. Correctional clients' cognition is viewed in terms of the relation between their attributes and behavior and their perception of patterns and rules to determine how they evaluate, explain, interpret, and understand their own positive and negative experiences as well as peace and conflict (including their crimes). In other words, effective counseling and interventions help clients develop more accurate cognitions about themselves, others, environments, patterns and rules governing the reality of interaction by recognizing the discrepancy between the human reality and their perceptions.

5. Social cognition takes the form of interaction schemas or a holistic cognitive system because only by accurately representing social reality can offenders function effectively in balancing interactions with reality.

Interaction Schemas Versus Relational Schemas

Research in social psychology has demonstrated that individuals' cognitions (including those of correctional clients) that regulate their evaluations, explanations, interpretations, adjustment and other psychological activities in their mental and interpersonal interactions take the form of **interaction schemas**—interaction-based cognitions that may be defined as generic cognitive representations of interpersonal reality and events. These schemas may be developed and maintained by repeated interaction experiences (Safran & Segal, 1990).

Although the concepts *interaction schemas* (Sun, 2005c) and *relational schemas* (Baldwin, 1992; Chen, Boucher, & Tapias, 2006) are related, interaction schemas are much broader than relational schemas.

The term **relational schemas** reflects simple interactions in close relationships, whereas the term *interaction schemas* refers to a more complex dynamic that includes: (1) cognitions of the self, others, and their mental structures and processes (including how the interacting persons evaluate, perceive, receive, validate, invalidate, adjust, and react to one another's communications); (2) the thinking, feelings, and attitudes of others; and (3) the evolving situations that facilitate and block human interactions. In other words, the expression of interaction schemas covers mental representations of both positive and close social relations and distressful human interactions (e.g., offenders' cognitive distortions of the victims and mental presentations of interpersonal traumas and childhood experience of abuse; see Ward, 2000).

Relational schemas view the regularities and patterns of interpersonal relationships in terms of interpersonal scripts—the elaborate sequence of behaviors of interacting individuals and describe how they interact in a situation (Baldwin, 1992). On the other hand, rather than regarding representations of the self and others in isolation, interaction schemas identify regularities between interacting individuals as perceived patterns, rules, and criteria that govern, transcend, and regulate interactions and explain why people interact the way they do (Sun, 2005c). These social–cognitive schemas, principles, and beliefs may include learned scientific knowledge as well as standards that we regard as controling and regulating interpersonal reality: morality, love, social desirability, aggression, and/or being right, beautiful, positive, or desirable (see more detailed discussion of these concepts later in this chapter).

Individuals use interaction schemas to encode, evaluate, categorize, and explain newly encountered interpersonal stimuli (interpersonal actions and communications) in order to retrieve relevant information from memory and to guide behavior in social interaction (Berscheid, 1994). The schemas administer individuals' thoughts, feelings, and behavior in social interactions through their mental expectations of people, including expectations about what will be required of them and how the interacting partners will act, think, feel, and behave (Snyder & Stukas, 1999). Researchers have demonstrated this phenomenon through the self-fulfilling prophecy. Investigations show that in situations where one person (the perceiver), having adopted beliefs about another person (the target), acts in ways that cause the behavior of the target to appear to confirm these beliefs. This prophecy is best exemplified by demonstrations in actual social situations. For instance, teachers having expectations of particular types and levels of academic performance from students in their classroom proceed in ways that elicit performances that corroborate these initial expectations. In a study on getting-acquainted conversations, participants who expected perceptual and behavioral confirmation of the stereotyped assumption indicated that physically attractive people have socially appealing personalities (Snyder & Stukas, 1999).

Offenders' Interaction Schemas

Offenders' interaction schemas are strongly influenced by their mental representations of the environment, the self, and others. Examples of "others" include all people who are actually (as perceived by the offenders) interacting with them—from family members such as father, mother, spouse, brothers and sisters to peers, teachers, children, friends, enemies, law enforcement officers, prosecutors, judges, correctional officers and counselors, and other staff. The way the offenders mentally represent and organize information about others (e.g., the victims, individuals who abused them in the past, legal personnel, and/or correctional counselors) has a direct effect on how they perform in correctional counseling and other programs.

Sex Offenders' Implicit Theories About Their Victims

According to Ward (2000), the results from this growing research field demonstrate that sexual offenders' cognitive distortions include underlying causal (implicit) beliefs or theories about their offenses and their victims that appear to be relatively coherent. They consist of a number of interlocking components related to viewpoints and attitudes rather than unrelated, independent cognitions. The implicit-theory approach suggests that a relatively small number of maladaptive implicit interaction schemas about the self and others may have a profound impact on sex offenders' criminal behavior and emotional and social adjustment. In particular, the contents of offenders' interaction schemas have the characteristics that both misconstrue their victims' mental state and justify their sex offenses by blaming the victims.

For example, sex offenders, or at least child molesters, depict children as being sexually provocative and as having benefited from the experience of sexual abuse. The offender's theory of the victim contains a misrepresentation of the victim's desires (needs, wants, and preferences), beliefs, and attitudes. Child molesters also have beliefs that legitimize sexual involvement with children and function to maintain offending. Child molesters, most particularly those men offending against other than family members, see children in sexual terms, as wanting sex, as not being harmed by sexual contact with an adult and therefore themselves as not really being responsible.

In addition, rapists' beliefs about their sex offenses are characterized by cognitions of aggression and dominance. Their cognitive distortions, frequently identified by researchers and clinicians, include "women who get raped get what they deserve," "women like to be dominated and controlled." They portray women as sexual aggressors and blame women for flirting with the offender. Blaming the victim, justifying offending, or excusing sexually abusive behavior are all examples of their cognitive distortions of interpersonal reality.

The Cognitive Distortions of Prejudice-Motivated (Hate) Offenders

Sun's (2006) analysis of research on hate crime shows that, like other offenders, hate offenders' cognitions about their victims and crimes are distorted. One of the distortions is self-serving bias, which tends to characterize people's explanations for their undesirable actions (i.e., making them desirable and reasonable from the agent's viewpoint; Bodenhausen, Macrae, & Hugenberg, 2003; Davidson, 1990; Fiske & Taylor, 1991, 2008). In addition, hate offenders' explanations for their crimes have the characteristics of blaming their victims and blaming differences in group membership as the cause of their offenses. These attributions misrepresent the social reality of what actually causes the crimes. Empirical research has shown that the mental state of hate offenders involves using victim memberships to justify and rationalize hate crime, including applying such methods as denials of injury to the victim, denial of responsibility, condemnation of the condemners, and "appeal to higher loyalties" by claiming a so-called "racial" motivation behind their criminal actions and other activities (Byers, Crider, & Biggers, 2004). Although these techniques of neutralization were first documented in criminological research (Minor, 1981), these concepts have been a focus of social–cognition research known as attribution theories.

Childhood Trauma and Offenders' Distorted Interaction Schemas

Research has confirmed that early childhood traumas have a profound influence on individuals' mental health well into adulthood (Elze, Stiffman, & Dore, 1999; Koch, Douglas, Nicholis, & O'Neill, 2006) and the likelihood they will become offenders (e.g., Burn & Brown, 2003; Hunter & Becker, 1994; Renshaw, 1994).

For example, most mentally disordered offenders were victims of abuse in childhood (Sun, 2005a), and most offenders suffer PTSD (posttraumatic stress disorder) (Koch et al., 2006). Davis and Leitenberg (1987) found that adolescent sex offenders had witnessed greater family violence and had experienced more physical and sexual abuse than nonsexual adolescent offenders. In addition, adolescents who have been sexually, physically, and/or emotionally abused as children show less empathy than nonabused children. They have trouble recognizing appropriate emotions in others and have difficulty taking another person's viewpoint (Burn & Brown, 2003). Furthermore, the results of Renshaw's (1994) investigation showed a strong relationship between offenders' childhood sexual victimization and the number of victims. In a study with 40 convicted child sexual offenders, participants completed an interview that included a polygraph and several psychological tests. The 20 offenders who had been sexually abused as children reported almost three times as many victims as the 20 participants who had not been sexually abused. In other words, children who are sexually victimized are at a much higher risk of becoming sexual offenders.

Furthermore, an important part of delinquents' cognitions that aggravate their involvement with offenses and their conflicts with the justice system is their perception that their parents were unfair and nonobjective in administering discipline. That explains why inconsistent or physically harsh discipline in the home (e.g., slapping, hitting, and punching) and emotional abuse (frequently screaming at the child, calling the child insulting names, excessively criticizing) and neglect (a gross lack of proper supervision and physical care) not only produce distorted interpersonal cognitions but also create the wrong guidelines for youths to solve interpersonal conflicts. The youths' perception of their parents' unfair interactions are confirmed in research by Smith and Kerpelman (2002), who studied adjudicated adolescent girls (aged 11–16 years) and their mothers (aged 32–44 years) and examined their perceptions of their relationship quality and communication styles. The results show that the common theme in the perceived relationship involves the daughter's complaints (for example, that the mother doesn't listen), lack of respect for the daughter and/or frequent misunderstandings.

How do we explain the observations that negative early childhood experiences consistently serve as an important precursor to committing abuses and offenses against others?

By reviewing the results of research in the fields of information processing, social learning, and self-regulation theories, Baer and Maschi (2003) maintained that trauma led to serious delinquency because adolescents whose lives were damaged by trauma developed more dysfunctional cognitive schemas than nontraumatized individuals who regulate how they perceive, encode, and react to social cues. The childhood traumas appear to have contributed to offenders' distorted interaction schemas (in addition to the emotions of anger and guilt) that they use to evaluate, explain, interpret, and adjust the self's interpersonal experiences and actions. The distorted cognitions that guide their psychological activities may include the beliefs that aggression and violence are the norms that govern interactions between the self and others (see Ward, 2000).

Supportive Relations and Hostile Relations

Offenders' interaction schemas about their relations with others can be grouped into two categories: (1) supportive relations and (2) hostile relations. Certainly there are many relations in between, but focusing on these two types of perceived relations will clarify the characteristics of perceived interpersonal reality.

Supportive relations include any type of interaction perceived as mutually beneficial and fair by clients. Offenders often have positive and pleasant feelings attached to this type of perception. Although most offenders have gone through abusive relations and have dysfunctions in their current interpersonal interactions, they may have a few supportive and positive relations from which they can draw strength.

It should be noted that perceived supportive relations may not always be prosocial. For example, one of the most consistent predictors of juvenile delinquency is peer association. With 246 boys living in inner-city Chicago neighborhoods as their research participants, Henry, Tolan, and Gorman-Smith (2001) examined the interaction among three variables: (1) family dynamics, (2) peer associations, and (3) antisocial behavior. They found that associating with delinquent friends, particularly those who engage in violent behavior, coupled with the low emotional connection within the family, is the strongest predictor for individual antisocial activities. In particular, adolescents who experienced low emotional support and inconsistent discipline from their parents, compared with youths from families characterized by warm interpersonal relationships and consistent discipline, reported having more deviant friends and being involved with more violent and nonviolent delinquent behavior. It can be argued that association with delinquent peers leads to antisocial activities because of the person's misperceptions of their peers' opinions when making decisions about what to do on a daily basis and about their lives as a whole.

Hostile relations are formed by the clients' cognitions of their interactions with others that are perceived as aggravating conflict and a sense of frustration or invalidation as well as being abusive, painful, and/or degrading (see Scarvalone, Fox, & Safran, 2005). Offenders have negative, hurt, or aversive feelings attached to this type of perception.

For example, they may have mental representations of several hostile relations, including their memories of childhood traumas (abusive relations), and their schemas about current conflicts with some correctional staff (maybe inaccurately assumed), other inmates, and/or some family members. In a conflict relationship, both partners' mental representations of the interpersonal situation include: (1) the available defense and approaches by the self; (2) the perceived available defenses and approaches by the interacting partner; and (3) interactions between both partners' defenses and approaches in terms of effectiveness.

Correctional counselors need to understand how offenders mentally represent others and whether their interaction schemas are distorted or accurate because they use the interaction schemas as guidelines to encode, evaluate, explain, construe, and adjust their experiences. The schemas include interactions with others, regulating their performance in correctional settings, and understanding and mitigating the conflicts they have experienced. Therefore, increasing the client's accurate interaction schema is a focus of correctional counseling.

Validation and Invalidation

The contents of interaction schemas include the perceived validation and invalidation in the process of communication between the self and others. They are two important mental components of interaction-based cognitions (see Leahy, 2005; Lesley, Buysse, & Ickes, 2005; Sillince, 1993). **Validation** in interaction can be defined as the processes in which a person's communications and messages (including intentions, desires, evaluations, judgments, and emotions) are recognized, accepted, encouraged, and confirmed by others, whereas **invalidation** refers to the process in which a person's communication, intentions, and judgments are denied, dismissed, or nullified by others. Both the validation and invalidation in interaction are perceived; therefore, individuals' cognition of the two processes may be accurate or distorted.

Leahy (2005) noted that the early experience of validation or invalidation when attempting to connect with others contributes to the success or failure of normal growth and emotions. Because many clinical clients received invalidations from others, therapists should understand the importance of validation as a central component of treatment. The validation/invalidation experience begins during infancy and early childhood and lasts a lifetime. From early on, humans' attempts at attachment or emotional connection are either nurtured (validated) or deflected (invalidated) through interacting with parents or others. The survey by Krause, Mendelson, and Lynch (2003) confirmed these observations. With the data from 127 participants who completed a series of self-report questionnaires, they found that a history of childhood emotional invalidation (i.e., psychological abuse and parental punishment, minimization, and distress in response to negative emotion) was strongly associated with chronic emotional inhibition and psychological distress in adulthood (i.e., ambivalence over emotional expression, thought suppression, and avoidant stress responses, as well as depression and anxiety symptoms).

Understanding the issues of validation and invalidation as parts of interaction schemas has at least four implications for correctional counseling:

1. **The experience of validation and invalidation serves as a source of the clients' emotions.** Emotion is defined as the awareness of the discrepancy between the experiences of validation or invalidation of the cognitive system that guides a person's expectations about social reality. Invalidation occurs when individuals use their distorted cognitive system to (1) anticipate events; (2) regulate psychological activities; and (3) test perceptions (Sillince, 1993).

2. **Marital distress or dissension can also be examined from the perspective of validation and invalidation.** Lesley et al. (2005) reported that there are either support or conflict interactions in marriage. Support interactions are epitomized by substantial behavioral similarities (i.e., validation/facilitation behaviors and neutral problem-solving behaviors) whereas conflict interactions are initiated and sustained by invalidation/antagonistic behaviors. In addition, partners' interaction-based cognition (e.g., feeling understood, satisfied) was especially affected by types of validation/facilitation interacting behaviors.

3. **The failure or ineffectiveness of some psychological practices may be engendered by the therapist's inability to validate the patient's feelings, values, and thoughts.** This inability thus becomes a significant impairment to both the therapy and the resolution of emotional difficulties. In addition, the clients and their emotional schemas may interfere with obtaining validation.

4. **Some correctional clients' dysfunctions in interpersonal domains involve their misunderstanding of the issue of validation and invalidation in situations of power disparity** (Sun, 2001). A repeated theme in correctional counseling revealed by clients involves childhood traumas of being sexually or physically abused in a situation where the abuser (the powerful adult) had punitive power over the child (the victim). The victims are afraid to communicate how they feel because they believe that the powerful adult, who generally dislikes unpleasant stimuli, may treat any negative communication as a sign of provocation and would retaliate against the victim. The nature of the issue, however, involves the victims' uncertainty about the validity of their approach. They are more likely to believe that the powerful side can invalidate the victims' truth or justice as long as the powerful side is willing to deny, palliate, or justify their wrongdoing or to undermine the veracity or fairness of the victims' approach. In other words, the victims have not discovered a connecting force that cannot be invalidated by the powerful side. The same issue still faces many correctional clients who misunderstand how to overcome the interpersonal abyss or disconnection between the self and others or how to turn their unilateral truth and justice into bilateral truth and justice.

Emotions as Relational Phenomena

Bergner (2003) developed the theory of **emotions as relational phenomena**, which maintains that emotions are to be viewed as a specific class of perceived relationships between oneself and a person, object, event, or state of affairs, rather than as inherently private affective or feeling states or experiences. The notion of relational emotions suggests a far greater range of therapeutic options than the traditional view.

For example, typical emotional concepts such as "love," "anger," "fear," and "sadness," form an appraisal of the relations between the self and other entities rather than indicating unique, internal, subjective human experiences. Take love as an example. Love is far more than a feeling state. It involves an interaction between individuals characterized by intimacy, commitment, and passion (Bergner, 2003). The same is true for negative emotions. According to Sun (2001), the nature of mental conflicts involves not only positive and negative self-concepts, but also a profound sense of distrusting others. In addition, most psychological symptoms (such as anger, guilt, depression, stress, anxiety, and self-doubt) are the result of a failed attempt to understand and overcome the self's disconnection from interpersonal reality rather than from the problem in oneself.

Bergner (2003) argued that although we tend to attribute emotional traits to individual persons in clinical practice and in everyday life, assuming the individuals are friendly, hostile, generous, fearful, or envious persons, in reality our evaluation of emotional traits is based on comparing the targets with the *average* person. In other words, we describe a person's emotional traits in relation to others.

In addition, the appraisal of the self's relations with other entities (e.g., a person, an event, or state of affairs) generates relevant motivation about how to interact or relate with others or situations. For example, to see something as a *danger* to me produces a motivation to escape or avoid it. To see something (e.g., being insulted or cheated) as a *provocation* to me provides the justification to be hostile or defensive (Bergner, 2003). In short, emotions are based on perceived relationships, and they serve as a source for interpersonal motivation.

The Self in Relation to Others

The discussion of interaction schemas entails the notion of the **self in relation to others** but it does not imply that individuals, including correctional clients, lack self-reflectiveness and the motivation to pursue self-knowledge, self-enhancement, and self-improvement. *Self-reflectiveness* involves people's mental processes of reflecting on their personal efficacy, the soundness of their thoughts, the validity of their actions, and the meaning of their actions and pursuits (Bandura, 2006). *Self-knowledge* refers to the desire for accurate and certain evidence of attributes and, in particular, for evidence that validates self-assessment. The need for self-knowledge is rooted in a need for consistency, uncertainty reduction, and/or the ability to predict and control the environment.

Self-enhancement refers to the desire for positive feedback about the self and for self-protection. *Self-improvement* refers to the desire to see oneself as increasingly close to some higher criteria of truth and value (Banaji & Prentice, 1994; Schlenker & Weigold, 1992).

Examining the issue of interaction schemas helps us to understand that self-awareness, self-knowledge, self-enhancement, and self-improvement take place only in interacting with others; the self is defined and evaluated only in relation to other entities such as criteria, standards, and social or human contexts.

It is problematic to assume that self-evaluation is determined by the self's criteria, as suggested by the *self-discrepancy theory* (Higgins, 1987). This theory assumes that people hold self-beliefs (actual-self) as well as beliefs about possible selves (the ideal-self and the ought-self, which serve as self-guides or standards motivating people to achieve a match between the guides and their actual self). It should be noted that the phrases *ideal-self* and *ought-self* refer to a person's perceived standards or criteria. Although they are subjective, the perceiver views them as representing more general rules governing human interaction. Therefore, they are not the self's standards but are related instead to perceived patterns that, if followed, can secure their valid approaches and overcome invalidation in social interactions. In addition, these criteria are shaped and defined by a culture or social values that the perceiver identifies with. In other words, although individuals compare themselves with their subjective criteria or standards, they must believe that perceived criteria represent reality concerning general patterns between themselves and others in social environments. They are aware that they cannot change these criteria at will.

Offenders' Social Cognition and Perceived Patterns

Research in psychology (e.g., Fiske & Taylor, 1991, 2008; Snyder & Stukas, 1999; Ward, 2000) showed that **social cognitions** include mental representations of interactions among social entities (e.g., the self, others, events, situations). We need to understand that individuals' interaction schemas contain their perceived patterns (standards, rules, criteria, norms, regulations, knowledge of human behaviors and other belief systems) that define, govern, and regulate interaction.

These patterns are much broader than the term "script," which refers to "how" individuals act in social situations or a temporary sequence of social interactions (Baldwin, 1992). The perceived patterns, however, involve the individual's mental representation of "why" the self and others act the way they do and why they have certain experiences. In other words, the perceived patterns governing social entities and their interaction denote individuals' implicit or explicit understanding and explanations of the causal structures of everyday experiences, the world, and human behavior (Keil, 2006).

According to Cialdini and Goldstein (2004), regardless of the types of criteria (scientific or moral) that people use, they always implicitly assume that the criteria are true patterns governing the reality of social interaction, because people are primarily motivated to form accurate perceptions of social reality. They react accordingly in order to develop and preserve meaningful social relationships and to maintain a favorable self-concept. A person's desire to respond appropriately to a dynamic social situation demands an accurate perception of reality. One inaccurate perception, cognition, or behavior could mean the difference between an experience of frustration or success, or between the experience of invalidation and the encounter of validation. In addition, all individuals are assumed to be able to act like scientists, forming hypotheses, testing them, and discarding those that fail to predict or confirm their expectations of the results. Throughout their lives, people develop a succession of increasingly accurate theories of the world and the mind (Ward, 2000).

Although individuals may believe that their interaction schemas are accurate representations of social reality, their beliefs may be distorted or inaccurate. This is an epidemic problem for the offender population. For example, Ward (2000) argued that sexual offenders' cognitive distortions emerge from underlying causal theories about the nature of their victims rather than from unrelated, independent beliefs. The offenders have implicit theories and beliefs that are relatively coherent and organized. Although their perceptions of their victims are inaccurate and severely distorted, they use the schemas like scientific theories to explain other people's actions and to make predictions about the world.

Perceived criteria or patterns may take the form of moral and value judgments. Personal moral standards that serve as guides and deterrents for conduct are linked to self-sanctions when individuals apply standards of right and wrong to monitor, judge, and regulate their conduct and the conditions under which it occurs (Bandura, 2006). According to Cialdini and Goldstein (2004) and Sun (2009), people use moral standards or social norms as explanatory patterns for social events and experiences because they assume that moral judgments represent scientific patterns regulating social reality. They use the relations (consistency or inconsistency) between moral or social norms and the target's (the self or others) attributes to understand and respond to social situations. That is why perceived (or misperceived) social norms or moral standards have been found to influence a range of behaviors in a myriad of domains.

It is important to understand the issue of perceived patterns and norms in social cognition because all internal and external communications (e.g., self-assessment and judgment, attribution, and adjustment and interpersonal communication) convey information about the target's relations (consistency/inconsistency) with the perceived criteria (see the more detailed discussion later in the chapter). Although offenders may not have accurate knowledge of legislation or ordinance, they do have moral standards and rules provided by their subcultures and learning experiences. It has been documented that a group's norms, rules, and moral standards serve to justify the actions of its individual members—in particular, when these actions are in conflict with established social norms and legislation. Offenders can even use the rules of conformity to benefit gang activities (Sun, 1993a). Conformity refers to the act of changing behavior to match the responses of others. Individuals who conform may have both informational and normative conformity motivations. Gang members who commit criminal activities with their group may assume that the majority of people have accurate knowledge of reality (informational motivation) or they want to obtain social approval from other members (normative conformity motivation). Both involve using interaction schemas to regulate actions (Cialdini & Goldstein, 2004; Sun, 1993a).

Interaction Schemas and the Regulation of Criminal Behavior and Other Psychological Activities

We need to understand that individuals' psychological activities (evaluation, explanation, and adjustments), which can be either functional or dysfunctional in the mental and interpersonal domains, are administered by their interaction schemas. The schemas consist of three cognitive components: (1) individuals' cognitions about the self, others, and environments (including physical and social contexts, and evolving situations that facilitate and block human interactions); (2) perceived patterns, norms, and other standards; and (3) perceived consistency and inconsistency between the targets (self and others) and the criteria. The interaction-schemas approach can be used to examine the psychological cause of criminal behavior, interpersonal conflict and harmony, negative self-concepts and emotional well-being from a unique perspective, as well as to suggest new directions for correctional intervention.

Distorted Interaction Schemas: A Psychological Cause for Criminal Behavior

The Meanings of Cognitive Distortions
Interaction schemas include cognitive structures and processes (knowledge, reasoning, perceiving, and decision-making) about the self, others, environments, and patterns and rules. Individuals' misconceptions of parts or the whole of the interrelated systems result in **cognitive distortions**.

The meaning of distorted interaction schemas consists of two dimensions: (1) an objective discrepancy between the perceptions of the self and others and of the patterns governing interactions and the human reality; and (2) the perceiver's unawareness of the discrepancy of his or her cognitive distortions.

In terms of the objective discrepancy with reality, offenders' cognitions may misrepresent reality about the self, others, and patterns or truth regulating human interaction. Their distorted cognition about the self involves inaccurate self-assessments (Barriga, Landau, Stinson, Liau, & Gibbs, 2000). Their distorted cognition about *others* involves misperceiving the intentions, needs, feelings, thinking, mental validation or invalidation of interpersonal communications, and actions of the victims, correctional staff, and others (Byers et al., 2004; Lakey, 1992; Saradjian & Nobus, 2003). For example, a correctional client may perceive the counselor's intention to help as a sign of hostility or manipulation.

The misconceived patterns that regulate interactions between the self, others, and situations consist of false assumptions about which principles are the guiding force for effective interaction with others and situations, assuming and applying invalid approaches as valid ones in dealing with human conflicts. The typical examples include offenders' preference for employing the rules of their intimate group (e.g., their gang affiliations) to define the legality or morality of their behavior rather than to follow the rules of society (Sun, 1993a). In addition, violent offenders tend to impose their desires, orders, or commands on others or on situations, with no consideration of the invalidation of their interacting with others and/or the operating situation (Blackburn, 1998). For example, offenders may believe that if they perceive their interactions (e.g., aggression and defense) as valid or invalid based on their internal judgments, the interacting other(s) will see the offenders' communications in the same way. Similar thinking may explain some clients' tendency to avoid communicating "negative" emotions or comments, not out of fear, but from the belief that being nice (the perceived pattern) is the only valid principle to follow and connect with those whose anger and intimidation have hurt their victims.

The subjective dimension of the offenders' cognitive distortions refers to the perceivers' unawareness that the cognitions that regulate their relations with the self and with others operate on a different level of awareness about human reality. Namely, offenders apply their distorted cognitions to their psychological activities because they assume that their knowledge of social reality is accurate. It is not only correctional clients who tend to have misconceptions with respect to their explanatory understandings: all people tend to think they understand the world in far more detail than they really do (Keil, 2006).

The subjective dimension of the offenders' cognitive distortion is important both for research and for treatment because although studies have shown the correlation between offenders' cognitive distortions and their crimes (Ward, 2000), the meaning of cognitive distortions was defined from the viewpoint of the researchers and/or victims. One of the issues overlooked in the investigations is whether the offenders are aware of their cognitive distortions related to their offenses or indeed whether they recognize their distorted cognition at all.

It can be argued that the offenders are not only unaware of their cognitive distortions about social entities (the self, others, and their victims) but use their beliefs that mismatch reality to guide their interpersonal actions and offenses. Social cognitive research has shown that people are motivated to minimize the disparity between their belief of "what is true" about human reality and the actual "truth." In other words, if they had true self-awareness about the discrepancy between their cognitions and reality, they would revise their perceptions (Sun, 2005b).

Cognitive Distortions and Crimes

Studies on the cognitive cause of criminal behavior show that offenders' distorted interaction schemas (which include misrepresenting the self, others, and patterns governing human interactions) generate criminal behavior. The following sections examine the association between offenders' distorted interacting schemas and three types of crime: (1) sex offenses, (2) hate crime, and (3) general aggression and violence.

Sex Offenses   Investigating the cognitive distortions in the self-report statements of clergymen who had sexually abused children, Saradjian and Nobus (2003) found that the offenders used their religious role and perceived relationship with God to justify their crimes and minimize the sense of guilt after offending, and to maintain a positive sense of self. Additionally, although all offenders tend to have cognitive distortions and misrepresentations about the needs, motivations, feelings of their victims (e.g., child molesters depict children as being sexually provocative and as having benefited from the experience of sexual abuse) (Ward, 2000), extrafamilial child molesters were more likely to endorse beliefs regarding the appropriateness of sexual contact with children (Hayashino, Wortele, & Klebe, 1995).

Lakey's (1992) study on male juvenile sex offenders (16 years of age and younger) showed that an undercurrent of misinformation and distorted belief permeated their cognitive systems. For example, they had distorted cognitions about the self (e.g., an inflated image of their abilities, insight, and knowledge). Their distorted knowledge about others included such misconceptions as "all adolescents are promiscuous." If a seated female crosses her legs, she is masturbating. The size of a penis is directly related to the size of the circle of its owner's hands or feet. In addition, they viewed family-taught values as sacred and above the law. They considered themselves disloyal to their families if they did not integrate family-taught values into their own systems, even if those rules and values were inappropriate or immoral. These boys assumed that their own faulty attitudes were universally held among their peers.

These studies clearly indicated that offenders' cognitive distortions that promote their involvement in sex crimes contain: (1) their faulty schemas about the self (inflated image of abilities, insight, and knowledge); (2) misrepresentations of their victims (describing children as being sexually provocative and as having benefited from the sexual offenses); and (3) false beliefs concerning rules and patterns that regulate human interaction and the offenders' relations with the patterns (e.g., clergymen who had sexually abused children used their religious role and perceived relationship with God to justify their crimes and minimize the sense of guilt after offending, and to maintain a positive sense of self).

Hate Crime   Empirical research shows that hate offenders' cognitions involve prejudice, which is a type of distorted cognitive schema about their victims. The indicators of prejudice may include: (1) erroneous generalization and oversimplification about the victims; (2) the formation of social attitudes toward the victims before or despite objective evidence; and (3) other inaccuracies in categorizing, evaluating, and explaining the victims' attributes (Sun, 1993b, 2006). Offenders' schemas contain misrepresented patterns or norms by which they rationalize and justify their hate, attitudes, and behavior. They use the victim and their own memberships to justify and rationalize hate crime, including blaming the victims and claiming that their illegal acts are performed on behalf of a certain race or religion (Byers et al., 2004; Sun, 2006).

General Aggression and Violence   A study by Barriga et al. (2000) showed that incarcerated juvenile delinquents showed higher levels of cognitive distortion (self-serving and self-debasing) than control groups. Most notably, self-serving cognitive distortions were specifically associated with delinquent or illegal behaviors (e.g., rationalizing their illegal acts by blaming the victims or situations), whereas self-debasing cognitive distortions were related to their mental conflicts (including anxiety about possible failures, exaggerating or personalizing negative experiences in the athletic, academic, and social areas).

Huesmann's (1988) cognitive-scripts model suggests that social behavior is controlled largely by cognitive scripts learned from daily experience. Individuals who have poorly integrated internal standards against aggression or who are convinced that violence is a way of life are more likely to incorporate aggressive scripts for their behavior. Dodge (1993) found that children prone to violence are more likely to have a hostile-attribution bias (interpreting ambiguous actions as hostile and threatening) than their less aggressive counterparts.

Guerra and Slaby's (1990) study revealed that after incarcerated delinquents in a maximum-security state juvenile correction facility participated in a cognitive mediation training (CMT) program, they showed increased skills in solving social problems and decreased endorsement of beliefs supporting aggression.

The results again demonstrate that offenders' distorted cognitions consist of their inaccurate interaction schemas that serve as the psychological mechanism for regulating their offenses.

Regulating Interpersonal Activities Through Interaction Schemas

The perspective of interaction schemas suggests a distinctive way to examine interpersonal activities. According to this approach, most of our intentional interpersonal actions or communications and related decision making (goal-setting, actions to take, and methods to use) are determined by our evaluation of the relations (consistency and inconsistency) between our patterns or standards and the attributes of a target (the self or other persons). The result of the evaluation determines both how we encode human communications (e.g., acceptance, rejection, or denial) and how we evaluate, explain, and predict the self's and interacting others' actions and experiences. For instance, people's passive interpersonal activities, such as withdrawal and fear (the perception of being defenseless when faced with either internal imprecation or external retaliation) result from perceiving their attributes or behavior as deviating from their mental criteria (Sun, 2009).

In contrast, individuals' active interpersonal engagements (such as love, compassion, acceptance, or the belief of being invincible and impervious to injury) are generated by viewing their attributes as consistent with their internal guidelines or interaction schemas. Their experiences of frustration or invalidation in interpersonal situations prompt them either to see the self as out of the ordinary or to see the individual with whom they are interacting as "abnormal." Either way, people use the target person's relations with their mental interaction schemas to understand and balance their interactions (Sun, 2009).

The perceived standards and the subsequent comparing and evaluating processes regarding the attributes of the self and interacting others are the regulators of our interpersonal activities as a result of two factors:

1. Intentional interpersonal actions or communications and related decision making (goal-setting, actions to take, and methods to use) depend on anticipated validity of the interactions (i.e., the actions and methods can realize the goal by overcoming possible invalidations) (Cantor & Kihlstrom, 1989).

2. The perceived validity of the communications (actions, methods, and goals) is decided by the belief that they match the interpersonal reality, the subjective form of which involves perceived patterns or standards (Cialdini & Goldstein, 2004).

Similarly, offenders' interpersonal actions that cause interpersonal conflicts can be understood as administered, at least in part, by their cognitions, which misrepresent the social reality concerning the self, others, and patterns or rules that govern social interaction (Sun, 2005b).

Offenders' interpersonal communications that are guided by distorted interaction schemas may produce two types of interpersonal conflict:

1. They may uphold others' confidence in aggression because their interactions with others, which involve violence or the avoidance of expressing authentic communications (e.g., they repress "negative" feelings of being hurt, and thus mollify, rather than admonish the aggressor) validates the others' misperceptions of the interpersonal reality.

2. They may jeopardize others' amity and affection for them when they fail to receive and validate others' desire for connection and friendship. In both situations, their interactions or communications generate or reinforce the self and others' misperceptions of interpersonal reality, which initiate interpersonal conflicts.

Mental Conflict and Distorted Interaction Schemas

According to the perspective of interaction schemas, various symptoms of mental conflict (including depression, anxiety, self rejection and alienation, guilt, perceived vulnerability to embroilment and adversity, and incapacity to expurgate past hurts) are associated with negative self-concepts and repeated frustration, failure, and other negative experiences, but they are caused neither by negative self-concepts nor by destructive encounters. Rather, mental experiences (mental conflict and well-being) are engendered by the person's mental system, including the types of perceived patterns and criteria by which the client evaluates the self and explains the self's experiences (Sun, 2009).

This observation indicates that offenders' mental experiences are mediated by perceived relations (consistency and inconsistency) with their mental standards or patterns. Just as positive assessments of the self (self-confidence, jubilation, and tranquility) arise from the perceived consistency between a person's attributes and the guiding principles he or she subscribes to, negative evaluations and related emotional suffering (low self-esteem, diffidence, guilt, unworthiness, fear, depression/anxiety, self-blame, and anger) are decided by the person's perceived deviation from those principles. Experiences of success prompt individuals to see their own attributes and actions as consistent with the patterns governing social reality, but experiences of frustration pressure them into adjusting their actions or attributes by directing their attention to the discrepancy from the internal criteria. This line of reasoning is consistent with clinical observations of the offender population and nonoffenders (Sun, 2001, 2005c).

Counseling and Interventions from the Perspective of Interaction Schemas

According to the model of interaction schemas, individuals experience mental, interpersonal, and other types of conflict because they use their distorted cognition of human reality (including their inaccurately perceived patterns, criteria, and norms) to evaluate the self's and others' attributes and actions. Therefore, counseling and treatment for mental, interpersonal conflicts involve helping clients alter their distorted interaction schemas.

For treatment personnel and correctional counselors, the appropriate approach involves knowing how to invalidate the false beliefs of clients by communicating information about a new reality that is beyond their mental invalidation in the social interaction and counseling process. This allows perceivers to see the discrepancy between their internal and external systems and adjust their mismatched cognitive system.

Counselors need to discern how interpersonal trauma experienced by offenders in their childhoods, which may have contributed to their cognitive distortions of social reality, promoted their involvement in criminal activities and substance abuse (Elze, Stiffman, & Dore, 1999; Fergusson & Horwood, 1998). Counselors need to understand how dysfunctional social interactions validate the offender's false belief about social reality. The meaning of validation is defined by the contents of the messages that are within the person's level of understanding, rather than by its values (e.g., being negative or positive). Offenders maintain their distorted cognition because communication from others or the environment has not changed their perceived reality.

To help clients understand and solve interpersonal conflict, counselors need to help clients see others' conflict-aggravating actions as guided by conformity to their internal, distorted cognitions of their interpersonal reality (including misrepresenting the clients' mental processes and situational context). Clients need to know that any methods backed by fear, coercion, intimidation, violence, and belligerence in dealing with human conflicts are counterproductive because the method of violence only validates cognitive distortions of others about the validity of aggression.

Therefore, this cognitive approach to interpersonal conflict resolution emphasizes the importance of communication. It is necessary to discern the self's cognitive discrepancy with human reality (the self's misperception of the minds and actions of others). It is also necessary to convey (through action and nonaction) that thinking, feelings, motivation, intentions, and actions are misrepresented in the cognition of others.

In addition, clients can be taught to invalidate and transform aggression in others by detecting the aggressors' cognitive deficiency in this area. For example, if the acrimony of others is guided by their cognitive unawareness of the client's psychological reality (how he or she evaluates, feels, perceives and corresponds to the others' aggression), the most appropriate strategy to invalidate their cognitive distortions is to communicate the client's feelings, needs, and evaluation and expectations of the aggressors. In addition, clients can learn that disengagement and detachment in conflict situations can deflect encroachments of others by contradicting the perceptions and expectations of those who exacerbate the situation. These methods include applying calm to subdue those who are obstreperous and using stillness to overcome heat (Sun, 1995).

The perspective of interaction schemas suggests a different approach to treating offenders' mental conflict. This approach shows the importance of understanding the self, but it views treatments that repress or change negative belief about the self as insufficient in healing mental or emotional injuries. Focusing on the positive aspects of the self may temporarily insulate individuals from their emotional anguish but doing so is not a panacea for mental conflict. Negative self-concepts are the symptoms rather than the psychological source of the conflict.

Rather than emphasizing a change in offenders' negative self-concepts and on re-examining the ratio of their achievements to their failures, the interaction-schemas model advocates that mental conflict (anxiety, depression, chagrin, guilt, diffidence, self-alienation) is generated by distorted cognitions about the reality of interaction (rather than simply about the self). These distortions are used as the criteria to evaluate and explain experiences. The solution to mental conflict and the strategy for creating peace (e.g., high self-confidence and esteem, psychological well-being and/or joy) is to revise the cognitions of human reality and discern the true patterns governing psychological activities. This approach includes learning how to interact with those individuals whose mental cognitions match human reality (including the reality of the perceiver's mental structure and processes). It is necessary to discern and invalidate the mental cognitions that deviate from reality. Moreover, abiding by human reality and natural patterns includes differentiating between blockages and opportunities such as knowing when to engage and when to detach from conflict (Sun, 2009).

Communicating thoughts and actions with interacting partners can revise others' actions by invalidating their distortions, because in social interactions, the self-thinking and actions are the contents of others' perceived reality or social environments. The thinking and actions of others are also part of the self's perceived reality (Bandura, 2006).

Why People Need Interaction Schemas

There are several reasons why cognitions take the form of representing the patterns of interactions between the self, others, and the situation rather than symbolizing the self or the other person in isolation:

1. We are social animals who construe the world in terms of interdependence. Our cognitive processes are geared toward discerning and recognizing familiar patterns of human interaction. We evaluate behavioral options in terms of our own needs and motives, and understand our partners' needs and predict their motives (Rusbult, Van, & Paul, 2003). Only by understanding the patterns can we realize the purpose of our social cognitions. The fundamental purpose of these cognitions is to balance our internal and external relations by understanding the mundane and monumental issues that we confront in everyday life. To achieve this goal, our schemas must mirror the reality of social interactions. These schemas, which function as cognitive maps to help us navigate through our social interactions, include our perceived interaction rules that govern ourselves and others, and the outcome of such interactions (validation and invalidation) (Baldwin, 1992; Cantor & Kihlstrom, 1989; Sun, 2009; Snyder & Stukas, 1999).

2. We are not just products of our life circumstances. As human agents we have the capacity to adapt and transcend the limitations of our immediate environment by shaping our life circumstances and the course our lives take. We create social systems and, conversely, these systems organize and influence our lives (Bandura, 2006).

3. We view both our consistency and inconsistency in our belief systems (values, principles, and standards) as the vehicle for understanding the reality of mental and human interaction. We assume that the internal criteria or schemas mirror universal law(s) regulating our interactions with others and in situational contexts. Consequently, any deviation from our mental standards is used to explain our experience of obstruction or invalidation, whereas maintaining our link with internal oneness is believed to enable us to overcome any invalidation generated by the self or others and by adversities. Oneness will validate our negotiations and communication with the mental and interpersonal entities.

4. Correctional clients' distorted interaction schemas serve as the psychological cause of the dysfunction in their mental, interpersonal, and other domains. To use cognitive therapies from the perspective of interaction schemas, correctional counselors need to focus their efforts on appraising and modifying offenders' inaccurate interaction schemas or cognitions that guide their psychological activities (evaluations, explanations, interpretations, and adjustments of their mental and social experiences).

Summary

Advances in social cognitive research indicate that social cognition takes the form of interaction schemas rather than cognitions of the self and other entities in isolation. Therefore, offenders' cognitive distortions include the misrepresentations of the self, others (including the victims), perceived patterns and norms of human interaction, and the relations between their perceived patterns/norms and their attributes. Their interaction schemas determine how they evaluate, explain, interpret, and understand their own criminal behavior as well as positive and negative experiences.

Social cognition represents a holistic cognitive system because social reality is an interconnected system and only by accurately representing social reality can individuals function effectively in balancing their interactions with reality.

Key Terms

Cognitive distortions

Emotions as relational phenomena

Hostile relations

Interaction schemas

Relational schemas

Self in relation to others

Social cognition

Supportive relations

Validation and invalidation

Discussion Questions

1. What are the purposes of offenders' cognitions? Just to make themselves feel better or to balance their interactions with others and their environments?

2. How do offenders' childhood traumas influence their distorted cognitions of social reality?

3. What is the psychological source of mental conflicts?

References

Baer, J., & Maschi, T. (2003). Random acts of delinquency: Trauma and self-destructiveness in juvenile offenders. *Child and Adolescent Social Work Journal, 20,* 85–98.

Baldwin, M. W. (1992). Relational schemas and the processing of social information. *Psychological Bulletin, 112,* 461–484.

Banaji, M. R., & Prentice, D. A. (1994). The self in social contexts. *Annual Review of Psychology, 45,* 297–332.

Bandura, A. (2006). Toward a psychology of human agency. *Perspectives on Psychological Science, 1,* 164–180.

Barriga, A. Q., Landau, J. R., Stinson, B. L., Liau, A. K., & Gibbs, J. C. (2000). Cognitive distortion and problem behaviors in adolescents. *Criminal Justice and Behavior, 27,* 36–56.

Bergner, R. M. (2003). Emotions: A relational view and its clinical applications. *American Journal of Psychotherapy, 57,* 471–490.

Berscheid, E. (1994). Interpersonal relationships. *Annual Review of Psychology, 45*, 79–129.

Blackburn, R. (1998). Criminality and the interpersonal circle in mentally disordered offenders. *Criminal Justice and Behavior, 25*, 155–176.

Bodenhausen, G. V., Macrae, C. N., & Hugenberg, K. (2003). Social cognition. In T. Millon & M. J. Lerner (Eds.), *Handbook of psychology* (Vol. 5, pp. 257–282). Hoboken, NJ: Wiley.

Burn, M. F., & Brown, S. (2003). A review of the cognitive distortions in child sex offenders: An examination of the motivations and mechanisms that underlie the justification for abuse. *Aggression and Violent Behavior, 11*, 225–236.

Byers, B., Crider, B. W., & Biggers, G. K. (2004). A study of hate crime and offender neutralization techniques used against the Amish. In P. B. Gerstenfeld & D. R. Grant (Eds.), *Crimes of hate: Selected readings* (pp. 118–129). Thousand Oaks, CA: Sage Publications.

Cantor, N., & Kihlstrom, J. F. (1989). Social intelligence and cognitive assessments of personality. In R. S. Wyer, Jr. & T. K. Srull, *Social intelligence and cognitive assessments of personality* (pp. 1–59). Hillsdale, NJ: Lawrence Erlbaum.

Chen, S., Boucher, H. C., & Tapias, M. P. (2006). The relational self revealed: Integrative conceptualization and implications for interpersonal life. *Psychological Bulletin, 132*, 151–179.

Cialdini, R. B., & Goldstein, N. J. (2004). Social influence: Compliance and conformity. *Annual Review of Psychology, 55*, 591–621.

Davidson, D. (1990). Paradoxes of irrationality. In P. K. Moser (Ed.), *Rationality in action: Contemporary approaches* (pp. 449–464). New York, NY: Cambridge University Press.

Davis, G. E., & Leitenberg, H. (1987). Adolescent sex offenders. *Psychological Bulletin, 101*, 417–427.

Dodge, K. A. (1993). Social-cognitive mechanisms in the development of conduct disorder and depression. *Annual Review of Psychology, 44*, 559–584.

Elze, D., Stiffman, A. R., & Dore, P. (1999). The association between types of violence exposure and youths' mental health problems. *International Journal of Adolescent Medicine and Health, 11*, 221–255.

Fergusson, D. M., & Horwood, L. J. (1998). Exposure to interparental violence in childhood and psychosocial adjustment in young adulthood. *Child Abuse and Neglect, 22*, 339–357.

Fiske, S. T., & Taylor, S. E. (1991). *Social cognition* (2nd ed.). New York, NY: McGraw-Hill.

Fiske, S. T., & Taylor, S. E. (2008). *Social cognition: From brains to culture* (3rd ed.). New York, NY: McGraw-Hill.

Guerra, N. G., & Slaby, R. G. (1990). Cognitive mediators of aggression in adolescent offenders: II. Intervention. *Developmental Psychology, 26*, 269–277.

Hayashino, D. S., Wortele, S. K., & Klebe, K. (1995). Child molesters: An examination of cognitive factors. *Journal of Interpersonal Violence, 10*, 106–116.

Henry, D. B., Tolan, P. H., & Gorman-Smith, D. (2001). Longitudinal family and peer group effects on violence and nonviolent delinquency. *Journal of Clinical Child Psychology, 30*, 172–186.

Higgins, E. T. (1987). Self-discrepancy: A theory relating self and affect. *Psychological Review, 94*, 319–340.

Huesmann, L. R. (1988). An information processing model for the development of aggression. *Aggressive Behavior, 14*, 13–24.

Hunter, J. A., & Becker, J. V. (1994). The role of deviant sexual arousal in juvenile sexual offending: Etiology, evaluation, and treatment. *Criminal Justice and Behavior, 21*, 132–149.

Keil, F. C. (2006). Explanation and understanding. *Annual Review of Psychology, 57*, 227–254.

Koch, W. J., Douglas, K. S., Nicholis, T. L., & O'Neill, M. L. (2006). *Psychological injuries: Forensic assessment, treatment, and law*. New York, NY: Oxford University Press.

Krause, E. D., Mendelson, T., & Lynch, T. R. (2003). Childhood emotional invalidation and adult psychological distress: The mediating role of emotional inhibition. *Child Abuse and Neglect, 27*, 199–213.

Lakey, J. F. (1992). Myth information and bizarre beliefs of male juvenile sex offenders. *Journal of Addictions and Offender Counseling, 13*, 2–10.

Leahy, R. L. (2005). A social-cognitive model of validation. In P. Gilbert (Ed.), *Compassion: Conceptualizations, research and use in psychotherapy* (pp. 195–217). New York, NY: Routledge.

Lesley, L., Buysse, A., & Ickes, W. (2005). Conflict and support interactions in marriage: An analysis of couples' interactive behavior and on-line cognition. *Personal Relationships, 12*, 23–42.

Minor, W. W. (1981). The neutralization of criminal offense. *Criminology, 18*, 103–120.

Renshaw, K. L. (1994). Child molesters: Do those molested as children report larger numbers of victims than those who deny childhood sexual abuse? *Journal of Addictions and Offender Counseling, 15*, 24–32.

Rusbult, C. E., Van, L., & Paul, A. M. (2003). Interdependence, interaction, and relationships. *Annual Review of Psychology, 54*, 351–375.

Safran, J. D., & Segal, Z. V. (1990). *Interpersonal process in cognitive therapy.* New York, NY: Basic Books.

Saradjian, A., & Nobus, D. (2003). Cognitive distortions of religious professionals who sexually abuse children. *Journal of Interpersonal Violence, 18*, 905–923.

Scarvalone, P., Fox, M., & Safran, J. D. (2005). Interpersonal schemas: Clinical theory, research, and implications. In M. W. Baldwin (Ed.), *Interpersonal cognition* (pp. 359–387). New York, NY: Guilford Press.

Schlenker, B. R., & Weigold, M. F. (1992). Interpersonal processes involving impression regulation and management. *Annual Review of Psychology, 43*, 133–168.

Sillince, J. A. A. (1993). There is more to emotion than goal attainment. *Genetic, Social, and General Psychology Monographs, 119*, 491–513.

Smith, S. L., & Kerpelman, J. L. (2002). Adjudicated adolescent girls and their mothers: Examining relationship quality and communication style. *Journal of Addictions and Offender Counseling, 23*, 15–29.

Snyder, M., & Stukas, A. A., Jr. (1999). Interpersonal processes: The interplay of cognitive, motivational, and behavioral activities in social interaction. *Annual Review of Psychology, 50*, 273–303.

Sun, K. (1993a). The implications of social psychological theories of group dynamics for gang research. *Journal of Gang Research: An Interdisciplinary Research Quarterly, 1*, 39–44.

Sun, K. (1993b). Two types of prejudice and their causes. *American Psychologist, 48*, 1152–1153.

Sun, K. (1995). How to overcome without fighting: An introduction to the Taoist approach to conflict resolution. *Journal of Theoretical and Philosophical Psychology, 15*, 161–171.

Sun, K. (2001, March). *The Implications of understanding the interpersonal and mental disconnections for correctional counseling.* Paper presented at the annual meeting of the Academy of Criminal Justice Sciences, Washington, DC.

Sun, K. (2005a). Mentally disordered offenders in corrections. In R. Muraskin (Ed.), *Key correctional issues* (pp. 120–127). Saddle River, NJ: Pearson Prentice Hall.

Sun, K. (2005b, March). *The importance of understanding offender cognitive distortions in correctional assessments.* Paper presented at the annual meeting of the Academy of Criminal Justice Sciences, Chicago, IL.

Sun, K. (2005c, May). *Anxiety reduction, interaction schemas, and negative cognitions about the self.* Poster presented at the annual meeting of the American Psychological Society, Los Angeles, CA.

Sun, K. (2006). The legal definition of hate crime and the hate offender's distorted cognition. *Issues in Mental Health Nursing, 27*, 597–604.

Sun, K. (2009). Using Taoist principle of the unity of opposites to explain conflict and peace. *The Humanistic Psychologist, 37*, 271–286.

Ward, T. (2000). Sexual offenders' cognitive distortions as implicit theories. *Aggression and Violent Behavior, 5*, 491–507.

Chapter 7

Counseling Processes

There are **three phases of the counseling process** for nonoffender populations (Hepworth & Larsen, 1993; Hepworth, Rooney, Rooney, Strom-Gottfried, & Larsen, 2006): (1) assessment, (2) intervention, and (3) termination/follow up.

- **Phase 1**: Counselors' activities during the assessment phase generally include client engagement, which is intended to start a therapeutic relationship of trust between the client and the counselor (Ivanoff, Blythe, & Tripodi, 1994); interviewing; exploration of the clients' issues—making direct observations of the nonverbal behavior of the clients and of interactions between the clients and others; obtaining collateral information about the clients from relatives, physicians, and other professionals; making formal and informal assessments; and planning (establishing rapport, formulating a multidimensional assessment of the problem, enhancing motivation of client(s) when inadequate, mutually negotiating goals to be accomplished, and formulating a contract).

- **Phase 2**: During the intervention phase, therapists focus on performing case management (matching available resources with the client's needs areas and coordinating the services) and changing the client's dysfunctions in their mental (e.g., distorted social cognitions), medical, interpersonal, family, and other areas by employing various psychological models and resources. Intervention may include one or a combination of three purposes: (1) *remediation*, which entails the elimination or amelioration of existing problems; (2) *prevention*, which attempts to control a dysfunction before it develops; and (3) *restoration*, which aims to rehabilitate clients whose functioning has been impaired by physical, mental, or

113

other difficulties (Hepworth & Larsen, 1993). Monitoring an improvement in the client's condition should begin as soon as the intervention is implemented in order to obtain information about the extent of progress toward treatment goals or intervention objectives (Ivanoff, Blythe, & Tripodi, 1994).

- **Phase 3**: The termination phase will occur when both the therapist and the client conclude that the counseling goals have been achieved, although some follow up may be necessary to determine whether the client is maintaining the progress made earlier in order to consolidate the result.

Counseling Processes for the Offender Population

The counseling processes for involuntary clients (offender population) incorporate most of the components of the counseling practice for nonoffender clients, but they have the following unique characteristics:

1. The first stage of the helping process is most important because involuntary clients generally enter initial interviews with negative and perhaps hostile feelings (Brodsky, 2011; Hepworth & Larsen, 1993). On the other hand, because a higher percentage of correctional clients are offenders who return to the correctional system for new convictions, counselors may already have some information about the clients based on previous experiences working with them.

2. For correctional counselors, both assessment and intervention are ongoing processes at each meeting with clients who either serve their time in incarceration or in the community. There are always new issues in the client's dysfunctions (e.g., violations of supervision conditions, infractions or breaches, interpersonal conflicts, family conflicts, and/or mental disorders). Updating previous assessments may be needed whenever new information about the client becomes available. Information about the offenders in community corrections may come from law enforcement, social service agents, family members, employers, and other agents that are related to offenders in some way.

3. The concept of termination has a different meaning in correctional counseling. More often than not, the counseling process for a correctional client in prison is terminated not because the counselor has reached the treatment goals but because the client must be transferred to another correctional institution. For security reasons, the counselor is not allowed to inform the client about the transfer until the day before. In other words, correctional counselors in prison settings can seldom complete treatments as planned. Counselors should pay particular attention to the issue of treatment termination because it tends to elicit a wide variety of feelings and behaviors. According to Baum (2005), the more clients believe that they have attained their therapeutic goals and they have the choice in the termination, the more positive feelings and reaction they have toward the termination. On the other hand, clients

are inclined to show great resistance, anger, rage, anxiety, and frustration regarding treatment termination when the termination is abrupt and is outside their control and desire. Sadly, treatment termination in correctional settings is often unexpected and happens beyond the control of the offender. To prevent or alleviate the client's rage and negative behavior in relation to the termination, prison or jail counselors need to inform him or her about unanticipated counseling termination at an early stage of intervention and to prepare to handle the negative reactions when they occur. Treatment plans for offenders in community corrections are also subject to other factors. Some clients may stop coming to the required treatment programs because of lack of motivation or because of having committed new offenses, thus again being processed by the criminal justice system.

Issues in Correctional Assessment

According to Brodsky (2011), and Ivanoff, Blythe, and Tripodi (1994), counselors need to know that obstacles to effective engagement and practice with offenders may come from three sources: (1) practitioners or counselors, (2) offenders, and (3) environments.

Practitioner-generated obstacles include the counselors' mismatched beliefs and emotions about the client population (e.g., anger toward and anxiety about the clients), inappropriate professional expectations (e.g., interpreting offenders' silence, hostility, or unwillingness as suggesting that clients devalue them or see them as lacking in skills), and inadequate training and preparation.

Offender-generated obstacles consist of the offender's dysfunctional mental mechanisms that impede the formation of the helping relationship, including reluctance, unwillingness, noncompliance, and hostility toward therapy or being overagreeable or extremely cooperative (this type of behavior also indicates a lack of successful engagement). In addition, offenders may practice malingering and deception.

Environmental obstacles such as social–political atmospheres that devalue counseling and treatment as well as unsupportive agencies and settings may all generate obstacles for successful engagement with involuntary clients.

Before counselors interview clients, they should thoroughly review previously administered, structured screening instruments for offender classification and assessment. These appraisals may be performed by correctional staff members at the reception center of state or federal correctional institutes or other facilities. Additional information about clients may include current crime convictions, sentence, infractions, and current symptoms of physical, mental, and emotional disorder. This information about the offender is typically stored in the database of the correctional institution.

Prior to performing assessments and interviews, counselors need to inform clients about the purpose of the evaluation and the associated limits on confidentiality according to the policy of the correctional institution. The counselors should involve the clients in formulating their treatment or supervision (in community corrections), including plans to reduce their defiance.

Brodsky and Lichtenstein (1999) suggest that when conducting therapy with offenders, who usually feel distrust, resentment, sadness, or anger toward the justice system and/or the counselor, counselors or therapists should avoid asking two types of questions that are detrimental to successful therapy with unwilling clients.

The first type includes routine greeting questions, such as "How are you?" and "How have you been doing?" This type of question is not productive with involuntary clients because they do not generate any concrete information. Some clients construe these questions as a form of inspection by the state, with the counselor acting as an agent of the state. In addition, if therapists ask the questions, and clients answer them, clients may come to believe that the essence of therapy rotates around such exchanges. This type of question will not help therapy because it cannot change the distorted cognitions of the client. Therapeutic changes result from therapist interventions that use honesty and compel direct feedback to change the client's perception of reality or the world, of others and of themselves.

The second type of question to be avoided with involuntary clients is a "why" question: "Why did you commit the crime?" or "Why don't you say anything?" The question "why" tends to be a blind alley question that distracts offenders from personal exploration and problem solving and forces them to generate an understanding of the cause-and-effect relationship for their actions or experiences. Avoiding such questions does not imply that the counselor is not interested in uncovering the causes of the client's dysfunction. On the contrary, the counselor needs the whole counseling process to find the answer.

Assessing **responsivity**—the degree of a client's readiness for counseling, defined as willingness to participate, ability to improve, and confidence to succeed (Loos, 2002)—is a necessary step in evaluating a client's issues and performing target interventions. The responsivity principle refers to delivering treatment programs in a style and manner that correspond to the ability and learning style of the correctional client (Andrews & Bonta, 2003).

As discussed previously, cognition takes the form of interaction schemas, including self-concept, perceived others and situations, and perceived patterns or norms that govern human interaction. Therefore, in addition to assessing offenders' dysfunction in the legal, interpersonal, substance abuse, family, employment, education, mental health, and other areas with standard instruments, counselors need to explore how clients misrepresent themselves, others, situations, and interactions between such entities. Only by understanding clients' distorted interaction-based cognitions that hinder their efforts to evaluate and overcome conflict can correctional counseling help them develop mental well-being and functional behavior.

The assessment of self-concept includes how clients view themselves in relation to others and how they evaluate and explain their emotional distress or interpersonal and situational conflicts. For example, clients are often unaware that false beliefs about themselves and others put them in conflict situations.

Counselors need to know how clients mentally represent others and their mental processes (cognitions, emotions, intentions, and motivations). The others include not only victims but also correctional staff and officers, family members, friends, and acquaintances or people who have shaped a client's life in some significant way (e.g., either their abusers or their mentors). Clients' cognitions comprise their perceptions of how others judge and explain their mental processes and actions. For example, they are often unaware that others may misperceive their viewpoint, understanding, expectations and standards, needs, and reasons regarding an interpersonal interaction, assuming that their knowledge of the self is the same in the minds of others.

Understanding clients' erroneous or inaccurate cognitions of others and their mental processes can help detect the sources of both their mental conflicts (e.g., childhood trauma) and their dysfunction in interpersonal conflict resolution.

Counselors must assess what principles, norms, and criteria the offenders regard as guidelines for evaluating, explaining, and adjusting their interpersonal experiences of validation, invalidation, and actions. For instance, although some offenders believe aggression and coercion are the guiding principles of their interpersonal actions (Blackburn, 1998), other offenders may follow the rules and believe that compliance with prison regulations is the way to evaluate themselves and others. Offenders' cognitive distortions about norms may also manifest themselves as ignorance of the statutes for illegal behavior (e.g., seeing family rules as superior to other norms; see Lakey, 1992).

Issues in Correctional Interventions

Eclecticism

Eclecticism is defined as the process of selecting concepts and strategies from various theories—from conventional cognitive-behavioral therapy, social learning model, self-efficacy, art therapy, and other social science approaches—for use in a single approach. It also refers to flexibility in applying a variety of methods (e.g., individual counseling, group modality) and the extensive use of combinations of verbal, visual, and kinesthetic media during the process of counseling (Loos, 2002).

Goal Setting and Cognitive Capacity

Realistic goals promote greater participation than moderately difficult and vague goals because they guide attention, effort, and action toward specific targets (Locke & Latham, 2006).

Goal setting with the client is often the first step in correctional interventions. The goal of a particular correctional intervention is determined by both the issues of the offender to be addressed (e.g., cognitive distortions, poor impulse control) and the therapeutic model employed by the counselor or therapist. In other words, the goal of treatment and intervention should be both meaningful (in the client's understanding) and measurable. The counselor can document the progress and results of intervention. For example, the main goal of cognitive-behavioral therapy is to modify maladaptive cognitive, emotional, and behavioral responses to the self and one's environment, including developing problem-solving skills. All these changes are measurable (Erickson & Achilles, 2004; Foster & Crain, 2002).

In addition, for goals to be enacted by offenders, counselors must be aware that realizing goals depends not only on offenders' motivations but also on their ability and skills. Motivation activates offenders' existing cognitive spectrums but it cannot make them perform tasks about which they have limited or no knowledge or skills. For example, a counselor may set up the goal that the offender needs to obtain a GED diploma. To help the client achieve such a goal, the counselor must gauge his or her learning capacities and may need to assist the offender in obtaining some related learning, memorizing, and thinking techniques.

Helping Clients Discern and Express Their Feelings

How should counselors help clients to become aware of and to express their feelings from a relational perspective? Helping clients to recognize such feelings is one of the most time-honored and broadly accepted clinical endeavors. Emotion plays a significant role in the counseling process. Feelings exist and are neither subordinate to nor dependent on cognition or behavior. All healing processes, growth, and change are accompanied by feelings (Loos, 2002). From the relational perspective of emotion, helping clients to be aware of what they are feeling remains in many circumstances an appropriate practice. However, this relational approach focuses on helping clients discern their feelings (anger, fear, or love) in the context of their interactions with other persons, events, and states of affairs (Bergner, 2003).

Motivational Interviewing

Motivational interviewing (**MI**) is an intervention technique that has great potential for use in the adult corrections arena. Although it is called "interviewing," it is best implemented during the intervention phase rather than the assessment phase (Hettema, Steele, & Miller, 2005; Miller & Moyers, 2005).

Motivational interviewing is a method to help clients work through hesitation and commit to change. It emphasizes and honors client autonomy and the ability to choose whether, when, and how to change. Although some clients are often ready to take action to overcome their dysfunctions and to take action in the right direction, others still have an involuntary attitude about their behaviors or attitudes.

The basic MI technique explores the client's own arguments for change. Four principles guide this approach:

1. The MI therapist seeks to evoke the client's desire, ability, reasons, and need for change—and responds with reflective listening. Clients thus hear themselves explaining their own motivation for change, and hear the reasons reaffirmed again by the counselor. Accurate empathy is crucial to obtaining an accurate understanding of the client's own perspective.

2. The therapist helps clients recognize the discrepancy between their current behaviors and their important goals or values.

3. The therapist diffuses clients' resistance and directs them back toward the intrinsic motivation for change.

4. The therapist supports clients' self-efficacy and conveys the message that clients are capable of change, with confidence in their desire and capacity to grow in positive directions. This process strengthens clients' motivational and verbal commitment to change, particularly when it is combined with a specific plan for implementing change.

The Therapeutic Relationship

Although the selection of counseling models and methods is important for performing effective counseling and intervention, the way counselors and offenders interact may be more crucial. The concept of the **therapeutic relationship** is based on Carl R. Rogers' (1902–1987) theory of person-centered counseling and the need for positive regard. For Rogers, the client is basically active and self-actualizing. A good therapeutic relationship includes such attitudes as warmth, liking, respect, sympathy, and acceptance (Pervin & John, 1997). Loos (2002) maintained that, as suggested by Rogers, feelings play a vital role in an individual's wholeness of being. Counselors can expand their ability to bring about change by consciously incorporating emotion into the counseling process. The validity of empathy, warmth, and genuineness has been established by research. From the cognitive perspective, feelings are also cognitions, because the feelings-based counseling process conveys a new interpersonal reality for the clients of which they were previously unaware.

Yalom (1998) suggested that it is the relationship between the client and therapist that generates healing power. Thus, developing a collaborative working relationship with the client is essential, particularly with offenders in corrections. They are involuntary clients whose attitudes toward counseling and supervision range from total rejection to complete acceptance. A positive therapeutic alliance builds feelings of safety and trust, both of which appear to be necessary for therapeutic change.

There are four interrelated features that belong in a successful therapeutic relationship that facilitates change and influences the outcome in correctional counseling: (1) empathy, (2) warmth, (3) genuineness, and (4) withholding judgment.

Empathy

Empathy has been defined as the cognitive ability to understand the emotional or cognitive status of others and to have an emotional or affective concern for others. A typical example of empathy involves role playing and perspective taking. The emotional or affective process consists of an observer's demonstration of empathic concern and ability to experience the distress of another person (Manger, Eikeland, & Asbjornsen, 2001).

Empathy in counseling is found to be positively related to increases in problem-solving skills in delinquent children (Kendall & Wilcox, 1980), leading to increased self-control by the end of treatment and at follow up. Empathy entails accurately detecting the feelings of a client and is a strong predictor of both abstinence and controlled drinking in clients with alcohol addiction.

Warmth

Therapists display **warmth** through acceptance, caring, and support and by showing real concern for clients, being sensitive to their needs and feelings, and making them feel comfortable. McLeod (1990) found that the therapists who showed interest, offered encouragement and reassurance, instilled hope, and offered practical assistance in increasing problem solving and coping were seen by their clients as being most helpful. Warmth also constitutes a type of affective intervention.

Genuineness

Therapists convey **genuineness** by portraying themselves in a "real" and consistent manner and by not being distrustful or self-protective. They are also comfortable and honest, and they are interested in interacting with clients. Clients rated the sincerity and respect of the therapist as important, and both have been linked to a beneficial treatment outcome. Showing respect indicates to clients that therapists accept and value them. Helping professionals need to value their clients as unique human beings (Suppes & Wells, 1991).

Withholding Judgment

Withholding judgment is related to the three features of a therapeutic relationship discussed previously, but it emphasizes helping offenders to become better persons regardless of their crimes and other dysfunctions, assisting them to take responsibility for their involvement in crime and other detrimental activities and for changing their maladaptive thinking and behavior. Withholding judgment does not mean that clients do not need to work on their illegal, irresponsible, or exploitative behaviors or attitudes. It entails the awareness of several verbal barriers to communication. These obstacles include moralizing by the counselor (by using "should" or "ought"), prematurely advising and giving suggestions or solutions before discovering the true problems, lecturing, criticizing or placing blame, threatening, or counterattacking (Hepworth & Larsen, 1993). This value is particularly important when working with offenders who have been convicted of heinous crimes (e.g., child molestation, sexual assault). Practitioners who bring their personal feelings about the offenses (e.g., disgust, animosity, and traumatic emotions) into the counseling process need to be reminded about the mental boundary in practice (Lazur, 1996).

Why Therapeutic Relationships Are Important

Horvath (2000) has suggested that the way in which the client perceives the therapist's behavior is what influences the outcome. Orlinsky, Grawe, and Parks (1994) found that in the majority of the clinical studies they had reviewed on sex offenders, it was the clients' estimate of the therapists' features that correlated with positive treatment outcomes. Due to the sensitive nature of their problems, clients need to be able to self-disclose without fear of rejection or judgment. Clients need to feel accepted, regardless of their previous behaviors.

Issues in Counseling Women Offenders

Currently, women make up 6.9% of the prison population, 12.9% of the jail population, 23% of probationers, and 12% of parolees. Although both male and female offenders generally come from similar low socioeconomic backgrounds, with low educational attainment and inadequate job skills, researchers have proposed a gender-sensitive (responsive or specific) approach in counseling women. This is because women offenders have different pathways through which they are involved in crime and carry different issues for assessment and intervention/treatment (Salisbury, Van Voorhis, & Spiropoulos, 2009; Spjeldnes & Goodkind, 2009; Van Wormer, 2010). Correctional counselors must better listen to, understand, and react to women's unique experiences.

First, there are unique social, family, and psychological factors that push women into conflict with the criminal justice system. Most of the offenses for women involve property crimes (e.g., fraud, larceny, or pretty theft), drug abuse violations, driving under the influence, prostitution, and other nonviolent crimes. There is a strong link between female crimes and dysfunctional interpersonal relationships, which include a significant history of victimization through sexual abuse, domestic violence, emotional trauma, parental stress, and lack of safety. The inability to modify these dysfunctional relationships further aggravates their mental conflicts, depression, substance abuse, and anger/hostility (Salisbury, Van Voorhis, & Spiropoulos, 2009; Van Wormer, 2010).

Second, assessment for women offenders should include the following salient issues in addition to evaluating the standard risk and needs issues (e.g., Calhoun, Bartolomucci, & McLean, 2005; Van Wormer, 2010):

1. Clients' dysfunctional interpersonal relationships (e.g., sexual, emotional and/physical abuse, victimization in domestic violence), with particular attention given to how the negative and unhealthy relationships lead to the crime involvements

2. Other family issues (e.g., pregnancy-related issues; most women offenders are primary caregivers to a child or other dependent)

3. Their current mental illnesses (e.g., symptoms of depression, anxiety, and psychosis), including co-occurring mental disorders, such as the presence of a mental disorder and substance-related disorder, as well anger/hostility issues

4. Their healthcare needs (women offenders have higher rates of HIV/AIDS and hepatitis C than male offenders)

5. Uncovering clients' strengths and positive values (particularly through their personal narratives) that give them hope and help them deal with adversities in life

Third, gender-sensitive treatments/interventions need to include the following strategies (Calhoun, Bartolomucci, & McLean, 2005; Spjeldnes & Goodkind, 2009; Van Wormer, 2010):

1. Build and maintain a therapeutic and trusting relationship between the counselor and client(s).

2. Group counseling is a preferred treatment modality over individual therapy because relationships serve as the focal concern of women, and group processes help clients, who carry the experience of trauma, abuse and hurts, to foster support for one another, learn and practice authentic interpersonal communication, and start healing processes by developing genuine connections with others.

3. The emphasis is put on both helping clients heal from abuse and trauma and empowering them to recognize and use their strengths to start a crime-free life.

4. Comprehensive programs are used to help incarcerated and reentry female offenders, including a case management approach that combines psychotherapy (e.g., cognitive behavioral therapy, group therapy, motivational interviewing), education, training in employment and coping skills, health care, substance abuse treatment, conflict resolution methods, parenting skills, housing assistance, and employment-related help.

Issues in Counseling Juvenile Offenders

Police made about 2.11 million arrests of persons younger than age 18 in the United States in 2008. At the national level, 10% of the arrests for murder and 25% of the arrests for robbery, burglary, larceny-theft, and motor vehicle theft involved juvenile offenders in 2008 (Puzzanchera, 2009). Juvenile offenders have not only intensified the crime problem but also consumed a large proportion of resources for social welfare, the justice system, education, and mental health services (Tarolla, Wagner, Rabinowitz, & Tubman, 2002). Counselors and juvenile probation officers in the juvenile justice system and social workers in the social services field are generally responsible for performing assessment and intervention for youth involved in various offenses or delinquent activities.

Assessment for Juvenile Offenders

Research has demonstrated that delinquency is determined by the interplay of five types of interconnected risk factors, including individual variables, family dynamics, peer influences, schools, and communities (Howell & Egley, 2005; Tarolla et al., 2002). Therefore, the assessment for juvenile offenders generally focuses on the following five areas:

1. The individual risk factors include antisocial attitudes and beliefs, drug use or abuse, poor academic achievement, mental disorders, cognitive distortions (e.g., hostile attribution bias), developmental delay or disruption, immature

cognitive development and moral reasoning, impulsivity, low ability to learn from experiences, sensation seeking, irritability, low empathy, and poor social problem-solving skills. The experiences of trauma and abuse (physical, sexual, and emotional) should be fully appraised because research has shown strong direct correlations among abuse and neglect, co-occurring mental health and substance use disorders and delinquency with the population of adolescents (especially girls) in the juvenile justice system (Veysey, 2008). Additionally, intellectual functioning and academic aptitudes and achievement levels are often included in the assessment process (Hoge, 2008).

2. The family risk factors include parental deviance (e.g., drug abuse, criminal activity), inadequate parental monitoring and discipline, family violence and abuse, parental conflict, and emotional neglect, maladaptive and coercive family interactions that reinforce aggression and deviant behavior but punish honest communications among family members.

3. The peer factors include affiliation with delinquent peers or gangs.

4. The school risk factors include poor academic environments and other unsafe and unhealthy conditions, and prevalence of bullying and other interpersonal conflicts at school.

5. The delinquency-prone communities are characterized by criminal subculture, frequent residential transition, high exposure to violence, and the lack of community organizations that facilitate positive growth for youth.

Although the assessment is risk-focused, counselors must also evaluate and understand the client's strengths that can serve as protective factors. Guerra, Williams, Tolan, and Modecki (2008) maintain that it is necessary to understand both the risk factors that increase the likelihood of delinquent behavior and the protective factors that decrease and/ or buffer the probability of delinquent behavior. Both risk and protective factors can be identified within the individual and within the other systems. For example, at the individual level, strengths refer to personal competencies, a positive identity, self-regulation skills, problem-solving skills, prosocial beliefs, hopefulness for the future, academic merits, and vocational skills.

Intervention for Juvenile Offenders

Because juvenile offenders have unique risk and needs areas, the following interventions are typically applied to treat them.

Family Therapy

Family therapy is a generic term that embraces a variety of family-based therapeutic approaches to delinquency or other family problems. The fundamental principle that governs family therapy emphasizes that the interdependency of family members (particularly parents and children) characterizes both the family structure and processes. Therefore, changes in individual family members and their interaction and communication patterns will impact the entire group. Family problems, such as delinquency, abusive relationships, and substance abuse result from dysfunctions in the family system. To deal with delinquency, the counselor first helps family members identify and analyze both dysfunctional and functional aspects of the family system, then engages them in reducing or eliminating factors within the family that exacerbate and promote the involvement in delinquency (e.g., the conflict-ridden milieu, parental drug abuse, negative communication patterns). Concrete therapeutic techniques include creating and maintaining parent/adolescent authentic interactions and communications, parent training (e.g., increasing their use of positive support and reinforcement for their children's prosocial behaviors and monitoring and deterring deviant behavior), and social skills training for youth. The purpose of family therapy is to develop a family environment that increases resiliency for all involved, facilitates communication and problem solving, and nurtures hope and potentials for youths (Guerra, Kim, & Boxer, 2008; Nahum & Brewer, 2004; Tarolla et al., 2002).

Cognitive-Behavioral Therapy
Cognitive-behavioral therapy (CBT) maintains that a person's distorted cognition (evaluations, explanations, and interpretations) of social reality regarding the self, others and situations regulates his or her antisocial behavior. The therapeutic techniques for youth offenders include discerning and modifying their maladaptive thoughts and behaviors, learning and rehearsing problem-solving skills, anger management, perspective taking, and reinforcing positive conduct (Tarolla et al., 2002). One type of cognitive distortion for youth offenders involves their hostile attributional styles that are supportive of aggressive reaction by biased attentions to and explanations of internal and external stimuli. It is particularly true for juvenile offenders with callous-unemotional (CU) traits. They also show lack of empathy, guilt, and remorse for their violent behavior (Boxer & Frick, 2008).

Cognitive-behavioral therapy is often combined with aggression replacement training for juvenile offenders, which is a type of anger management program that includes social skills training and a moral reasoning component. This program intends to help youths recognize the harmful consequences of their aggressive and antisocial behavior and understand the feelings of others (Tarolla et al., 2002).

Dealing with Gang Issues
Research has shown that risk factors for gang membership are similar to delinquency risk factors, including individual, family, school, peer group, and community risk variables (Wyrick & Howell, 2004). For example, at the individual level, conduct disorder at a very early age, drug or alcohol use, precocious sexual activity, and negative life events all predict future gang membership. The gang-prone family structure includes broken

home, poverty, child abuse or neglect, poor parental supervision, excessive control-based discipline, and gang involvement of other family members. The school risk factors consist of low academic performance, hatred toward learning, negative labeling of youth by teachers, and unsafe school environments. Association with delinquent peers is one of the strongest predictors of gang membership. The community risk factors include area poverty, neighborhood drug use, gang-concentrated neighborhood and community disorganization (e.g., lack of informal social control and support). Therefore, interventions with youth gang members can target these areas by enhancing the protective factors at the individual (e.g., individual counseling), family (e.g., parental education, family therapy), school (e.g., implementing safe school/healthy students programs), peer (e.g., increasing adult supervisions of peer associations), and community levels (e.g., enhancing community organizations). In short, a comprehensive approach to gang prevention, intervention, and suppression is needed. There is no single program that can solve complicated gang problems (Howell & Egley, 2005; Wyrick & Howell, 2004).

Ethical Dilemmas in Corrections

Four Types of Ethical Dilemmas

As part of the network of helping professionals who are trained in psychology, social work, counseling or other mental health fields, correctional counselors working in the federal, state, county, or other local correctional settings may often face **ethical dilemmas**—problems generated by the two roles they perform (the helping professional and the enforcer of the correctional policies of the government) and by two codes of ethics that overlap but are also distinct from each other.

Ethics is a discipline within philosophy that studies the moral principles of human conduct. Ethical principles are defined as standards of conduct or action in relation to others (Remley & Herlihy, 2005). The organizations governing all helping professionals in psychology, social work, and counseling have their own ethical standards and professional guidelines for how members should perform their duties. Correctional organizations and federal and state correctional systems also have policies, ethical standards, and guidelines for their employees. The two systems may not always agree with each other. Only by understanding the differences can counselors perform their correctional role without sacrificing their professional ethical principles.

The basic ethical principles embraced by the helping professionals are based on six core values: (1) service; (2) social justice; (3) self-determination; (4) importance of human relationships; (5) integrity; and (6) competence (see National Association of Social Workers, 1999; Remley & Herlihy, 2005; Suppes & Wells, 1991; Toriello & Benshoff, 2003). Although both the helping professions and the correctional system share the same goals of promoting and maintaining integrity (honesty and responsibility) and competence for their members through training, education, and supervision, interpretations differ regarding the other four ethical issues as follows:

1. The helping professionals' primary goal is to provide services to people in need and to address social problems. The service consists of two factors: beneficence and nonmaleficence. **Beneficence** refers to promoting the client's growth and well-being or holding the client's interests as primary. **Nonmaleficence** involves an obligation not to inflict harm on others intentionally (Harper, 2006). This ethical value suggests that helping personnel should help rather than control clients. However, correctional institutes are not mental health or social service agencies and mental health professionals working in correctional settings have dual roles (both as treatment staff and as enforcers of the DOC or other governmental policies). They are compelled to comply with the needs of the institution as primary, are considered correctional officers first and foremost, and are expected to engage in custody-oriented activities (e.g., assisting in the evening count, searching for contraband in inmates' property, pat-searching all inmates). This requirement may undermine traditional therapeutic goals and the relationship between the therapist and inmate, compromising the therapist's credibility and efficacy (Weinberger & Sreenivasan, 1994). Clinical practitioners may find themselves in a disciplinary hearing where they are expected to promote the interests of the correctional institution that may be opposed to those of individuals served by the counselors or therapists (Ivanoff & Smyth, 1997).

2. Helping professionals are responsible for **social justice** and challenging social injustice. Following this ethical principle entails pursuing social change, particularly for vulnerable and oppressed individuals and groups of people. As discussed previously, it is not uncommon for counselors to encounter the misconduct of correctional employees or other forms of injustice (such as discrimination) in correctional settings. As described by Van Wormer (1999), the dilemma is that when the helping staff advocate on behalf of clients to fight injustice, they may have to resign from their positions on some occasions because the practice is inconsistent with the culture and practice of the correctional institution.

3. Another core value of the helping professions is the principle of **self-determination** or **autonomy in practice**. It suggests that people have an inherent need to control their lives and strive for psychological growth. Because offenders in corrections are involuntary clients, they are required to do many things against their self-determinations (e.g., participating in correctional programs and following supervising conditions and requirements). Although counselors seek to enhance offenders' capacity and their opportunity to change and to deal with their own needs, counselors must be aware that the needs of the correctional institution and the community as well as the public's need for protection and the society's

interests are no less important. For example, most correctional institutions have policies governing an offender's right to refuse medication based on the U.S. Supreme Court's ruling in *Washington v. Harper* (1990). The Court held that although inmates have a protected constitutional interest in avoiding the forced dispensation of psychotropic drugs, this interest must be balanced against the state's interest in prison safety and security. In other words, inmates can exercise their self-determination regarding medication as long as doing so will not create risk or harm to themselves, others, or the institution.

4. Helping professionals view human relationships as an important vehicle for change. Strengthening relationships promotes the well-being of individuals, families, social groups, organizations, and communities. Counselors need to know that not all relationships are appropriate for correctional clients. Correctional institutions may have policies that encourage offenders to have some relationships (e.g., to keep contact with their family members) but forbid them from having other relationships (e.g., contact with the victims, crime partners, or inmates who have been transferred to other institutions).

How to Deal with Ethical Dilemmas

Correctional counselors need to realize that ethical dilemmas usually reflect the conflict between the prevailing ideology of the correctional administration that emphasizes security and custodial concerns, and the values and missions of the helping professional organizations that emphasize treatment and advocacy (Weinberger & Sreenivasan, 1994).

Some researchers (e.g., Sales & Shuman, 1996; Schultz-Ross, 1993) maintain that the dilemmas occur on the interface between the mental health model (e.g., psychiatry), law, and corrections. The law is based on a strict definition of right and wrong and on absolute judgments of guilt, with an emphasis on incapacitation and social control goals. In contrast, the goal of mental health models is based on medicine and the view that proper treatment will restore the patient to a basic, well-adapted state. The medical position or treatment model is concerned with the offender as an individual and with "treatability."

In addition, the codes of ethics of both the helping professional organizations and correctional institutions may lack guidance for dealing with ethical dilemmas, resolving ethical disputes, or capturing the complexity of the issues. A systematic approach for reaching ethical resolutions may include the following steps: (1) identifying the dilemma and all possible options; (2) identifying the consequences of those options; (3) reviewing ethical guidelines and the principles involved; and (4) deciding on the apparent best course of action (Toriello & Benshoff, 2003).

Hepworth and Larsen (1993) suggest managing ethical dilemmas in social services by considering one priority: that the rights to life, health, well-being, and the necessities of life take precedence over rights to confidentiality and opportunities for wealth, education, and recreation. In addition, when a policy is unjust or otherwise harms the well-being of clients or therapists, then violation of laws, policies, or procedures may be justified.

In addition to these ethical dilemmas, correctional counselors must be aware that discrimination and prejudice in criminal justice systems remain major types of unethical conduct in such areas as law enforcement, the sentencing of juvenile and adult offenders, and corrections (e.g., Hart, Larsen, Litton, & Sullivan, 2003; U.S. Commission on Civil Rights, 2000).

Summary

Typical counseling processes consist of three phases: (1) assessment, (2) intervention, and (3) termination/follow up. Offender assessment needs to include the appraisal of the client's responsivity, cognitions of the self and others, and the types of principles, norms, and criteria that offenders regard as guidelines for evaluating, explaining, and adjusting their interpersonal experiences of validation, invalidation, and actions.

Counselors must recognize that obstacles to effective engagement with offenders may come from practitioners or counselors, offenders, and environments.

To engage in intervention for the offender, therapists can employ various psychological models and resources. Emotion plays a significant role in the counseling process. Motivational interviewing (MI) is a method to help clients work through hesitation and commit to change.

A good therapeutic relationship includes such attitudes as empathy, warmth, respect, and acceptance/withholding judgments.

The gender-sensitive approach is necessary in counseling women offenders because they have different pathways through which they are involved in crime and hold different issues for assessment and intervention/treatment. Counselors also need to pay attention to unique risk and needs areas of juvenile offenders by reducing the risk factors for delinquency and enhancing protective factors.

Correctional counselors working in the federal, state, county, or local correctional settings often face or experience ethical dilemmas or conflicts generated by the two roles they perform (e.g., as helping professional and as enforcer of the correctional policies of the government) and by the two types of codes of ethics that overlap but are also different from each other in some ways.

Key Terms

Beneficence and nonmaleficence

Eclecticism

Empathy

Ethical dilemmas

Genuineness

Motivational interviewing

Responsivity

Therapeutic relationship

Three phases of counseling processes

Warmth

Withholding judgment

Discussion Questions

1. What are the main activities and issues in the assessment phase?

2. What are the issues in the termination stage of correctional counseling?

3. What are the two types of questions to be avoided at the assessment stage?

4. Discuss the importance of helping clients discern and express their feelings.

5. What are the five types of risk factors for juvenile delinquency?

References

Andrews, D. A., & Bonta, J. (2003). *The psychology of criminal conduct* (3rd ed.). Cincinnati, OH: Anderson.

Baum, N. (2005). Correlates of clients' emotional and behavioral responses to treatment termination. *Clinical Social Work Journal, 33*, 309–326.

Bergner, R. M. (2003). Emotions: A relational view and its clinical applications. *American Journal of Psychotherapy, 57*, 471–490.

Blackburn, R. (1998). Criminality and the interpersonal circle in mentally disordered offenders. *Criminal Justice and Behavior, 25*, 155–176.

Boxer, P., & Frick, P. J. (2008). Treatment of violent offenders. In R. D. Hoge, N. G. Guerra, & P. Boxer (Eds.), *Treating the juvenile offender* (pp. 147–170). New York, NY: Guilford Press.

Brodsky, S. L. (2011). *Therapy with coerced and reluctant clients.* Washington, DC: American Psychological Association.

Brodsky, S. L., & Lichtenstein, B. (1999). Don't ask questions: A psychotherapeutic strategy for treatment of involuntary clients. *American Journal of Psychotherapy, 53*, 215–220.

Calhoun, G. B., Bartolomucci, C. L., & McLean, B. A. (2005). Building connections: relational group work with female adolescent offenders. *Women & Therapy, 28*(2), 17–29. doi:10.1300/J015v28n02_02

Erickson, S. J., & Achilles, G. (2004). Cognitive behavioral therapy with children and adolescents. In H. Steiner (Ed.), *Handbook of mental health interventions in children and adolescents: An integrated developmental approach* (pp. 525–556). San Francisco, CA: Jossey-Bass.

Foster, S. L., & Crain, M. M. (2002). Social skills and problem-solving training. In F. W. Kaslow, & T. Patterson (Eds.), *Comprehensive handbook of psychotherapy: Cognitive-behavioral approaches* (Vol. 2, pp. 31–50). Hoboken, NJ: Wiley.

Guerra, N. G., Kim, T. E., & Boxer, P. (2008). What works: Best practices with juvenile offenders. In R. D. Hoge, N. G. Guerra, & P. Boxer (Eds.), *Treating the juvenile offender* (pp. 79–102). New York, NY: Guilford Press.

Guerra, N. G., Williams, K. R., Tolan, P. H., & Modecki, K. L. (2008). Theoretical and research advances in understanding the causes of juvenile offending. In R. D. Hoge, N. G. Guerra, & P. Boxer (Eds.), *Treating the juvenile offender* (pp. 33–53). New York, NY: Guilford Press.

Harper, M. G. (2006). Ethical multiculturalism: An evolutionary concept analysis. *Advances in Nursing Science, 29*, 110–124.

Hart, J. L., Larsen, A. M., Litton, K. S., & Sullivan, L. J. (2003). Racial profiling: At what price? *Journal of Forensic Psychology Practice, 3*, 79–88.

Hepworth, D. H., & Larsen, J. A. (1993). *Direct social work practice: Theory and skills* (4th ed.). Pacific Grove, CA: Brooks/Cole.

Hepworth, D. H., Rooney, R. H., Rooney, G. D., Strom-Gottfried, K., & Larsen, J. A. (2006). *Direct social work practice: Theory and skills* (7th ed.). Belmont, CA: Thomson Brooks/Cole.

Hettema, J., Steele, J., & Miller, W. R. (2005). Motivational interviewing. *Annual Review of Clinical Psychology, 1*, 91–111.

Hoge, R. D. (2008). Assessment in juvenile justice systems. In R. D. Hoge, N. G. Guerra, & P. Boxer (Eds.), *Treating the juvenile offender* (pp. 54–75). New York, NY: Guilford Press.

Horvath, A. O. (2000). The therapeutic relationship: From transference to alliance. *Journal of Clinical Psychology, 56*, 163–173.

Howell, J. C., & Egley, A. (2005). Moving risk factors into developmental theories of gang membership. *Youth Violence and Juvenile Justice, 3*, 334–354. doi:10.1177/1541204005278679

Ivanoff, A., Blythe, B. J., & Tripodi, T. (1994). *Involuntary clients in social work practice.* New York, NY: Aldine De Gruyter.

Ivanoff, A., & Smyth, N. J. (1997). Preparing social workers for practice in correctional institutions. In A. R. Roberts (Ed.), *Social work in juvenile and criminal justice settings* (2nd ed., pp. 309–324). Springfield, IL: Charles C Thomas.

Kendall, P. C., & Wilcox, L. E. (1980). Cognitive-behavioral treatment for impulsivity: Concrete versus conceptual training in non-self-controlled problem children. *Journal of Consulting and Clinical Psychology, 48*, 80–91.

Lakey, J. F. (1992). Myth information and bizarre beliefs of male juvenile sex offenders. *Journal of Addictions and Offender Counseling, 13*, 2–10.

Lazur, R. F. (1996). Managing boundaries: Group therapy with incarcerated adult male sexual offenders. In M. P. Andronico (Ed.), *Men in groups: Insights, interventions, and psychoeducational work* (pp. 389–410). Washington, DC: American Psychological Association.

Locke, E. A., & Latham, G. P. (2006). New directions in goal-setting theory. *Current Directions in Psychological Science, 15*, 265–268.

Loos, M. D. (2002). Counseling the chemically dependent: An integrative approach. *Journal of Addictions and Offender Counseling, 23*, 2–14.

Manger, T., Eikeland, O., & Asbjornsen, A. (2001). Effects of social-cognitive training on students' empathy. *Swiss Journal of Psychology, 60*, 82–88.

McLeod, J. (1990). The client's experience of counseling and psychotherapy: A review of the literature. In W. Dryden & D. Mearns (Eds.), *Experiences of counseling in action* (pp. 66–79). London, UK: Sage Publications.

Miller, W. R., & Moyers, T. B. (2005). Motivational interviewing. In G. P. Koocher, J. C. Norcross, & S. S. Hill III (Eds.), *Psychologists' desk reference* (2nd ed., pp. 267–271). New York, NY: Oxford University Press.

Nahum, D., & Brewer, M. (2004). Multi-family group therapy for sexually abusive youth. *Journal of Child Sexual Abuse, 13*, 215–243. doi:10.1300/J070v13n03_11

National Association of Social Workers (1999). *NASW code of ethics.* Retrieved from http://www.socialworkers.org/pubs/code/code.asp.

Orlinsky, D. E., Grawe, K., & Parks, B. K. (1994). Process and outcome in psychotherapy: Noch einmal. In A. E. Bergin & S. L. Garfield (Eds.), *Handbook of psychotherapy and behavior change* (4th ed., pp. 270–376). Oxford, England: Wiley.

Pervin, L. A., & John, O. P. (1997). *Personality: Theory and research* (7th ed.). New York, NY: Wiley.

Puzzanchera, C. (2009). *Juvenile arrests 2008.* The Office of Juvenile Justice and Delinquency Prevention, Office of Justice Programs. Washington, DC. Retrieved from https://www.ncjrs.gov/pdffiles1/ojjdp/228479.pdf.

Remley, T. P., & Herlihy, B. (2005). *Ethical, legal, and professional issues in counseling* (2nd ed.). Upper Saddle River, NJ: Pearson/Merrill/Prentice Hall.

Sales, B. D., & Shuman, D. W. (1996). The newly emerging mental health law. In B. D. Sales & D. W. Shuman (Eds.), *Law, mental health, and mental disorder* (pp. 2–14). Pacific Grove, CA: Brooks/Cole.

Salisbury, E. J., Van Voorhis, P., & Spiropoulos, G. V. (2009). The predictive validity of a gender-responsive needs assessment: An exploratory study. *Crime & Delinquency, 55*, 550–585.

Schultz-Ross, R. A. (1993). Theoretical difficulties in the treatment of mentally ill prisoners. *Journal of Forensic Sciences, 38*, 426–431.

Spjeldnes, S., & Goodkind, S. (2009). Gender differences and offender reentry: A review of the literature. *Journal of Offender Rehabilitation, 48*, 314–335. doi:10.1080/10509670902850812

Suppes, M. A., & Wells, C. C. (1991). *The social work experience: An introduction to the profession.* New York, NY: McGraw-Hill.

Tarolla, S. M., Wagner, E. F., Rabinowitz, J., & Tubman, J. G. (2002). Understanding and treating juvenile offenders: A review of current knowledge and future directions. *Aggression and Violent Behavior, 7*, 125–144. doi:10.1016/S1359-1789(00)00041-0

Toriello, P. J., & Benshoff, J. J. (2003). Substance abuse counselors and ethical dilemmas: The influence of recovery and education level. *Journal of Addictions and Offender Counseling, 23*, 83–98.

U.S. Commission on Civil Rights (2000, November). *Revisiting who is guarding the guardians?: A report on police practices and civil rights in America.* Retrieved from http://www.usccr.gov/pubs/guard/main.htm.

Van Wormer, K. (1999). The strengths perspective: A paradigm for correctional counseling. *Federal Probation, 63*, 51–58.

Van Wormer, K. (2010). *Working with female offenders: A gender-sensitive approach.* Hoboken, NJ: John Wiley & Sons Inc.

Veysey, B. M. (2008). Mental health, substance abuse, and trauma. In R. D. Hoge, N. G. Guerra, & P. Boxer (Eds.), *Treating the juvenile offender* (pp. 210–238). New York, NY: Guilford Press.

Washington v. Harper, 494 U.S. 210 (1990).

Weinberger, L. E., & Sreenivasan, S. (1994). Ethical and professional conflicts in correctional psychology. *Professional Psychology: Research and Practice, 25*, 161–167.

Wyrick, P. A., & Howell, J. C. (2004). Strategic risk-based responses to youth Gangs Juvenile Justice, 9, 20–29. Retrieved from https://www.ncjrs.gov/pdffiles1/ojjdp/203555.pdf.

Yalom, I. D. (1998). *The Yalom reader: Selections from the work of a master therapist and storyteller.* New York, NY: Basic Books.

Chapter 8

Group Counseling in Corrections

The modality of group counseling has been widely used in correctional settings, dealing with such issues as anger management, conflict resolution, assertiveness training, substance abuse problems, childhood trauma, and sex offender treatment (Lazur, 1996; Springer, McNeece, & Arnold, 2003; Suppes & Wells, 1991). Group counseling helps members change their behavior, cope with or reduce their personal problems or rehabilitate themselves, facilitate self-improvement, and increase healing processes by facilitating the sharing of intense emotions and offering strong support for such sharing (Hepworth & Larsen, 1993; Hepworth, Rooney, Rooney, Strom-Gottfried, & Larsen, 2006). Because of its low cost and efficient use of time, group counseling is preferable in prison facilities where there is a scarcity of counselors and mental health professionals (Suppes & Wells, 1991).

The Basic Components of a Group

The sociological perspective defines a group as a collection of individuals who communicate with one another according to their role or status, specified by some implicit or unwritten rules or norms. It consists of interactions among leaders and followers, internal and external organizations (communicating with other groups and systems), implicit or written rules, levels of cohesion and consensus about the goal(s) and function of the group. This definition of group can be called the *external standards* of the group. It should be noted that groups differ from other types of social category that contain individuals who share common characteristics (such as age, levels of education) but have little influence on each other.

133

Another definition of *group* is based on its psychological dimensions. For example, the social–psychological definition of group involves not only the above external criteria but also some *internal standards*, such as whether the members perceive themselves to be of the same social category, share emotional involvement in this common definition of themselves, and achieve a degree of social consensus about the evaluation of their group and their membership (Sun, 1993).

Help-focused groups in general consist of three types: Treatment (therapeutic) groups, support groups (e.g., Alcoholics Anonymous), and task groups organized to complete given projects (Hepworth et al., 2006). The group issues examined in this chapter involve treatment groups that intend to improve members' functions in mental health, human relationships, legal, and other areas.

Group Leader

The group leaders in correctional settings may include one or two counselors or therapists. In general, the leader's role in a group can be described as facilitating the attainment of group and individual goals and ensuring the continuation of the group. The group leader is both an observer and participant in the group. The leader stores information about sequences or cyclical patterns of behavior, or connects events that have occurred over long periods of time, and keeps in mind the original goals of the group (Yalom, 1998). A cotherapy model (i.e., the combination of a male and a female therapist or leader) may be more appropriate for a sex offender treatment program by providing a good model for appropriate behaviors between men and women. In addition, the presence of a woman during group discussions often discourages the practice of male "macho" attitudes (Mamabolo, 1996).

The main tasks of group leaders include: (1) providing the therapeutic structure and establishing and reinforcing group norms, which include actively assisting clients in translating their complaints into interpersonal issues; (2) monitoring interpersonal dynamics (level of participation of the members, their communication patterns and nonverbal behavior, and feeling tone); and (3) facilitating productive interaction and helping the group reflect on its own process (see I. D. Yalom, 1998; V. J. Yalom, 2005). Productive interaction includes constructive confrontations, which involve identifying members' feelings, thoughts, and behavior that deviate from group standards and contribute to their difficulties. It is the group leader who must help members focus on the original goals. The leader must also have the flexibility to address various tensions and new issues that may emerge in group processes—for example, conflicts among group members for control and dominance, aggressive members who do not respect and honor the rules of the group, and any deep emotional issues (e.g., sadness, anger) triggered by group processes. Lazur (1996) defines the leader's role in regulating people's interactions within the group as the management of internal boundaries, in contrast to the management of external boundaries, which involves balancing the relation between the group and other agencies (e.g., correctional staff or other personnel).

A common error of group leaders is to practice some form of individual psychotherapy in group settings while failing to use group dynamics to help the counseling process (Yalom, 2005).

When a group leader manages the group too strictly, it may undermine the group process. For example, Page, Campbell, and Wilder (1994) found that therapy groups for alcohol and drug abusers can be more therapeutic when leaders interact in a less formal way with group members. Namely, the members were given opportunities to confront leaders as well as other members. Beech and Fordham (1997) also showed that overcontrolling leaders had a detrimental effect upon the group climate.

Group Norms and Rules

Group norms and rules refer to written or spoken, explicit or implicit expectations and beliefs shared by members about how they should behave as group members. Most of these rules, expectations, and possible consequences of their violations are generally initiated by the leader and are then discussed and approved by the majority of the members at the first session of group counseling. The group may observe the following common rules (see Ireland, 2004; Mamabolo, 1996; I. D. Yalom, 1998; V. J. Yalom, 2005):

1. Group members are expected to actively participate and communicate. They must engage in self-disclosure (e.g., revealing their thinking, feelings, experiences, observations, and impressions), listen to and be interested in what others say, ask questions, and give honest, sincere feedback to other members.

2. Members are required to follow the rule of **confidentiality**—to keep all information shared in the group confidential. This rule is fundamental and will enable each individual in the group to reveal their experiences and share their feelings more readily with other members. There is only one exception to this rule: if participants reveal information about a risk of harming themselves or others or threatening the safety or security of the institution, such information about a possible or an ongoing offense will be reported by the leader to the appropriate authorities.

3. Group members are typically asked to show commitment to working on their issues through the group process, which includes attending group sessions, taking personal responsibility for personal change, and completing homework or assignments (if any).

Group Cohesion

A group environment in which members feel comfortable and are able to trust the therapist and one another results in **group cohesion**—a concept that can also be simply defined as the attractiveness of a group for its members. The cohesion or cohesiveness involves the feeling that group members are valued and unconditionally accepted and supported by other members. Cohesiveness is a necessary precondition for other therapeutic factors to function optimally (Yalom, 1998).

Research has shown that group cohesiveness is viewed as a central healing factor. Group cohesion was found to increase the amount of between-session, therapy-relevant discussions and client participation during sessions. Beech and Fordham (1997) gave the Group Environment Scale to members and leaders of 12 sexual offender treatment groups. The results indicated that the atmosphere of a group strongly influenced treatment change. A successful group was highly cohesive, well-organized, and administered with a helpful and supportive leadership style. Such a group also encouraged the open expression of feelings, produced a sense of group responsibility, and instilled a sense of hope in its members.

Differences Between Group Therapy and Individual Therapy

Group therapy differs from individual therapy in the following ways:

1. The group serves as a major healing agent because it is a social microcosm mirroring social interactions in the real world (Yalom, 2005).

2. The group as an environment for social interaction helps to rectify members' distorted cognitions of interpersonal reality and develop new and accurate cognitions about social reality.

3. Group processes help participants to release feelings that block social performance and to gain support from others (Yalom, 2005). Groups offer many advantages over individual therapy, including encouraging members to share their feelings, learning to trust others in the group, learning to accept their own painful, mixed feelings about their deviant behavior, increasing self-awareness, and promoting commitment to treatment settings. Group members can confront one another directly and immediately in an authentic manner (Suppes & Wells, 1991).

In short, group therapy is both an effective counseling method and an efficient use of therapeutic resources. The clients' symptoms and underlying difficulties largely result from their misperceptions of interpersonal reality and patterns governing interpersonal relationships. The group process, therefore, helps the members to become more aware and modify their maladaptive interpersonal cognitions and behaviors through authentic interactions, including honest feedback, the feeling of support and belonging, sharing personal experiences, and a new understanding of others (Yalom, 2005).

The Group Counseling Process

Before organizing a therapeutic group, the group leaders need to develop a plan for **group counseling**. This plan should specify the goals of the group, its norms and rules (to be shared and approved by its members), the length of group therapy, meeting schedule, location, and the number of potential members. The optimum group size for psychotherapy is between 6 and 10 clients and 1 or 2 therapists (Yalom, 2005). Some extra members (no more than 12 to 14) may be necessary at the beginning because a few individuals will withdraw in the early sessions.

The leaders need to actively recruit members for the group. Although some groups consist of referred involuntary members (e.g., probationers who are mandated by courts to participate in drug abuse treatment programs), groups in prison are generally initiated by counselors, and their members are offenders who want to join the groups. For this type of voluntary group program, counselors need to conduct interviews to assess the applicants' motivations and responsivity and select suitable members. Although their willingness and commitment to group counseling processes are the main factors to be considered, some researchers suggest that the selection should focus on eliminating clients who want to join but are not appropriate for group counseling. This type of individual may include the "expert," who appears to know the answer to everyone's problems in the group, and the "monopolizer," who tends to dominate group processes by talking only about his or her issues. In addition, clients who are not able to function well enough to tolerate the emotional intensity of group encounters should be put on the exclusion list. These offenders may benefit more from private individual sessions (Yalom, 2005).

Like individual counseling, group counseling processes generally consist of three basic stages: (1) assessment, (2) intervention, and (3) termination. Depending on the issues to be worked out in the group, **assessment** can be conducted either with formal instruments or informal responses from the members. Although the group leader usually predetermines the goals of a group program—for example, substance abuse treatment, social skills training, anger management, and the treatment of sexual deviance—the members' functions and conditions with respect to the goals remain to be evaluated and revealed through the group process. Group-based **interventions** differ from individual counseling in that they involve the full participation of group members who serve both as clients and therapist(s) to help one another become more aware of and modify their maladaptive interpersonal cognitions and behaviors through authentic interactions (Yalom, 2005). At the **termination**, the leader evaluates the group's accomplishments. Participants comment on what the program meant to them and how to maintain whatever progress they obtained in the program and offer suggestions for improving the group processes in the future. Termination in group counseling differs from individual therapies in that most group programs conclude according to the originally scheduled timetable (e.g., 12 or 15 weeks) and seldom postpone the termination schedule because some individual members need additional time to work on their issues (Mamabolo, 1996; Ireland, 2004). These members may still receive individual counseling and therapies.

Stages of group process can also be examined from the perspective that views the development of a group as the progression from its formation through maturity to disintegration. This perspective typically regards the group process as consisting of five stages, each of which is characterized by different emotional and behavioral issues and interpersonal dynamics (Brabender & Fallon, 2009; Springer et al., 2003). Although there is lack of consensus about the contents of the five stages, the following five major issues related to the stages are found in most of the research on group psychotherapy (see Brabender & Fallon, 2009; Springer et al., 2003):

1. Group members feel anxious and distrust one another and there is little communication or sharing information among them. This type of dynamic is typically found at the formation stage of the group.

2. Group members struggle for attention, dominance and/or control in the group process. For example, some members may rebel against the group leader by refusing to follow requirements, or they may engage in conflict with one another. Another example is that an offender may try to draw all attention to the self by exaggerating his or her crime story. These phenomena are generally observed at the second stage.

3. Group members start to disclose emotions and personal information, listen and give help to each other, feeling benefitted from the participation. This stage may be called the intimacy stage.

4. Group members develop a stronger sense of cohesion and emotional connection with one another, feeling that they can be natural and authentic in the group. They work on the target issues effectively. This indicates that they have reached the fourth stage.

5. Finally, each group member must separate from the group when it is time for termination. Most members will have some emotional reactions at this stage.

It needs to be emphasized that these five stages are the ideal group development. In reality, particularly in prison settings, many factors (e.g., offender characteristics, prison restraints, limited time, interpersonal conflicts) may interrupt the process.

Summary

Group-based interventions differ from individual counseling in that they involve the full participation of group members who serve both as clients and therapists to help one another become more aware of and modify their maladaptive interpersonal cognitions and behaviors through authentic interactions.

The basic components of a group include leaders, members, and rules, as well as the levels of cohesion and consensus about the function and goal(s) of the group. The leader's role in a group can be described as a set of actions that facilitate the attainment of group and individual goals and ensure the continuation of the group. Group norms and regulations for correctional group programs include confidentiality, respect for others, active participation, and the commitment to complete the program.

The cohesiveness of a group is defined as a group environment in which members feel comfortable and are able to trust the therapist and one another.

Key Terms

Assessment

Confidentiality

Group cohesion

Group counseling

Group norms and rules

Interventions

The main tasks of group leaders

Termination

Discussion Questions

1. What types of individuals are not appropriate for group programs?
2. What are the advantages and limitations of group counseling in comparison to individual counseling?

References

Beech, A., & Fordham, A. S. (1997). Therapeutic climate of sexual offender treatment programs. *Sexual Abuse: Journal of Research and Treatment, 9*, 219–237.

Brabender, V., & Fallon, A. (2009). *Group development in practice: Guidance for clinicians and researchers on stages and dynamics of change.* Washington, DC: American Psychological Association. doi:10.1037/11858-000

Hepworth, D. H., & Larsen, J. A. (1993). *Direct social work practice: Theory and skills* (4th ed.). Pacific Grove, CA: Brooks/Cole.

Hepworth, D. H., Rooney, R. H., Rooney, G. D., Strom-Gottfried, K., & Larsen, J. A. (2006). *Direct social work practice: Theory and skills* (7th ed.). Belmont, CA: Thomson Brooks/Cole.

Ireland, J. L. (2004). Anger management therapy with young male offenders: An evaluation of treatment outcome. *Aggressive Behavior, 30*, 174–185.

Lazur, R. F. (1996). Managing boundaries: Group therapy with incarcerated adult male sexual offenders. In M. P. Andronico (Ed.), *Men in groups: Insights, interventions, and psychoeducational work* (pp. 389–410). Washington, DC: American Psychological Association.

Mamabolo, L. M. (1996). Group treatment program for sexually and physically assaultive young offenders in a secure custody facility. *Canadian Psychology, 37*, 154–160.

Page, R. C., Campbell, L., & Wilder, D. C. (1994). Role of the leader in therapy groups conducted with illicit drug abusers: How directive does the leader have to be? *Journal of Addictions and Offender Counseling, 14*, 57–66.

Springer, D. W., McNeece, C. A., & Arnold, E. M. (2003). *Substance abuse treatment for criminal offenders: An evidence-based guide for practitioners.* Washington DC: American Psychological Association.

Sun, K. (1993). The implications of social psychological theories of group dynamics for gang research. *Journal of Gang Research: An Interdisciplinary Research Quarterly, 1*, 39–44.

Suppes, M. A., & Wells, C. C. (1991). *The social work experience: An introduction to the profession.* New York, NY: McGraw-Hill.

Yalom, I. D. (1998). *The Yalom reader: Selections from the work of a master therapist and storyteller.* New York, NY: Basic Books.

Yalom, V. J. (2005). Group psychotherapy: An interpersonal approach. In G. P. Koocher, J. C. Norcross, & S. S. Hill III (Eds.), *Psychologists' desk reference* (2nd ed., pp. 388–393). New York, NY: Oxford University Press.

Chapter 9

Anger Management

Anger management is needed for both offender and nonoffender populations whose anger is a prominent feature of their clinical disorders (e.g., posttraumatic stress disorder; see Novaco, 2002). Anger management programs in prison have at least two benefits: (1) reducing violence in prison and (2) decreasing aggressive or criminal behavior following release (Ireland, 2004).

Anger is defined as a negative, tumultuous emotion, subjectively experienced as an arousal state of hostility toward someone or something perceived to be the source of an aversive event (Novaco, 2002). A precursor of both impulsive and premeditated violence and aggression, anger as an emotion develops early in life. Research shows that infants' expression of anger emerges with their cognitive changes at 6 months of age, when infants begin to understand cause-and-effect relations (see Loeber & Hay, 1997). They show signs of rage and manifest aggression when encountering frustrations in the social world. By 12 months, actions that lead to conflict with older individuals start to provoke either protest or retaliation.

How Anger Regulates Aggression

Anderson and Bushman (2002) noted that anger plays several causal roles in *aggression*, which can be defined as any action directed toward another individual that is carried out with the mental state (intent, negligence, or recklessness) to cause harm.

1. Anger reduces inhibitions against aggression in at least two ways. Anger serves as a decision rule in the person's mind to justify his or her aggressive retaliation. In addition, it is a turbulent emotion that may interfere with a person's higher-level

cognitive processes, including undermining moral reasoning and judgment that normally control aggressive acts.

2. Anger allows individuals to carry an aggressive intention over time, because anger maintains or increases their focus on the provoking events, heightening their mental processing of those events, and therefore improving the recall of those events.

3. Like other emotions, anger serves as an information cue for individuals. It informs them about causes, effects, responsibility, and possible methods (e.g., retaliation) of responding to the source of anger. For example, if anger is triggered in a vague social situation, the anger experience itself helps explain the ambiguities in a hostile way.

4. Anger sets up or leads to aggressive thoughts, scripts (i.e., the perceived sequence of a social situation), and related physical responses in the situation. The angry person tends to use the anger-related cognitive structures to interpret and respond to the situation in a violent way. One related consequence of the many associations between anger and cognitive structures is that offenders frequently occupy themselves with anger-related stimuli but ignore neutral stimuli.

5. Anger functions as a motivational factor by energizing behavior and increasing arousal levels. This physical stimulation, coupled with aggression-related knowledge structures, increases the likelihood of aggression.

Anger Management Techniques

The most frequently used procedure for anger management is known as **stress inoculation** by cognitive-behavioral therapy (Chemtob, Novaco, & Hamada, 1997; Novaco, 2002).

This anger treatment approach involves *stress inoculation*—the cognitive restructuring and the learning of arousal reduction and behavioral coping skills, obtained through reappraising anger and augmenting a self-monitoring capacity. This procedure for anger management consists of the following key components (Chemtob, Novaco, & Hamada, 1997; Novaco, 2002):

1. Clients are taught about the link between anger, stress, and aggression.

2. Clients start to engage in self-monitoring the frequency, intensity, and situational triggers of their anger.

3. Clients cognitively create a personal anger-provocation hierarchy (identifying situations that create more anger and those that produce less anger).

4. Clients learn arousal reduction techniques such as gradual muscle relaxation, breathing-focused relaxation, and guided imagery training. (One of the typical relaxation methods involves meditation, such as the one described in **Exhibit 9-1**.)

EXHIBIT 9-1: A Simple Meditation Technique for Anger Management

Correctional clients may be taught to practice a simple meditation technique known as the wisdom-lotus Qigong method. Derived from a branch of Chinese Buddhism, it is a relaxation and visualization technique that shares a similar principle with traditional Chinese medicine about healing. The method recognizes that the connection between the internal system (body and mind) and the external system (universe) leads to well-being and healing, whereas pain manifests the internal and external disconnections. The meditation technique is intended to create the connection and eliminate the disconnections.

The following selected exercises of wisdom-lotus Qigong represent one method to calm the mind. This technique can be practiced either indoors or outdoors, in standing or sitting positions. The process may take 15 minutes or longer, depending upon the need of the individual.*

1. Imagine that the Sun moves from a distance to you and then encases you; feel the warmth and brightness for one minute.

2. Imagine that the Sun shrinks to the size of a golf ball inside your belly area behind your navel; it still has warmth and brightness; let it stay there for 1 to 3 minutes.

3. Visualize a giant shining lotus (any color) that travels from a distance to you; you sit on the lotus; feel the light in the bright ball inside your belly coming out from all directions and connecting with the petals of the lotus; internally focus on the scene for 1 to 3 minutes.

4. Visually shrink the lotus to the size of a golf ball and mentally put it inside your belly behind the navel area.

5. Move the lotus in a circle from the center of the belly to the outside (counterclockwise seven or nine times and then clockwise seven or nine times); when moving the lotus counterclockwise, the circles become bigger each time; when moving the lotus clockwise, the circles become smaller each time until the lotus returns to the original location.

6. Focus on the lotus inside your belly for 1 to 3 minutes and then finish.

*Note that this practice may not be suitable for mentally disordered clients.

5. Clients learn to revise their cognitive schemas about anger, including changing their attentional focus from anger-provoking thoughts to perceptions associated with peace and joy, modifying evaluations of situational stimuli (e.g., identifying positive aspects of an apparently negative event), and giving self-instructions.

6. Clients learn about behavioral coping skills in communication, such as respectful assertiveness and strategic withdrawal or disengagement from conflict situations.

7. Clients practice the cognitive and arousal regulatory and behavioral coping skills at the same time as visualizing and role playing progressively more intense anger-arousing scenarios.

Ireland (2004) suggested that these anger management techniques are best implemented in 12 group sessions with each session focusing on one of the following tasks:

1. Clients learn about the general contents of the sessions, rules of the program, and the importance of using anger diaries.

2. They identify triggering factors and situations and obtain an understanding of the consequences of temper loss.

3. They realize that angry behavior tends to annoy others, and they learn the importance of body language in signaling anger.

4. They substitute aggressive with nonaggressive body language.

5. They understand the importance of aggressive thoughts in producing violence before, during, and after an angry incident.

6. They learn to use nonangry thoughts before, during, and after angry incidents and to self-praise following the successful control of anger.

7. They understand the importance of physical arousal in relation to angry behavior and learn to control and minimize the arousal.

8. They learn relaxation techniques to help handle physical tension.

9. They practice nonangry behavior toward others.

10. They learn to express anger appropriately.

11. They recognize and deal with criticism, insults, and peer pressure in a constructive way.

12. They identify various high-risk situations and prevent lapse/relapse.

Anger Management for Overcontrolled Offenders

Williams and Poijula (2002) stressed that cognitive approaches are not sufficient for effective anger management. Clients should be given opportunities to express anger through verbal communication or using pictures that describe their feelings and related body sensations. Davey, Day, and Howells (2005) further criticize the typical anger management programs that are intended to increase a client's capacity to inhibit and control angry responses. The processes have largely been concerned with the identification, assessment, and treatment of offenders who both experience and express high anger in dysfunctional or antisocial ways. However, this type of anger management program has overlooked an important subgroup of violent offenders whose chronically overcontrolled anger serves as an important antecedent for their violent responses. Their anger problem is distinct from those who are impulsive in their responses to anger.

The anger problem for **overcontrolled offenders** involves one of two characteristics: (1) a low level of experiencing angry thoughts, feelings, hostility, and overt aggression because of anger suppression; or (2) a strong control or self-regulation of an internal anger reaction, but ruminating about provocations and being preoccupied with violent fantasy after being assaulted or bullied. The association between the inhibition of anger and violence can be explained by the traditional Freudian notion that emotions such as anger that are kept in check will exceed the person's psychological capacity to control and eventually manifest themselves in undesirable ways.

Therefore, counselors should avoid seeing all offenders as having a similar anger problem. In particular, therapists need to pay attention to the following issues related to those who cannot feel or express anger:

1. As a group, overcontrolled offenders tend to be particularly low in treatment readiness and in participating in group processes. Therapists must understand the difficulty in engaging these individuals and that they should seek information about how the client's previous learning experiences (e.g., childhood emotional invalidation and chronic emotional inhibition) influence his or her current repression or low experience of anger.

2. If counselors teach specific anger control strategies to those who already overuse these strategies, the results are likely to be at best futile and at worst counterproductive because these methods will fail to address the client's maladaptive anger control style.

3. Counselors need to help clients recognize that the repression of experiencing or expressing anger is another type of abnormality. Avoidant coping will lead to psychological distress and antisocial responses under stressful life circumstances. For these types of violent offenders, appropriate interventions address their denial of anger or their rumination about anger-provoking events, assisting them to develop skills to experience or express anger in an appropriate way.

In short, counselors need to view violent offenders as heterogeneous in terms of the emotional and situational antecedents for their violent acts. In addition counselors need to further differentiate between offenders with problems of inhibited anger experience and those who restrain anger expression.

Another anger management technique is the method of developing or expanding alternative (more accurate) cognitions about interpersonal reality. According to the model of interaction schemas, dysfunctional responses and emotions are generated by distorted interaction schemas. Inappropriate anger is the result of cognitive distortions. Therefore, counselors can teach clients to control anger by helping them to evaluate, perceive, interpret, and react to frustrations, to others, and to events in an alternative or more accurate way.

Perceiving the source of anger in a more accurate manner suggests that anger may be produced by clients' misrepresentations of the intentions and motivations of others. Research shows that perceivers' emotional reactions (e.g., anger) to an assumed harm-doer are based on a consideration of the motives, or state of mind, attributed to the person (Miller, 2001).

The perpetrator's state of mind includes two components: (1) intentionality and (2) predictability. *Intentionality* refers to whether acts of harm are unintentional or intentional; the former causes less anger and less retaliation than the latter. *Predictability* describes whether the harm is predictable or not and in keeping with the person's capacity. The victim will still have some degree of anger toward the perpetrator of unintentional but foreseeable harm (Miller, 2001). An offender's anger may result from misperceiving the two components of the other's mind. If clients learn that their cognitions of the mental state of others is distorted, they will diminish their anger.

In addition, this alternative cognition approach argues that for every problem, there are *always* multiple and more constructive solutions and for every goal or need, there are *always* multiple ways to achieve it (Sun, 1995). Correctional clients often experience frustration and related anger because they misinterpret their limited knowledge of situations and methods as the complete understanding of reality, unaware of alternative perceptions and reactions with respect to the target issues. This idea can be illustrated with an example.

Larry, an inmate at a correctional facility, came to his counselor for advice about how to deal with a correctional officer. Larry indicated that he was very angry with the officer because every time Larry returned from the infirmary to his cell (Larry needed medical treatment three times a week at the prison clinic), the officer usually delayed opening the cell door. Typically, after the inmate shouted his cell number he had to wait for 5 minutes before the officer used the automatic control to open the door. Larry told his counselor that he would have to resort to aggression and hurt the officer if this practice continued. The counselor found out that aggression was the only response Larry knew in dealing with interpersonal conflicts, and he was unaware that there are more constructive ways (e.g., peaceful conversation or communication) that can resolve such conflicts. After learning and rehearsing the new cognitive skills, Larry talked directly with the officer. Following the honest exchange of opinions, the officer stopped the postponing practice and Larry's anger was greatly reduced.

This method works because the client's misperceptions of social realities exacerbated his anger-related psychological activities (e.g., perceiving, construing, and reacting to provoking stimuli) at the beginning, but the counseling approach developed and expanded his cognitive repertoire.

Factors Influencing the Effectiveness of Anger Management Programs

The gender of the participants, the duration of anger management programs, and the therapeutic relationship between the counselor and client may all impact program effectiveness.

The gender of the participants is found to influence the success of the program in several ways. For example, comparing 50 female prisoners with 121 male inmates enrolled in anger management programs, Suter, Byrne, Byrne, Howells, and Day (2002) found that disrespectful treatment, frustrations in meeting's one's needs, and interpersonal irritations aggravated both male and female offenders' anger experiences and expressions. However, the women offenders showed more resentment toward perceived unfairness and injustice they had experienced than the men. In addition, the male inmates were less expressive of their anger than the female inmates. Furthermore, although only 12% the female participants were convicted of violent crimes (in contrast with 54% of the male participants), they demonstrated a higher level of anger than the men. Therefore, anger management issues may not be directly related to violent crime the offender is involved with.

A relatively short anger management program may also jeopardize its success. For example, Heseltine, Howells, and Day (2010) observed that after participating in a 20-hour anger management program, the participating offenders showed no significant improvement in anger experience and expression than the control group, though they did demonstrate more awareness about the issue of anger.

Therapeutic alliance (a positive work relationship between the counselor and the client) is found to predict treatment success in correctional settings. Howells and Day (2003) noticed that the lack of therapeutic alliance in some of the anger management programs impedes their success, which is typically produced by a mandatory requirement for participation coupled with the participants' unwillingness.

Perceived Injustice as a Source of Anger

The focus of anger management is to help offenders develop the cognitive and behavioral skills to monitor their thinking and regulate their responses (Chemtob et al., 1997; Novaco, 2002). Correctional counselors need to be aware, however, that clients' anger may result from perceived injustice about the misconduct of some correctional staff. The overwhelming majority of correctional staff and officers are professionals who safeguard justice and respect, promote, and contribute to a workplace that is safe, healthy, and free of harassment and the abuse of power. Unfortunately, violations of the institutional code of ethics do happen in correctional settings.

The wrongdoing of staff generates anger because injustice (e.g., disrespectful treatment) is a common determinant of both anger and aggression (Miller, 2001). The reason for this is that injustice violates the concept of entitlement. One of the entitlements involves an individual's right to be treated in a way that fosters positive self-regard by virtue of his or her humanity.

This right consists of two expectations: (1) *interpersonal sensitivity*, which involves the belief that individuals are entitled to polite and respectful treatment from others, and (2) *accountability*, which involves the belief that individuals are entitled to explanations for the actions of others that have consequences for them. When those expectations are violated by personnel working in the justice system, it influences an offender's perception of fairness and generates negative emotions, including anger. Some examples of disrespect include unjustified accusation and blaming, failure to admit an error, giving orders in an inappropriate tone, and illegal misuse of status and power (Miller, 2001).

Summary

Anger management programs in prison have at least two benefits: (1) reducing violence in prison and (2) decreasing aggressive and criminal behavior following release.

A typical anger management program is conducted through the procedure of stress inoculation, which focuses on cognitive restructuring and the learning of arousal reduction and behavioral coping skills, through reappraising anger and augmenting self-monitoring capacity.

Anger management for overcontrolled violent offenders, however, addresses their denial of anger or their rumination about anger-provoking events, assisting them to develop skills to experience or express anger in an appropriate way.

Offenders' anger may result from their perceived injustice related to misconduct of some staff members.

Key Terms

Aggression

Anger

Overcontrolled offenders

Stress inoculation

Discussion Questions

1. Describe the differences in anger management between undercontrolled and overcontrolled offenders.

2. How does perceived injustice serve as a source of anger?

References

Anderson, C. A., & Bushman, B. J. (2002). Human aggression? *Annual Review of Psychology, 53*, 27–51.

Chemtob, C. M., Novaco, R. W., & Hamada, R. S. (1997). Cognitive-behavioral treatment for severe anger in posttraumatic stress disorder. *Journal of Consulting and Clinical Psychology, 65*, 184–189.

Davey, L., Day, A., & Howells, K. (2005). Anger, over-control and serious violent offending. *Aggression and Violent Behavior, 10*, 624–635.

Heseltine, K., Howells, K., & Day, A. (2010). Brief anger interventions with offenders may be ineffective: A replication and extension. *Behavior Research and Therapy, 48*, 246–250. doi:10.1016/j.brat.2009.10.005

Howells, K., & Day, A. (2003). Readiness for anger management: Clinical and theoretical issues. *Clinical Psychology Review, 23*, 319–337. doi:10.1016/S0272-7358(02)00228-3

Ireland, J. L. (2004). Anger management therapy with young male offenders: An evaluation of treatment outcome. *Aggressive Behavior, 30*, 174–185.

Loeber, R., & Hay, D. (1997). Key issues in the development of aggression and violence from childhood to early adulthood. *Annual Review of Psychology, 48*, 371–410.

Miller, D. T. (2001). Disrespect and the experience of injustice. *Annual Review of Psychology, 52*, 527–553.

Novaco, R. W. (2002). Anger control therapy. In M. Hersen & W. Sledge (Eds.), *Encyclopedia of psychotherapy* (Vol. 1, pp. 41–48). Amsterdam, The Netherlands: Academic Press.

Sun, K. (1995). How to overcome without fighting: An introduction to the Taoist approach to conflict resolution. *Journal of Theoretical and Philosophical Psychology, 15*, 161–171.

Suter, J. M., Byrne, M. K., Byrne, S., Howells, K., & Day, A. (2002). Anger in prisoners: Women are different from men. *Personality and Individual Differences, 32*, 1087–1100. doi:10.1016/S0191-8869(01)00105-2

Williams, M. B., & Poijula, S. (2002). *The PTSD workbook*. Oakland, CA: New Harbinger.

Chapter 10

Mentally Disordered Offenders in Corrections

Although correctional mental health counselors and other mental health professionals (psychologists, psychiatrists, social workers, and mental health nurses) are responsible primarily for mentally disordered offenders, other correctional staff and probation or parole officers often have a portion of their offender caseloads with current diagnoses of mental disorders.

The Prevalence of Offenders with Mental Disorders

Several recent surveys (Bureau of Justice Statistics [BJS], 1999, 2001a, 2006; Steadman, Osher, Robbins, Case, & Samuels, 2009) show a growing population of mentally disordered offenders in the correctional field. For example, at midyear 2000, on average, 1 in 10 state inmates were receiving psychotropic medication. At least 1 in 8 state inmates were involved in mental health therapy or counseling. Five states (Hawaii, Maine, Montana, Nebraska, and Oregon) have nearly 20% of inmates who receive psychotropic medications. The latest BJS report (2006) which was based on recent surveys of inmates in state and federal correctional facilities and local jails, indicated that more than half of all prison and jail inmates, including 56 percent of state prisoners, 45 percent of federal prisoners, and 64 percent of local jail inmates, had a mental health problem (ranging from minor mental health issues to severe psychiatric symptoms) within the 12-month period. It should be

Sun, Key, "Mentally Disordered Offenders in Corrections," in Muraskin, Roslyn (Ed.), Key Correctional Issues, ©2005, pp 120–127. Adapted by permission of Pearson Education, Inc., Upper Saddle River, New Jersey.

noted that the findings were based on the inmates' self-reports, but the information about the recent mental health problems and clinical diagnoses was conveyed to the interviewees by mental health professionals and the results demonstrated the rising trend reliably.

How Offenders with Mental Disorders End Up in Corrections

The issue of the mental disorder of an offender may arise at any point in the criminal process from arrest or trial, to sentencing, during incarceration, and in community corrections (Cohen, 1996). The movement of offenders with mental disorders through the criminal justice system may start when a person is arrested for a crime and is charged and arraigned. If the defendant seems mentally disordered, the court orders an evaluation of competence to stand trial. Defendants who are found to be incompetent to stand trial (such as being unable to understand the legal process against them or to assist a lawyer in the preparation of a defense) will then be ordered to be treated to competence before the trial begins. Defendants who are found not guilty by reason of insanity are committed to a secure hospital administered by the State Department of Health and Social Services. Defendants who are found guilty are sent to corrections (Maier & Fulton, 1998). The state prison systems typically screen inmates for mental disorders at a reception/diagnostic center before placement in a state facility (BJS, 2001a).

The phrase **mentally disordered offenders** has actually been used to describe four categories of individuals in the criminal justice system (Dvoskin & Patterson, 1998; Heilbrun & Griffin, 1998): (1) not guilty by reason of insanity (NGRI)—the mental disorder at the time of their offenses renders them criminally not responsible for the offense; (2) incompetent to stand trial (IST); (3) mentally disordered sex-offenders; and (4) mentally disordered inmates. In this chapter, the term *mentally disordered offenders* refers mainly to the sentenced offenders serving time in prison or the community.

Counseling Issues for Mentally Disordered Offenders

Mentally disordered offenders are a diverse group with a wide range of treatment needs. To begin with, the offenders are diagnosed as having active psychiatric or psychotic symptoms on the basis of DSM-IV-TR (*The Diagnostic and Statistical Manual of Mental Disorders, 4th edition, Text Revision*). For example, the survey by Steadman et al. (2009) of 822 adult male and female inmates in five jails located in Maryland and New York showed that the 16.6% of the inmates had current serious mental disorders (including major depressive disorder, bipolar disorder, and schizophrenia). Noticeably, the rate of the serious mental disorders for the women inmates was 31.0%, whereas the rate for the male inmates was 14.5%. In addition, research has demonstrated that mentally disordered offenders have clinical problems similar to those of other offenders, including aggression and problems of institutional management, criminal predilection, skills deficits, substance abuse, estrangement from family and friends, and serious health conditions such as HIV/AIDS, tuberculosis, and hepatitis (Conly,

1999; Rice & Harris, 1997). Furthermore, this population is more susceptible to environmental stressors. For example, incarceration conditions, such as overcrowding and noise, can aggravate existing mental disorders or develop new ones (Sowers, Thompson, & Mullins, 1999).

Mentally disordered offenders generally have more than one mental disorder and need a broad range of services. This offender population also shows high rates of substance dependence or abuse. Recent studies show that 74 percent of state prisoners and 76 percent of local jail inmates with a mental health problem were dependent on or abusing drugs or alcohol in the year before their admission to corrections (BJS, 2006). More than 80% of mentally ill inmates have a criminal history, including previous incarcerations and probation sentences. Some of them are reluctant to admit their need or to seek treatment. They can be unwilling to engage in a therapeutic alliance with mental health practitioners. Additional issues for offenders with mental disorders in community corrections include their difficulty remembering to take medication or to keep medical appointments (Lurigio, Rollins, & Fallon, 2004).

Pertinent Legal Issues for Mentally Disordered Offenders

The **dual status of mentally disordered offenders** refers to the overlap between their status as both the offender and the mentally disordered patient (Rice & Harris, 1997). Methods of interpreting the relations between the two aspects of the offender population characterize major issues and conflicts in legal decisions, staff interactions, and treatment models.

History of the Law

The evolving legal context related to mentally disordered offenders can be categorized in three stages: (1) pre–civil rights movement; (2) the civil rights movement; and (3) 1980s–present (Hafemeister, 1998; La Fond, 1996).

At the time of the pre–civil rights movement, individuals with mental disorders could be taken into custody on the arresting officer's judgment. The mental health system had a comparable ability to cast a wide net, with broad civil-commitment criteria and few procedural protections. Treatment staff had great control over admission and release decisions. Offenders with mental disorders had virtually no voice of their own.

During the civil rights movement (the early 1960s to about 1980), a series of landmark legal cases reaffirmed individual constitutional rights that limited governmental authority, placing restrictions on using the mental health system to remove offenders with mental disorders involuntarily from the community.

These legal cases were based on the following premises: (1) *equal protection of the law:* a prison inmate should be given the same procedural protections as any other individual being civilly committed; (2) *responsibility:* judges or juries, rather than clinicians, should be primarily responsible for determining whether offenders should enter the mental health system; and (3) *treatment*: the least restrictive treatment environment should be employed (Hafemeister, 1998; La Fond, 1996).

From the 1980s to 1990s, however, judicial attitudes toward offenders with mental disorders changed. Courts abandoned rehabilitation as the primary purpose of criminal incarceration, adopted a just-desert theory, and became more reluctant to interfere with the administration of large state institutions, including mental hospitals (La Fond, 1996). The courts retreated from earlier assertions that all psychiatric patients have the same rights, permitting greater restrictions on the release of offenders with mental disorders, with the need to protect the community taking priority over the liberty interests of the offender. Offenders with mental disorders may be denied the opportunity to be placed in the least restrictive treatment setting, with the burden placed on them to show an absence of "dangerousness" (Hafemeister, 1998).

The Current Law

The federal constitutional obligation to provide mental health care to inmates suffering serious medical or mental health conditions results from a combination of the judicial interpretation of the Eighth Amendment and the due process clause of the Fourth Amendment (Metzner, Cohen, Grossman, & Wettstein, 1998). In spite of many changes in the legal context, the premises of the 1960s and 1970s do not appear to have been totally abandoned (Hafemeister, 1998). The current legal context reflects an attempt to balance two types of interest: (1) community protection; and (2) the constitutional rights of mentally disordered offenders.

An example of the current law is reflected in the **DeShaney principle** which maintained the government's obligation to provide health care (*DeShaney v. Winnebago Department of Social Services*, 1989). The state has a duty to provide necessary services to, and protect from injury, certain classes of persons in custody once they enter into a "special relationship" with the state.

In *Estelle v. Gamble* (1976), the Supreme Court held that responsible correctional staff must be *deliberately indifferent* to the *serious medical needs* of inmates before Eighth Amendment liability may apply.

In *Washington v. Harper* (1990), the Supreme Court ruled that although inmates have a protected constitutional interest in avoiding the forced dispensation of psychotropic drugs, this interest must be balanced against the state's interest in prison safety and security. In a more recent decision (*Kansas v. Crane*, 2002), the Supreme Court ruled that for states to incarcerate sex offenders after they have served their prison time, the states must show that these inmates have both a mental disorder and "serious difficulty" in controlling their behavior.

Recently, some Federal inmates challenged a federal statute that authorizes the Department of Justice to civilly commit mentally ill and sexually dangerous federal prisoners after serving their prison terms on the ground that the law was incongruous with the Constitution. In *United States v. Comstock* (2010), the Supreme Court held that the Constitution grants Congress the authority to enact the legislation regarding the civil commitment of certain federal prisoners or persons in federal custody (see Law & Frierson, 2010).

In addition, the changing legal context has influenced the growing problems of mentally disordered offenders in corrections. Recent changes in the law and courtroom proceedings make it more difficult to divert offenders with mental disorders into noncorrectional treatment programs. Many of the patients formerly taken care of in hospitals are now housed in prisons, because there is an increase in arrests related to drug offenses, and punishments for these offenses have become harsher and less flexible (Kupers, 1999; Sowers et al., 1999).

Mental Disorders and Violence

Considerable research has evaluated the correlation between mental disorder and violence. This issue has been the subject of political and scientific controversy for decades (Bonta, Law, & Hanson, 1998; Clear & Dammer, 2000; Harris & Lurigio, 2007; Perlin, 2001). After reviewing the relevant literature, Perlin (2001) and Rice and Harris (1997) concluded that there appears to be a greater-than-chance relationship between mental disorder and violent behavior, but mental disorders make only a trivial contribution to the overall level of violence in society. Bonta, Law, and Hanson (1998) performed a meta-analysis (i.e., a statistical technique that combines the results of two or more separate studies on a topic) of 64 longitudinal studies conducted between 1959 and the end of 1995. The results showed that the four major groups of predictors of recidivism (i.e., personal demographics, criminal history, deviant lifestyles history, and diagnosis/treatment for mental disorder) were the same for mentally disordered offenders as for nondisordered offenders. Clinical or psychopathological symptoms of mental disorders were either unrelated to recidivism or negatively related (Namely, offenders with mental disorders may actually have a lower recidivism rate than other offenders). Only the criminal history variables were the best predictors.

The *MacArthur Violence Risk Assessment* study (initially published in 1998), a major and comprehensive investigation with researchers from across the United States, has shed new light on the debate by examining specific risk factors for violence among psychiatric populations. The findings indicated that the mentally ill persons with the following characteristics have a risk for violent behavior (see Harris & Lurigio, 2007):

1. A co-occurring diagnosis of a substance use disorder, which was robustly predictive of violence.

2. Previous violence (based on self-report, arrest records, and hospital records), which was strongly correlated with future violence.

3. Persistent violent thoughts or daydreaming about harming others.

4. Anger or a generally "suspicious" attitude toward others.

5. Psychopathy or antisocial personality, which is related to the general propensity for violence in both psychiatric and non-psychiatric populations.

However, the following factors were *not* strong predictors of violence:

1. A diagnosis of schizophrenia, which was associated with a lower rate of violence than a diagnosis of a personality or adjustment disorder.

2. Delusions, the presence of which is not associated with violence.

When examining the issue of mental disorders and violence, researchers also suggest that it is necessary to pay attention to the following issues:

1. Mental disorders denote a range of dysfunctions in areas such as cognition, mood, somatoform, drug use, sexuality, personality, and life-span. Therefore, offenders with mental disorders can have either serious or minor symptoms, most of which have nothing to do with crime (Anckarsäter, Radovic, Svennerlind, Höglund, & Radovic, 2009).

2. The belief about dangerousness of mental illness may cause the believers to discriminate toward persons with mental illness by excluding them in social, job, human relationships and other opportunities, thus worsening their psychiatric conditions and exacerbating the likelihood of their aggressive behavior (Markowitz, 2011).

3. The fact that mentally disordered individuals are arrested and incarcerated in numbers that surpass their proportion in the general population may reveal their tendency to commit "survival" crimes. Mentally ill offenders tend to commit crimes against public order or minor property offenses that were more a reflection of marginal urban survival than a threat to the community (Lurigio et al., 2004).

Social Policies, Culture, Class, and Gender

Social policies, such as that of deinstitutionalization, which caused the release of thousands of mentally ill people from psychiatric facilities to the community, have contributed to the high prevalence of mental disorders in correctional facilities (Conly, 1999; Kupers, 1999; Markowitz, 2011). This policy was initially implemented in the United States in the 1960s, and the practice continued in the past five decades, with the intention to reduce the reliance on the state and county mental hospitals and to develop a treatment network of services in the community for individuals with mental disorders. Consequently, many psychiatric hospitals closed or admitted few patients to the facilities. This policy was also aimed at reintegrating clients into society and minimizing the stigma associated with psychiatric institutions (Wright, Gronfein, & Owens, 2000). However, this otherwise well-intended policy has exacerbated conditions for the mentally disordered and has contributed to their increased involvement in the criminal justice system. This is because of its coincidence with a lack of adequate social services, including cuts in public assistance, declines in the availability of low-income housing, and the limited availability of mental health care in the community. Consequently, many mentally ill persons end up in correctional facilities that lack appropriately trained staff and sophisticated screening procedures for handling persons with mental disorders. The mental health conditions of many incarcerated offenders may deteriorate and/or develop increased risk of suicide as the result of abuse or mishandling in that environment (Markowitz, 2011).

The issue of mentally disordered offenders in corrections can be examined in the cultural, class, and gender contexts of the offender population. According to the Bureau of Justice Statistics (2001b, 2001c), the general offender population in corrections already has a disproportionate number of African Americans, with more than a third of probationers, more than two out of five adults on parole, and prisoners who include 9.7% of all African American males between 25 and 29 years old. At year-end 2000, women represented 6.6% of all prison inmates, 22% of adult probationers and 12% of all parolees. In terms of social class, most offenders with mental disorders come from the economically disadvantaged segment of the society who reside in crime-prone neighborhoods, with significant family dysfunction and little treatment for their mental and substance use disorders in the past. They not only have experienced greater levels of stress and conflict, but also lack social and professional support and psychological coping efficacies that help mitigate the effects of stress and frustration (Markowitz, 2011).

Although the plight of mentally disordered women prisoners is no better than that of their male counterparts, harsher sentences, especially related to drugs, cause overcrowding in women's prisons (Kupers, 1999). Female inmates were also found to have higher rates of mental health problems than male inmates (BJS, 2006). Studies have shown that women in corrections have psychological needs and mental health problems that are different from those of men (e.g., Hartwell, 2001; Morash, Bynum, & Koons, 1998). For example, after comparing female mentally ill offenders (total number 76) and male mentally ill offenders (total number 385) in Massachusetts, Hartwell (2001) reported that although more than half of both male and female mentally disordered offenders did not complete high school, 20% of the mentally ill female offenders report some college education in comparison to 4% of the men. Female mentally ill offenders were also younger, more likely to have used social services, reported traumas and substance-abuse problems, and been diagnosed with personality disorders, than the male mentally ill offenders. The review by Morash et al. (1998) showed that female offenders were more likely to have suffered physical and sexual abuse (43%) than male offenders (12%) and more likely to have become addicted to drugs (54%) than their male counterparts (50%). In addition, female offenders were more concerned with interpersonal relationships than male offenders, as suggested by the self-in-relation theory (Manhal-Baugus, 1998). According to the theory, human connections are extremely important in women's psychological development and functioning. Studies have shown that women's involvement with crimes and abuse of illegal drugs, as well as their mental health problems, are typically initiated or aggravated by their negative experiences or frustrations in intimate relationships (Kupers, 1999; Messina & Grella, 2006; Miller & Meloy, 2006).

Assessment

Dvoskin and Patterson (1998) pointed out that mental health services for offenders either in custody or in the community can be placed into the following broad categories: *screening, evaluation, psychiatric treatment, rehabilitation, case management, medical treatments,* and *special treatment* (e.g., substance abuse treatment, sex offender treatment programs). When offenders with mental disorders serve their time in the community, however, additional issues such as housing, public assistance, education, and employment may arise.

In addition to standard assessment instruments (e.g., LSI-R) intended for all offenders, the mental health professionals (MHP) in corrections use the *Diagnostic and Statistical Manual of Mental Disorders,* (DSM-IV-TR), the mental health assessment tool compiled by the American Psychiatric Association in 2000. It is a guidebook for the MHP to measure major clinical disorders, such as schizophrenia, anxiety, mood disorders, and personality disorders. It also helps the MHP to record clients' functioning in other areas, including their general medical conditions, psychosocial problems, education, employment, housing, economic problems, problems with access to health-care services, interaction with the legal system, and global assessment of functioning.

Intervention and Treatment

There are two purposes involved in treating mentally disordered offenders: (1) reducing the risk of violence and (2) alleviating mental disorders through various types of interventions, including individual psychotherapy, group psychotherapy, psychotropic medication, acute hospitalization, substance-abuse treatment, and case-management of other needs areas (Rice & Harris, 1997). Counselors need to pay particular attention to the following issues when performing the interventions:

1. Counselors need to recognize that there are unique ethical and professional dilemmas for the MHP (e.g., psychologists, social workers, psychiatrists, correctional mental health counselors, and other therapists) in corrections (Kupers, 1999; Sales & Shuman, 1996; Schultz-Ross, 1993; Weinberger & Sreenivasan, 1994).

    The MHPs in corrections have dual roles (both as treatment staff and as enforcers of policies of DOC or other correctional institutions). As employees of the correctional institution, their primary responsibility is to maintain security, which means they may sometimes be required to act as correctional officers and engage in custody-oriented activities. This requirement creates strains on the traditional therapeutic goals and the relationship between the therapist and the individual inmate. In addition, the correctional policies dictate the degree of confidentiality by asking counselors to share clients' mental health information with administrative personnel. Additional conflicts may be generated by disagreement between the MHP and the custody staff who may differ in training, knowledge, viewpoint, and purpose in relation to assessment and interventions for mental disorders. For example, the MHPs may criticize the correctional environment as failing to contribute to restore clients' normal functions, and in many cases even aggravating offenders' dysfunctions. Alternatively, security personnel may view the treatment or counseling environment as overly lenient or as weakening the authority of officers and the punitive nature of the institution (Mobley, 2006).

2. Special tasks are involved in working with mentally disordered offenders serving time in the community. According to Lurigio et al. (2004), when mentally disordered offenders are released from prison, their reentry into the community is complicated by many factors. Therefore, effective reentry strategies for mentally ill offenders must begin with a comprehensive discharge plan that includes specific information on an inmate's needs for community-based treatment and services, employment, housing, and financial and social support. The scarcity of services for mentally disordered offenders serving time in rural areas should be taken into consideration. Once the offenders are living in the community, correctional staff should apply case-management techniques. These approaches help the offender population to access multiple services by integrating and coordinating different service domains, such as mental health and medical treatment, mandatory correctional supervision, substance-abuse treatment, housing, job training, and establishing and maintaining clients' eligibility for supplemental security income or social security disability insurance. In addition, correctional personnel should use the team approach that involves community correctional officers, case managers, and treatment providers who collaborate on decisions regarding the selection, supervision, treatment, and continuity of care for offenders with mental disorders in community corrections. Correctional staff should also be aware of possible cultural and language barriers between them and some mentally disordered offenders.

3. Correctional counselors must be familiar with the psychotropic prescriptions the clients are taking and the general effects of the medication on the client's thinking, perception, emotions, and behavior. The counselors need to communicate with psychiatrists or medical practitioners frequently to understand and manage the clients' mental health conditions. However, just knowing the medication involved is not enough for effective treatment of mentally disordered clients. Understanding the interpersonal cognitions of mentally disordered offenders is required for successful counseling.

4. Counselors need to be aware that mental disorders are not just biological or neurochemical issues. Although biological therapy such as medication may eliminate or alleviate symptoms, it does not solve the psychosocial problems or issues of a client (Maxmen & Ward, 1995). The psychosocial problems of the offender population require counseling intervention to focus on changing the clients' interpersonal cognitions (interaction schemas), rather than on simply modifying their perceptions of themselves.

Focusing on clients' interaction schemas is important because it has been well documented that dysfunctional social relationships, which prevent individuals from achieving positive goals or avoiding negative situations, can lead to crime (see Agnew, 1999; Mazerolle & Maahs, 2000). In addition, clinical observation reveals that offenders use invalid methods to handle interpersonal issues, such as applying violence or intimidation to get what they want, imposing their desires or commands on others or in situations without consideration of the reactions of the others or of the context. This is not because they have misconceptions about themselves, but because they misunderstand others (Sun, 2001). In contrast, building, rebuilding, and strengthening social relationships serve as a buffer against recidivism (Bazemore, Nissen, & Dooley, 2000). All negative social environments and dysfunctional social relations are mediated by one's interpersonal cognition (Fiske & Taylor, 1991).

Studies have consistently demonstrated a strong association between trauma and mental disorder (BJS, 1999; Elze, Stiffman, & Dore, 1999; Fergusson & Horwood, 1998). For example, surveys by the Bureau of Justice Statistics (1999) showed that rates of prior physical and sexual abuse were higher among the mentally disordered inmates (one-third of men and three-quarters of women in state prisons) than among other inmates or probationers. Elze et al. (1999) interviewed 792 youths (aged 14 to 18 years) in St. Louis and found that exposures to high rates of violence (including personal victimization and witnessing violent acts) in their families, communities, and schools were associated with symptoms of major mental health disorders (i.e., depression, post-traumatic stress disorder, conduct disorder, substance abuse or dependence). In the study by Fergusson and Horwood (1998), 1,265 youths at age 18 retroactively reported their exposure to interparental violence. Their findings showed that high levels of exposure to interparental violence were also associated with elevated rates of mental health problems, substance-abuse behaviors, and criminal offenses. On the basis of their clinical observations, Kupers (1999) and Sun (2001) suggested that the strong correlation between trauma and mental disorder for the offender population indicates the importance of the clients' interpersonal cognition. That is, offenders' mental disorders may be initiated and/or aggravated by the inability of their interpersonal cognitions to understand their traumas, which include interpersonal frustration and disconnection. In short, these findings support a social cognitive approach to understanding mental disorders.

Two Different Explanations for Mental Disorder

Counselors need to be aware that currently there are two different perspectives for explaining mental disorder: The biomedical explanation and the social cognitive explanation. They also suggest dissimilar treatments and interventions.

The biomedical explanation for mental disorders has become the mainstream during the past two decades. With the growing use of psychophysiological measures such as functional magnetic resonance imaging (fMRI), positron emission tomography (PET), electroencephalography (EEG), magnetoencephalography (MEG), and endocrine or genetic data, advocates for the biomedical approach argue that biological or neurological events underlie (are more fundamental than) than psychological events, including mental disorders. For example, it is pervasive to hear that "depression is a chemical imbalance" or "schizophrenia is a brain disease." Supporters of this approach maintain that the biochemical/neurological processes provide the true understanding of the human mind (see Miller, 2010).

On the other side of the debate, however, are scientists who are deeply skeptical of placing too much confidence in neuroscience and are offended by their premature claims (Diener, 2010). Some of the psychologists (e.g., Beck, 2010; Gernsbacher, 2010; Miller, 2010) have identified major problems with the claim that "biological events underlie the psychological events." Their rationales, which are supportive of the social cognitive approach, can be summarized as follows:

Although mental processes are associated with some biochemical/neurological operations, the data generated from psychophysiological measures (e.g., fMRI, EEG) only show that the mental functions and dysfunctions are correlated with neurobiological processes. However, correlation is not causation.

The biological approach has identified some neurological or chemical changes in the nervous system when people engage in mental activities, but it does not show that biological transformations generate psychological experiences. In fact, the reverse relation (psychological events cause biological events) is more likely. Researchers have observed that psychological activities, such as thinking, decision-making, problem solving and other cognitive function or dysfunction, emotional or motivational regulation, cause biochemical or brain changes. For example, reviews of studies of cognitive behavioral therapy or other learning activities (e.g., working-memory training) show that they lead to fMRI-recorded brain changes. Research has also shown that after aerobic exercise, there were structural and functional brain variations. One does not have depression because one has a chemical imbalance, it is equally likely that being depressed causes chemical imbalance (Miller, 2010). Both pharmacological and psychological treatments (e.g., psychotherapy) can lead to changes in brain activity, as assessed by positron emission tomography (PET) or EEG. In addition, PTSD-related trauma has been shown as cause brain changes (Bailey, 2002; Miller, 2010).

Besides, there is a common tendency to confuse *biological* with *innate* (Beck, 2010). A difference in the brain between two groups of people (e.g., persons with a mental disorder and persons without the mental disorder) does not imply that the difference is inherent. In fact, all learning experiences, cognitive activities, and learned behaviors will in some way change the brain. According to Beck (2010), nonexperts and the mass media are inclined to be "fooled" by scientific-sounding, but uninformative, neuroscience language because people tend to have blind, misguided confidence in biological data and find brain images and neuroscience language more convincing than results that make no reference to the brain.

Furthermore, there is no specific correspondence between brain states and psychological states. For instance, researchers readily interpret activation in the amygdala as reflecting the intense attachment, vigilant protectiveness, and empathy that characterize normal maternal attachment when the research subjects are mothers looking at photos of their children, whereas they construe activation in the same region as suggesting sexual/ aggressive behavior when the participants are boyfriends listening to sentences such as "my girlfriend gave a gorgeous birthday present to her ex-boyfriend" (See Gernsbacher, 2010). There is likely an indefinite set of potential neural implementations of a given psychological phenomenon. Conversely, a given neural circuit may serve different psychological functions at different times or in different individuals. In short, observations about biological phenomena can add our understanding about the complexity of mental experiences, but they cannot replace psychological explanations (Miller, 2010).

The emphasis that biological mechanisms determine psychological experiences also implies that the main intervention for mental disorders involves the use of psychiatric medication, which can modify neurological and biochemical activities in the brain.

On the other hand, mental health professionals who embrace the position that psychological operations underlie biochemical events focus on understanding the clients' social experiences and how they appraise, explain, understand, adjust, and react to the positive and negative experiences. This is not to say that medication cannot be helpful in alleviating psychiatric symptoms but it may also disrupt or disable normal brain function and impair higher human functions (Breggin, 2008). In addition, simply labeling mental disorders as a neurological problem may discourage the efforts to work with clients on his/her cognitive, emotional, and motivational issues and on how to understand and change dysfunctional interpersonal relationship, trauma, unemployment and other areas of conflict (Bailey, 2002).

Summary

Mentally disordered offenders in corrections generally have more than one mental disorder and a broad range of services needs. The dual status of such offenders refers to the overlap between their status as both offender and as mentally disordered patient. How to interpret the relations between the two aspects of the offender population characterizes major issues and conflicts in legal decisions, staff interactions, and treatment models. The federal constitutional obligation to provide mental health care to inmates suffering serious medical or mental health conditions results from a combination of the judicial interpretation of the Eighth Amendment and the Due Process Clause of the Fourth Amendment.

Social policies and recent changes in sentencing laws are largely responsible for the increase of mentally disordered offenders in corrections.

Mental health services for offenders either in custody or in the community can be broadly placed into the following categories: screening, evaluation, psychiatric treatment, rehabilitation, case management, medical treatment, and special treatment (e.g., substance abuse treatment, sex offender treatment programs). When offenders with mental disorders serve their times in the community, however, additional issues such as housing, public assistance, education, and employment may arise.

Counselors need to be aware that mental disorders are not simply biological issues.

Key Terms

DeShaney principle

Dual status of mentally disordered offenders

Mentally disordered offenders

Washington v. Harper

Discussion Questions

1. What are the characteristics of mentally disordered female offenders?

2. How and why do the MHP and the custody staff differ in their views of mentally disordered offenders?

3. What are the social sources of mental disorders?

4. What are the two different explanations for mental disorder?

References

Agnew, R. (1999). Foundation for a general strain theory of crime and delinquency. In F. R. Scarpitti & A. L. Nielsen, *Crime and criminals: Contemporary and classic readings in criminology* (pp. 258–273). Los Angeles, CA: Roxbury.

American Psychiatric Association (2000). *Diagnostic and Statistical Manual of Mental Disorders, Text Revision* (4th ed.). Washington, DC: Author.

Anckarsäter, H., Radovic, S., Svennerlind, C., Höglund, P., & Radovic, F. (2009). Mental disorder is a cause of crime: The cornerstone of forensic psychiatry. *International Journal of Law and Psychiatry, 32*, 342–347. doi:10.1016/j.ijlp.2009.09.002

Bailey, C. (2002). Is it really our chemicals that need balancing? *Journal of American College Health, 51*, 42–47. doi:10.1080/07448480209596328

Bazemore, G., Nissen, L. B., & Dooley, M. (2000). Mobilizing social support and building relationships: Broadening correctional and rehabilitative agendas. *Correctional Management Quarterly, 4*, 10–21.

Beck, D. M. (2010). The appeal of the brain in the popular press. *Perspectives on Psychological Science, 5*, 762–766. doi: 10.1177/1745691610388779

Bonta, J., Law, M., & Hanson, K. (1998). The prediction of criminal and violent recidivism among mentally disordered offenders: A meta-analysis. *Psychological Bulletin, 123*, 123–142.

Breggin, P. R. (2008). *Brain-disabling treatments in psychiatry: Drugs, electroshock, and the psychopharmaceutical complex* (2nd ed.). New York, NY: Springer.

Bureau of Justice Statistics, U.S. Department of Justice. (1999). *Mental health and treatment of inmates and probationers*. Washington, DC: Author.

Bureau of Justice Statistics, U.S. Department of Justice. (2001a). *Mental health treatment in state prisons, 2000.* Washington, DC: Author.

Bureau of Justice Statistics, U.S. Department of Justice. (2001b). *Advance for release: National correctional population reaches new high—grows by 126,400 during 2000 to total 6.5 million adults.* Washington, DC: Author.

Bureau of Justice Statistics, U.S. Department of Justice. (2001c). *Prisoners in 2000.* Washington, DC: Author.

Bureau of Justice Statistics. (2006). *Mental health problems of prison and jail inmates.* Retrieved from http://bjs.ojp.usdoj.gov/index.cfm?ty=pbdetail&iid=789

Clear, T. R., & Dammer, H. R. (2000). *The offender in the community.* Belmont, CA: Wadsworth.

Cohen, F. (1996). Offenders with mental disorders in the criminal justice-correctional process. In B. D. Sales & D. W. Shuman (Eds.), *Law, mental health, and mental disorder* (pp. 397–413). Pacific Grove, CA: Brooks/Cole.

Conly, C. (1999). *Coordinating community services for mentally ill offenders: Maryland's community criminal justice treatment program.* Washington, DC: National Institute of Justice.

DeShaney v. Winnebago Department of Social Services, 489 U.S. 189 (1989).

Diener, E. (2010). Neuroimaging: voodoo, new phrenology, or scientific breakthrough? Introduction to special section on fMRI. *Perspectives on Psychological Science, 5,* 714–715.

Dvoskin, J. A., & Patterson, R. F. (1998). Administration of treatment programs for offenders with mental disorders. In R. M. Wettstein (Ed.), *Treatment of offenders with mental disorders* (pp. 1–43). New York, NY: Guilford Press.

Elze, D., Stiffman, A. R., & Dore, P. (1999). The association between types of violence exposure and youths' mental health problems. *International Journal of Adolescent Medicine and Health, 11,* 221–255.

Estelle v. Gamble, 429 U.S. 97 (1976).

Fergusson, D. M., & Horwood, L. J. (1998). Exposure to interparental violence in childhood and psychosocial adjustment in young adulthood. *Child Abuse and Neglect, 22,* 339–357.

Fiske, S.T., & Taylor, S. (1991). *Social cognition* (2nd ed.). New York, NY: McGraw-Hill.

Gernsbacher, M. A. (2010). Stigma from psychological science: Group differences, not deficits-introduction to stigma special section. *Perspectives on Psychological Science, 5,* 687. doi: 10.1177/1745691610388767

Hafemeister, T. L. (1998). Legal aspects of the treatment of offenders with mental disorders. In R. M. Wettstein (Ed.), *Treatment of offenders with mental disorders* (pp. 44–125). New York, NY: Guilford Press.

Harris, A., & Lurigio, A. J. (2007). Mental illness and violence: A brief review of research and assessment strategies. *Aggression and Violent Behavior, 12,* 542–551. doi:10.1016/j.avb.2007.02.008

Hartwell, S. (2001). Female mentally ill offenders and their community reintegration needs: An initial examination. *International Journal of Law and Psychiatry, 24,* 1–11.

Heilbrun, K., & Griffin, P. A. (1998). Community-based forensic treatment. In R. M. Wettstein (Ed.), *Treatment of offenders with mental disorders* (pp. 168–210). New York, NY: Guilford Press.

Kansas v. Crane, 534 U.S. (2002).

Kupers, T. (1999). *Prison madness.* San Francisco, CA: Jossey-Bass.

La Fond, J. Q. (1996). The impact of law on the delivery of involuntary mental health services. In B. D. Sales & D. W. Shuman (Eds.), *Law, mental health, and mental disorder* (pp. 219–239). Pacific Grove, CA: Brooks/Cole.

Law, K., & Frierson, R. L. (2010). Constitutionality of the Federal Sex-Offender law. *Journal of the American Academy of Psychiatry and the Law, 38,* 615–617.

Lurigio, A. J., Rollins, A., & Fallon, J. (2004). The effects of serious mental illness on offender reentry. *Federal Probation, 68,* 45–52.

Maier, G. J., & Fulton, L. (1998). Inpatient treatment of offenders with mental disorders. In R. M. Wettstein (Ed.), *Treatment of offenders with mental disorders* (pp. 126–167). New York, NY: Guilford Press.

Manhal-Baugus, M. (1998). The self-in-relation theory and women for sobriety: Female-specific theory and mutual help group for chemically dependent women. *Journal of Addictions and Offender Counseling, 18*, 78–85.

Markowitz, F. E. (2011). Mental illness, crime, and violence: Risk, context, and social control. *Aggression and Violent Behavior, 16*, 36–44. doi:10.1016/j.avb.2010.10.003

Maxmen, J. S., & Ward, N. G. (1995). *Essential psychopathology and its treatment* (2nd ed.). New York, NY: Norton.

Mazerolle, P., & Maahs, J. (2000). General strain and delinquency: An alternative examination of conditioning influences. *Justice Quarterly, 17*, 753–778.

Messina, N., & Grella, C. (2006). Childhood trauma and women's health outcomes in a California prison population. *American Journal of Public Health, 96*, 1842–1848.

Metzner, J. L., Cohen, F., Grossman, L. S., & Wettstein, R. M. (1998). Treatment in jails and prisons. In R. M. Wettstein (Ed.), *Treatment of offenders with mental disorders* (pp. 211–264). New York, NY: Guilford Press.

Miller; G. A. (2010). Mistreating psychology in the decades of the brain. *Perspectives on Psychological Science, 5*, 716–743. doi: 10.1177/1745691610388774

Miller, S. L., & Meloy, M. L. (2006). Women's use of force: Voices of women arrested for domestic violence. *Violence Against Women, 12*, 89–115.

Mobley, M. J. (2006). Psychotherapy with criminal offenders. In I. B. Weiner & A. K. Hess (Eds.), *The handbook of forensic psychology* (3rd ed., pp. 751–789). Hoboken, NJ: Wiley.

Morash, M., Bynum, T. S., & Koons, B. A. (1998). *Women offenders: Programming needs and promising approaches.* Washington, DC: U.S. Department of Justice, Office of Justice Programs, National Institute of Justice.

Perlin, M. L. (2001). Hidden agendas and ripple effects: Implications of four recent Supreme Court decisions for forensic mental health professionals. *Journal of Forensic Psychology Practice, 1*, 33–64.

Rice, M. E., & Harris, G. T. (1997). The treatment of mentally disordered offenders. *Psychology, Public Policy and Law, 3*, 126–183.

Sales, B. D., & Shuman, D. W. (1996). The newly emerging mental health law. In B. D. Sales & D. W. Shuman (Eds.), *Law, mental health, and mental disorder* (pp. 2–14). Pacific Grove, CA: Brooks/Cole.

Schultz-Ross, R. A. (1993). Theoretical difficulties in the treatment of mentally ill prisoners. *Journal of Forensic Sciences, 38*, 426–431.

Sowers, W., Thompson, K., & Mullins, S. (1999). *Mental health in corrections: An overview for correctional staff.* Lanham, MD: American Correctional Association.

Steadman, H. J., Osher, F. C., Robbins, P., Case, B., & Samuels, S. (2009). Prevalence of serious mental illness among jail inmates. *Psychiatric Services, 60*, 761–765. doi:10.1176/appi.ps.60.6.761

Sun, K. (2001). *The implications of understanding the interpersonal and mental disconnections for correctional counseling.* Paper presented at the annual meeting of Academy of Criminal Justice Sciences, Washington, DC.

United States v. Comstock, 130 S. Ct. 1949 (2010).

Washington v. Harper, 494 U.S. 210 (1990).

Weinberger, L. E., & Sreenivasan, S. (1994). Ethical and professional conflicts in correctional psychology. *Professional Psychology: Research and Practice, 25*, 161–167.

Wright, E. R., Gronfein, W. P., & Owens, T. J. (2000). Deinstitutionalization, social rejection, and the self-esteem of former mental patients. *Journal of Health and Social Behavior, 41*, 68–90.

Chapter 11

Understanding and Treating Substance Abuse

Many offenders in corrections have substance abuse problems. However, a shortage of trained special therapists in the milieus has undermined both effective drug abuse treatment for correctional clients and their needs for reductions in recidivism (Mulvey, Schubert, & Chassin, 2010). To help correctional counselors understand and handle substance abuse problems, this chapter presents a summary of the related research.

Prevalence of Drug Abuse Problem

Nationally, crime rates continue to decline, whereas arrests for drug law violations continue to climb. In 2009, police made 1.6 million arrests for drug offenses or 13% of the total number of arrests (FBI, 2010). However, this number only included the offenses of drug possession or sales. Additionally, drug abuse is related to a large number of other offenses (e.g., stealing, robbery or burglary, or violent crimes) or to a lifestyle that predisposes the drug abuser to engage in illegal activity in illicit markets (Rand, Sabol, Sinclair, & Snyder, 2010). Meanwhile, the number of juvenile offenders and female offenders with substance abuse problems is increasing faster than the number of adult male offenders (National Institute on Drug Abuse [NIDA], 2006).

A recent survey by the Substance Abuse and Mental Health Services Administration (SAMHSA) (2010) showed that more than one-fifth (22.8%) of the 1.7 million adult offenders on parole or other supervised release from prison were current illicit drug users. 27.9% of the 5.1 million adults on probation reported current illicit drug use for the same time. In contrast, only 8.7% of the general population aged 12 or older were illicit drug users.

167

Definition of Addiction and Psychoactive Drugs

Addiction is commonly defined as a compulsive pattern of drug-seeking and drug-taking behavior that takes place at the expense of most other activities (Robinson & Berridge, 2003). Mere drug use does not constitute addiction. It must involve the component of pathological craving for *psychoactive drugs* (drugs that alter mood, perceptions and/or consciousness).

Inaba and Cohen (2007) suggest that according to their mental effects, psychoactive drugs can be classified into three categories: Uppers, downers, and all arounders.

Uppers (**stimulants**) include cocaine, amphetamines (meth, speed, crank, ice), diet pills, Ritalin, lookalikes, nicotine, and caffeine. At lower doses, these substances produce such effects as stimulation, confidence, aggressiveness, lack of hunger or thirst, faster heart rate, raised blood pressure, and alertness. At high doses with prolonged use, however, they generate neurotransmitter depletion, exhaustion, paranoia, psychosis, dehydration, unhealthy weight loss, and uncontrolled heart rate.

Downers (**depressants**) include opiates and opioids (opium, heroin, etc.), sedative-hypnotics, alcohol, and others. Although they can produce such desired effects as pain relief, sedation, anxiety control, muscle relaxation, suppression of inhibitions, and drowsiness, undesired effects generated by misuse include depressed respiration, slowed heart rate, constipation, slurred speech, unconsciousness, coma, and death.

All arounders (**psychedelics**), such as LSD, certain mushrooms, and marijuana, cause intensified and confused sensations as well as illusions, delusions, and hallucinations. Many of the psychedelics also cause stimulation, impaired judgment, and faulty reasoning.

It should be noted that not all harmful drugs are illegal. For example, alcohol and tobacco (with nicotine as its active ingredient) are partially responsible for millions of deaths and injuries per year in the United States, but their dangerous effects are less heeded than those of other psychoactive drugs (Milkman & Wanberg, 2005).

Etiology of Substance Abuse

The dominant explanation on the causality of substance abuse uses the **biopsychosocial model**, which views the problem as caused by the interaction among biological (biochemical and neurological), psychological (cognitive, motivational, and emotional) and social (e.g., family or other interpersonal conflicts, unemployment, poverty) systems (G. Miller, 2010). This approach suggests that each of the three systems plays a role in causing substance addiction, but has not elucidated how the multiple variables interact in initiating and maintaining addiction for the offender population. This author proposes that substance addiction represents a type of goal-directed action, and that it is best viewed as a maladaptive way to get desired mental experiences (e.g., pleasure, relief from pain, or altered consciousness) (Sun, 2011). This proposition is based on and can better incorporate research findings from four areas: (1) biochemical effects of psychoactive drugs, (2) how the mind regulates mental health, (3) basic human needs and cognitive understanding, and (4) initiating factors for substance abuse.

Biochemical Effects of Psychoactive Drugs

After psychoactive drugs enter the body through various channels (e.g., oral administration, injection, inhalation), the blood eventually carries them to the central nervous system (the brain and spinal cord). Psychoactive drugs become addictive partially because they mimic or modify the effects of neurotransmitters influencing the brain reward circuits that are important for regulating motivations related to survival, such as nutrients, water, sex, and safety. The repeated use of addictive drugs eventually changes how the brain functions and brain anatomy, which may help explain why addicts are at a high risk of relapse to drug abuse even after long periods of abstinence, and why they persist in seeking drugs despite deleterious consequences (Inaba & Cohen, 2007; Robinson & Berridge, 2003). In addition, defective genetic inheritance, in utero injuries and certain personality factors (e.g., impulsivity, low tolerance for frustration) can increase vulnerability to substance abuse (Finn, 2002; G. Miller, 2010).

Drug-generated desirable experiences, however, are brief and ephemeral because psychoactive drugs, including psychiatric drugs, vary in their toxicity and may disrupt or disable normal brain function in areas of the frontal lobes, limbic systems, and other structures by poisoning neurons or even destroying them. As the result, the drugs impair higher human functions, including emotional responsiveness, self-regulation, and autonomous or voluntary activity (Breggin, 2008).

The biochemical perspective can partially explain addiction, but it does not present a complete picture because individuals do not need external chemical sources for their moods and consciousness. The healthy mind, coupled with the healthy body, can produce all the neurotransmitters humans need for positive emotional experiences in a balanced way.

How the Mind Regulates Mental Health

Research in neuroscience and cognitive-behavioral therapy has demonstrated that although mental processes are associated with some biochemical/neurological operations, it is the mental activities such as thinking, decision making, problem solving and other cognitive functions, and emotional or motivational regulations that influence emotional well-being and related biochemical processes (G. A. Miller, 2010). In addition, positive human relationships, healthy foods and supplements, breathing exercises, meditation, and physical exercise can all improve mood and mental clarity by changing brain activities (G. A. Miller, 2010; Rossman, 2011). Other activities, such as hugging, sex, even deviant activities, are found to produce neurotransmitters (Milkman & Wanberg, 2005).

Basic Human Needs and Cognitive Understanding

Then the question is: if people themselves can produce and regulate the needed neurotransmitters, why do they resort to substance abuse?

In addition to considering biological mechanisms, we need to be aware that addiction is shaped by the interaction of two factors: (1) experiencing frustration and conflict in meeting one's basic needs, and (2) the inability of the mind to make sense of, explain, and handle frustration and conflict. This position is supported by research on human needs and on social cognition (e.g., Fiske, 2003; Ward & Mann, 2004).

It has been found that all intentional and important human actions manifest attempts to meet human needs, including life (health), mental peace, knowledge, excellence in performance, a sense of control (autonomy and self-directedness), friendship (including intimate, romantic, and family relationships), belonging, understanding, controlling, enhancing self, and trusting, spirituality, happiness and creativity. One of the most important needs involves developing cognitive control through understanding social reality. This is because human beings are active goal-pursuing individuals who are constantly seeking meaning in their social and mental experiences. Humans everywhere seek to develop an accurate understanding of their social context (e.g., Fiske, 2003; Ward & Mann, 2004).

Most of the offender population, who live in dysfunctional social, interpersonal, and physical contexts, have experienced both severe frustration in meeting those needs and the inability to accurately understand and handle conflict. For example, they have suffered interpersonal conflicts, family tensions, and/or other human tragedies, had experience with trauma and abuse (sexual, emotional, and/or physical), and domestic violence in the home, with few opportunities for legitimate employment. Juvenile offenders may have school difficulties, delinquent peer associations, and socioeconomic disadvantage (Milkman & Wanberg, 2005; Springer, McNeece, & Arnold, 2003). All of these factors become risk factors for substance abuse and criminal involvement when the offenders' cognitions (schemas) are unable to help understand their experiences accurately and to help them execute appropriate actions. Experienced frustration generates emotional pain that compels them to reduce it. Drugs serve as temporary relief from mental conflict.

The Initiating Factors

Some developmental, motivational, and social factors that cause juvenile offenders to engage in drug use/abuse include sensation seeking, thrill seeking. behavioral disinhibition, impulsivity, insecure attachment in infancy, parental mental health issues and substance abuse (serving as a bad role model), as well as peer pressure (Milkman & Wanberg, 2005; Wanberg & Milkman, 2010). The conditions that lead to or promote one's use of drugs at the outset may be called the **initiating factors** for drug abuse, but they are different from the more fundamental variables for continuing addiction, because initiating factors play less of a role in maintaining addiction (Sun, 2011).

Assessment

Accurate assessment is necessary for effective correctional intervention and treatment or referral. The methods of assessment for substance abuse may include the use of face-to-face interviews, psychological testing, drug testing, self-evaluation, collateral information (observations by family members or others), individualized rating scales, and standardized assessment instruments (Springer et al., 2003). Many relevant inventories are available. For instance, the ASAM Criteria, an assessment tool developed by the American Society of Addiction Medicine, are preferred by medical professionals and social workers (see Bradley & Ward, 2009; Gastfriend & Mee-Lee, 2011). The items in the assessment tools concentrate on the following five areas related to substance abuse (see Gastfriend & Mee-Lee, 2011; Milkman & Wanberg, 2005; Perkinson, 2002; Wanberg & Milkman, 2010):

1. The amount, frequency, and duration of drug abuse, including the types of substances, which may range from prescription drugs such as stimulants or sedatives to street drugs (such as marijuana and cocaine), to legal substances such as nicotine and alcohol.

2. Biomedical conditions and complications, acute intoxication and/or withdrawal complications, emotional/behavioral conditions and complications; personality disorders and other mental health problems.

3. Treatment acceptance/resistance, recovery situations, including the symptoms of relapse and continued drug abuse potential.

4. Social and environmental factors such as social and interpersonal circumstances, family history, abuse history (physical, sexual, emotional), financial status, employment or education. Examples include family difficulties, limited social skills, educational and employment problems, mental health disorders, infectious diseases, and other medical problems. For offenders who are reentering society, additional challenges and stressors may include reuniting with family members and complying with criminal justice supervision requirements. The unique issues for juveniles may involve fighting, stealing, vandalism, low school achievement, and early sexual activity.

   The assessment also needs to document the positive factors in the client's social, environmental and family settings, which play a role in preventing relapses. For example, family protective factors: (secure attachment, positive family interaction, and strong social ties), psychosocial protective factors (attachments to conventional individuals, a resiliency-strengthening community infrastructure) particularly benefit the needs of youths, promoting positive human development and facilitating their efforts to overcome substance abuse problems.

5. Individual psychological mechanisms (e.g., cognition, motivation, emotions, and attitudes) regarding substance abuse. The issues may include both the offender's deficient cognitions, behavior, and emotional trauma and protective factors such

as positive and conventional goals in life, functional interpersonal cognition and behavior, personal competence skills, positive relationship and empathy, healthy motivation, resiliency and emotional maturity against substance abuse, and involvement in constructive activities.

Screening and Diagnosis

It is important to separate *assessment* from *screening* and *diagnosis*, although the three activities are intimately related in process. **Screening** takes place before a comprehensive assessment and involves the use of a brief instrument or an informal interview to determine the likelihood that an individual has, or is at a high risk for substance abuse (Springer et al., 2003).

Diagnosis is typically made by using DSM-IV-TR (*The Diagnostic and Statistical Manual of Mental Disorders*, 4th edition, Text Revision) (American Psychiatric Association, 2000) following a complete assessment. The DSM-IV-TR lists three categories of substance-related disorders, including substance dependence, substance abuse, and substance-induced disorders (including substance intoxication and substance withdrawal). According to the DSM-IV-TR, the symptoms of substance dependence and substance abuse overlap, but there are some differences between the two diagnoses. The diagnosis of substance abuse emphasizes recurrent and significant harmful consequences associated with the repeated use of substances (e.g., repeated failure to fulfill major role obligations, recurrent use in physically hazardous situations, multiple legal and/or social and interpersonal problems). On the other hand, the criteria for substance dependence emphasize tolerance, withdrawal, or a pattern of compulsive use of substances. In addition, once the criteria for substance dependence are met, a diagnosis of substance abuse should not necessarily be made.

In this chapter, the term *substance abuse* is used to include any of the substance-related disorders. Although the diagnosis alone is not enough for treatment and intervention for addiction, it can help professionals communicate and share information with one another.

The Treatment Plan

Before mental health professionals engage in treatment for correctional clients with substance abuse problems, they should formulate an appropriate, realistic, and attainable treatment plan, which may include the following components (G. Miller, 2010; NIDA, 2006):

1. Identify the offender's unique conditions and status in corrections. For example, offenders at the reentry phase (transitioning back into the community from incarceration) have a higher risk for relapse than during incarceration because of available drugs and other temptations in the community (e.g., access to

alcohol or illegal drugs, witnessing others' drug abuse, and various stressors). In addition, the treatment plan should take into account the different treatment needs for women and juveniles in the justice system (NIDA, 2006). For example, incarcerated women are significantly more likely than incarcerated men to have severe substance abuse histories, as well as co-occurring physical health and mental health problems; they also experience other stresses created by the issues of childcare services and the lack of housing and employment. In addition to substance abuse, juvenile offenders' issues include academic failure, emotional disturbances, physical health issues, family problems, and a history of physical or sexual abuse. One-third of juvenile arrests involve teenage girls who report some form of emotional, physical, or sexual abuse.

2. Determine how to improve the client's psychological mechanisms (cognition, motivation, and emotions) regarding drug use. As discussed previously, substance abuse represents a maladaptive way to get desired mental experiences (e.g., pleasant state or relief from pain). Therefore, the plan needs to focus on developing cognitive competency and improving dysfunctional interpersonal contexts and other areas for the client. In addition, the plan should address how to amend attitudes, motivations, beliefs, and behaviors that support drug use, as well as problem solving and skill building for resisting drug use and criminal behavior.

    The treatment needs to integrate other issues related to substance abuse. For example, most correctional clients with drug abuse problems also need mental health treatment, requiring an integrated approach for treating the co-occurring mental health problems and substance use disorders. Additionally, drug abuse offenders suffer higher rates of infectious diseases, such as hepatitis, tuberculosis, and HIV/AIDS than the general population. Other stressors that aggravate an individual's risk for relapse include lack of housing and child care, medical, psychiatric, and/or social support services, and the need for vocational and employment assistance. The plan may take into consideration how families play an either positive or negative role in the recovery of substance abusing juveniles.

3. Prevent recidivism. Substance abuse treatment should be implemented with other interventions to prevent reoffending and ensure that it enhances correctional supervision requirements and the offender's accountability for his or her actions, because substance abuse is strongly correlated with criminal activity, denial of individual responsibility for one's actions, and blaming others or situations for the self's involvement in crime.

4. For medical professionals, the treatment plan may include pharmacotherapy, which is based on the medical model of neurobiological explanations of addiction.

For detailed discussion in this area, please refer to specialized sources (e.g., Inaba & Cohen, 2007).

Treatment Modalities for Addiction

Treatment modalities denote the common therapeutic approaches to the correctional population with substance abuse issues. They may be used individually or collectively (in group settings). These modalities include motivation-focused approaches (motivational interviewing and self-efficacy approach), cognitive-behavioral therapy (CBT), family therapy, and group therapy (including the therapeutic community). In reality, integration or eclecticism is the most popular theoretical orientation. *Eclecticism* involves the process of selecting concepts and strategies from various theories for use in a single approach. It also refers to flexibility in applying a variety of methods (e.g., individual counseling, group modality) and the extensive use of combinations of sound, visual, and kinesthetic media during the process of counseling.

Motivational Interviewing

Motivational interviewing (MI) in substance abuse treatment refers to an intervention method that instigates the client to change his or her drug abuse or other undesirable behavior by creating a perceived discrepancy between the client's present behavior and situations and the person's deeply held values and goals. Numerous studies have shown the effectiveness of MI for addictions (Glynn & Moyers, 2009).

The general procedures of MI include the following tasks (Glynn & Moyers, 2009; Hettema, Steele & Miller, 2005; Miller & Moyers, 2005):

1. Develop discrepancy. The MI therapist helps clients recognize the discrepancy between their current substance abuse behavior and their important goals or values that contradict the deviant behavior.

2. Seek to evoke the client's desire, ability, reasons, and need for dealing with his or her substance abuse problems and respond with empathy and reflective listening. The counselor thus reaffirms the client's reasons and desires for change. Accurate empathy, without judgment of or hostility to the client's viewpoint, is crucial to attaining accurate understanding and reiteration of the client's own perspective.

3. Diffuse resistance by helping the client examine the consequences of substance abuse and his or her mental struggles to handle the issues, directing the client back toward the intrinsic motivation for change.

4. Support the client's self-determination and choice, with confidence in the client's desire and capacity to improve in substance abuse and other dysfunctional areas. The counselor needs to see the self as a partner, rather than an expert, in collaboration with the client. This process strengthens the client's motivational

and verbal commitment to change, particularly when it is combined with a specific plan for implementing change.

Self-Efficacy

Self-efficacy is defined as individuals' confidence in their ability to organize and execute a given course of action to solve a problem or accomplish a task by mobilizing motivational and cognitive resources (Bandura, 2006). In other words, self-efficacy represents the core belief of the individual about his or her power to bring about change or exercise control over a variety of tasks by his or her actions. The model of self-efficacy can be applied to the different stages in providing substance abuse treatment.

In particular, Whittinghill, Whittinghill, Rudenga, and Loesch (2000) maintain that the following types of efficacy shape the phases of treatment for substance abuse, including resistance self-efficacy, harm-reduction self-efficacy, action self-efficacy, coping self-efficacy and recovery self-efficacy.

Resistance self-efficacy refers to an individual's perceived ability to resist attempts and persuasion to use alleged experimental substances for the first time. **Harm-reduction self-efficacy** denotes the ability to regulate the frequency and quantity of substance abuse and alcohol drinking after initial use. **Action self-efficacy** is closely related to harm reduction. It is defined as a person's belief about the self's ability to implement the behavior necessary to stop (or at least reduce) the use of a psychoactive drug. **Coping self-efficacy** refers to the person's competence to handle tempting and high-risk situations after successfully negotiating the action stage and achieving abstinence. **Recovery self-efficacy** is for individuals who want to manage setbacks or relapses after achieving sobriety and who need this type of self-efficacy to maintain long-term recovery.

Cognitive-Behavioral Therapy

Cognitive-behavioral therapy, which integrates the key components of behavioral and cognitive therapy, has demonstrated efficacy in reducing the use of alcohol and cocaine, particularly over the long term (Barry and Petry, 2009).

The behavioral approach is based on two types of learning theories: (1) classical (respondent) conditioning; and (2) instrumental (operant) conditioning. Both theories have been used to explain how learning experiences shape or promote deviant, antisocial, or undesirable behavior, including substance abuse. By the same token, the learning mechanisms can be used to control, treat, or minimize substance abuse. From this perspective, substance abuse is viewed as a type of reinforcement that sustains the dysfunctional behavior. Operant conditioning, classical conditioning, and social learning mechanisms can be employed to eliminate substance abuse by making the sight or smell of substances and drug use lose their reinforcing property.

Although cognitive therapy involves a diverse set of terms and procedures, it shares the basic postulate that cognition or thinking largely determines feelings and behavior. Three frequently used cognitive models for offenders with substance abuse problems focus on three different areas (Barry and Petry, 2009):

1. Revising a person's negative self-concept. This approach assumes that it is irrational or negative cognitive beliefs about the self, rather than negative activating experiences, that lead to negative emotional states (e.g., depression or anxiety) and dysfunctional behavior. The behavior includes a sense of defeat and the withdrawal of investment in people and in conventional goals, as well as an intensified sense of vulnerability. The purpose of cognitive therapy is to restructure the client's irrational/negative/distorted/automatic beliefs or schemas into rational, accurate, and positive ones.

2. Developing offenders' social skills and problem-solving skills to cope with craving and to be assertive, teaching clients to learn to identify and avoid high-risk situations and solve problems generated by stressful life events.

3. Helping offenders discern the connection between thoughts and outcomes. For example, clients learn that their thoughts of the desirable effect of a substance will lead to substance abuse. On the other hand, thinking about negative results of drug abuse such as inability to hold employment, interpersonal tensions, or financial problems can generate negative emotions and behavioral change (Milkman & Wanberg, 2005).

Cognitive therapy for substance abuse, however, needs to go beyond the goals of developing a positive self-concept and learning cognitive skills or other "how to do" things. Counselors need to help clients understand and modify their distorted interaction schemas, including their misperceived norms and rules and interpersonal reality that are used to evaluate, explain, and react to the self's experiences and social situations regarding substance abuse.

Family Therapy

Family therapy involves family members, particularly parents and children, in dialogue about substance abuse. The counselor first helps family members identify and analyze both dysfunctional and functional aspects of the family system, then engages them in reducing or eliminating factors within the family that exacerbate and promote the involvement in alcohol and other drug use (e.g., the conflict-ridden milieu, parental drug abuse) and in developing a family environment that increases resiliency for all involved, facilitating communication and problem solving, and nurturing hope and potential for youths (Milkman & Wanberg, 2005; Springer et al., 2003).

Group Treatment

Group treatment is the most commonly used mode of intervention with substance-abusing offenders (G. Miller, 2010; Springer et al., 2003). It can take the form of self-help/

support groups (e.g., Alcoholics Anonymous, Narcotics Anonymous, and Cocaine Anonymous), psychoeducational groups, and interactional therapeutic groups. Group treatment can be conducted in the community or within the prison/jail. Although there are more structural constraints, policies, and laws in an incarcerated setting than in the community, the group dynamics for helping offenders recover from drug abuse remain similar.

In addition to the basic characteristics of group dynamics (e.g., the leader's role, recruiting and engaging the members, group rules, group cohesion), group therapy differs from individual therapy in that group dynamics represent interpersonal contexts and a social microcosm mirroring social interactions in the real world. It serves as a healing agent by rectifying members' distorted cognitions of interpersonal reality and developing new and accurate cognitions about social reality. In addition, group processes help participants to release feelings that block social performance and gain support from others. Groups offer many advantages over individual therapy, including encouraging members to share their feelings, learning to trust others in the group, learning to accept their own painful, mixed feelings about their deviant behavior, increasing self-awareness, and promoting commitment to treatment settings. Group members can confront one another directly and immediately in an authentic manner.

For clients with substance abuse issues, the group serves as a healthy social environment in which members can exchange information, learn normal social interaction and problem solving as well as communication skills. Group helps them identify with others who are going through similar problems and understand their own attitudes toward addiction in the interpersonal process. People are made aware that they are not alone in their pain and struggles in overcoming drug abuse, and that they can be accepted by the others and be authentic in expressing and communicating their feelings and needs, developing both a sense of self-worth and belonging (NIDA, 2006; Perkinson, 2002; Springer et al., 2003),

In short, group therapy is both an effective counseling method and an efficient use of therapeutic resources. The clients' symptoms and underlying difficulties largely result from their misperceptions of interpersonal reality and patterns governing interpersonal relationships. The group process, therefore, helps the members to become more aware and modify their maladaptive interpersonal cognitions and behaviors through authentic interactions, including honest feedback, a feeling of support and belonging, sharing personal experiences, and a new understanding of one another (Yalom, 1998).

The **therapeutic community (TC)** is a highly specialized type of residential treatment program or group. Therapeutic communities have been used to treat a variety of disorders, including substance abuse and mental illness. The TC differs from other groups for drug treatment in the following ways (Springer et al., 2003; Stohr, Hemmens, & Dayley, 2005):

1. All community members serve as therapists and counselors in an around-the-clock learning and living residence facility.

2. It is a residential-based substance abuse treatment modality based on peer support for prosocial values and behaviors with client involvement in their own treatment.

3. Drug abuse is viewed as a disorder of the whole person; therefore, treatment should address all aspects of that person (e.g., trauma, emotional injuries, education, interpersonal communications, relationships, negative patterns of thinking, feeling, and behaving), with the main goal to develop not only a responsible drug-free lifestyle but also a positive, capable and law-abiding person.

4. Personal responsibility and mutual assistance are emphasized through peer interaction, support, acceptance, and insight.

Summary

A large number of offenders either are convicted of drug law violations or have substance abuse problems. The counselor needs to help clients understand that although substance abuse does involve unbalanced neurotransmitters in the neurological circuitry, it is more influenced by how the mind understands and deals with conflict. To perform effective treatment, the counselor needs to develop a realistic treatment plan according to the assessment of five areas, including the current drug abuse problems, mental health issues, previous treatment and relapse issues, both negative and positive social environmental factors, and the psychological mechanisms (cognition, motivation, emotions, and attitudes) regarding substance abuse. There are a variety of treatment models that can be used in treating substance abuse.

Key Terms

Three types of psychoactive drugs and their effects

Differences among assessment, screening, and diagnosis

Five areas in assessing substance abuse

Therapeutic community

Discussion Questions

1. Describe different explanations for substance abuse.

2. Do you agree that substance abuse and criminal behavior are caused by some common variables? How?

3. Describe four treatment modalities for substance abuse.

4. What do you think the government can do to stop substance abuse (in addition to enacting more drug laws punishing the violators)? Give your rationale.

References

American Psychiatric Association. (2000). *The diagnostic and statistical manual of mental disorders* (4th ed., text revision). Washington DC: Author.

Bandura, A. (2006). Toward a psychology of human agency. *Perspectives on Psychological Science, 1,* 164–180.

Barry, D., & Petry, N. M. (2009). Cognitive behavioral treatments for substance use disorders. In P. M. Miller (Ed.), *Evidence-based addiction treatment* (pp. 159–174). Burlington, MA: Academic Press.

Bradley, C., & Ward, K. (2009). Mental health and addictions: Legal and ethical issues for practice. In T. Maschi, C. Bradley, K. Ward, T. Maschi, C. Bradley, & K. Ward (Eds.), *Forensic social work: Psychosocial and legal issues in diverse practice settings* (pp. 183–195). New York, NY: Springer Publishing Co.

Breggin, P. R. (2008). *Brain-disabling treatments in psychiatry: Drugs, electroshock, and the psychopharmaceutical complex* (2nd ed.). New York, NY: Springer.

Federal Bureau of Investigation (FBI). (2010). *Crime in the United States 2009.* Washington, DC: U.S. Department of Justice. Retrieved from http://www2.fbi.gov/ucr/cius2009/arrests/index.html.

Finn, P. R. (2002). Motivation, working memory, and decision making: A cognitive-motivational theory of personality vulnerability to alcoholism. *Behavioral and Cognitive Neuroscience Reviews, 1*(3), 183–205. doi:10.1177/1534582302001003001

Fiske, S. T. (2003). Five core social motives, plus or minus five. In S. J. Spencer, S. Fein, M. P. Zanna, J. M. Olson, S. J. Spencer, S. Fein, . . . J. M. Olson (Eds.), *Motivated social perception: The Ontario symposium* (Vol. 9, pp. 233–246). Mahwah, NJ: Lawrence Erlbaum Associates Publishers.

Gastfriend, D. R., & Mee-Lee, D. (2011). Patient placement criteria. In M. Galanter, H. D. Kleber, M. Galanter, H. D. Kleber (Eds.), *Psychotherapy for the treatment of substance abuse* (pp. 99–123). Arlington, VA: American Psychiatric Publishing, Inc.

Glynn, L. H., & Moyers, T. B. (2009). Motivational interviewing for addictions. In P. M. Miller (Ed.), *Evidence-based addiction treatment* (pp. 159–174). Burlington, MA: Academic Press.

Hettema, J., Steele, J., & Miller, W. R. (2005). Motivational interviewing. *Annual Review of Clinical Psychology, 1,* 91–111.

Inaba, D. S., & Cohen, W. E. (2007). *Uppers, downers, all arounders: Physical and mental effects of psychoactive drugs* (6th ed.). Ashland, OR: CNS Publications, Inc.

Milkman, H. B., & Wanberg, K. W. (2005). *Criminal conduct and substance abuse treatment for adolescents. Pathways to self-discovery and change: The provider's guide.* Los Angeles, CA: Sage.

Miller, G. (2010). *Learning the language of addiction counseling* (3rd ed.) Hoboken, NJ: Wiley.

Miller, G. A. (2010). Mistreating psychology in the decades of the brain. *Perspectives on Psychological Science, 5,* 716–743. doi: 10.1177/1745691610388774

Miller, W. R., & Moyers, T. B. (2005). Motivational interviewing. In G. P. Koocher, J. C. Norcross, & S. S. Hill III (Eds.), *Psychologists' desk reference* (2nd ed., pp. 267–271). New York, NY: Oxford University Press.

Mulvey, E. P., Schubert, C. A., & Chassin, L. (2010). *Substance use and delinquent behavior among serious adolescent offenders* (NCJ 232790). Washington, DC: Office of Juvenile Justice and Delinquency Prevention. Retrieved from http://www.ncjrs.gov/pdffiles1/ojjdp/232790.pdf.

National Institute on Drug Abuse (NIDA). (2006). Principles of drug abuse treatment for criminal justice populations (NIH Publication No. 06-5316). Washington, DC: National Institutes of Health. Retrieved from http://www.drugabuse.gov/podat_cj/.

Perkinson, R. R. (2002). *Chemical dependency counseling: A practical guide* (2nd ed.). Thousand Oaks, CA: Sage.

Rand, M. R., Sabol, W. J., Sinclair, M, & Snyder, H. N. (2010). Alcohol and crime: Data from 2002 to 2008. Washington, DC: Bureau of Justice Statistics. Retrieved from http://bjs.ojp.usdoj.gov/index.cfm?ty=pbdetail&iid=2313.

Robinson, T. E., & Berridge, K. C. (2003). Addiction. *Annual Review of Psychology*, 5425–5453. doi:10.1146/annurev.psych.54.101601.145237

Rossman, J. (2011). *The mind–body mood solution: The breakthrough drug-free program for lasting relief from depression*. Emmaus, PA: Rodale Press.

Springer, D. W., McNeece, C. A., & Arnold, E. M. (2003). *Substance abuse treatment for criminal offenders*. Washington DC: American Psychological Association.

Stohr, M. K., Hemmens, C., Dayley, J., Baune, D., Kjaer, K., Gornik, M., & Noon, C. (2005). Residential substance abuse treatment programming: What do the inmates think? In B. Sims & B. Sims (Eds.), *Substance abuse treatment with correctional clients: Practical implications for institutional and community settings* (pp. 95–131). New York, NY: Haworth Press.

Substance Abuse and Mental Health Services Administration (SAMHSA). (2010). *Results from the 2009 National Survey on Drug Use and Health: Volume I. Summary of national findings* (Office of Applied Studies, NSDUH Series H-38A, HHS Publication No. SMA 10-4856 Findings). Rockville, MD: Author.

Sun, K. (2011, Nov.). *Understanding etiology of substance abuse: Separating the initiating factors from addiction variables*. Poster presented at the Annual Convention of American Society of Criminology. Washington, DC.

Wanberg, K. W., & Milkman, H. B. (2010). *Provider's handbook for assessing criminal conduct and substance abuse clients*. Los Angeles, CA: Sage.

Ward, T, & Mann, R. (2004). Good lives and the rehabilitation of offenders: A positive approach to sex offender treatment. In P. A. Linley & S. Joseph, (Eds.), *Positive psychology in practice* (pp. 598–616). Hoboken, NJ: John Wiley & Sons.

Whittinghill, D., Whittinghill, L., Rudenga, L., & Loesch, L. C. (2000). The benefits of a self-efficacy approach to substance abuse counseling in the era of managed care. *Journal of Addictions & Offender Counseling, 20*, 64–74.

Yalom, I. D. (1998). *The Yalom reader: Selections from the work of a master therapist and storyteller*. New York, NY: BasicBooks.

Chapter 12

Restorative Justice and Correctional Counseling

In addition to helping and counseling correctional clients, counselors or community correctional officers (particularly juvenile probation counselors) may be involved in assisting or facilitating an emerging program known as *restorative justice*, which represents a relatively new and alternative approach to administering justice to adult and juvenile offenders in community or in incarceration in the United States. Restorative justice promotes the goal of justice and a new method of dispensing justice, focusing on serving victims whose needs are often overlooked in the retribution-oriented system and bringing together all parties affected by the harm or wrongdoing (e.g., offenders and their families, victims and their families, other members of the community, and professionals). It is also intended to solve the conflict and heal the wounds of the parties affected by the offense (Katz & Bonham, 2009; Umbreit, & Armour, 2010; Van Wormer, 2004).

Four Characteristics of Restorative Justice

Research shows that restorative justice has four main characteristics (see Fred, 2005; Gumz & Grant, 2009; Katz & Bonham, 2009; Van Wormer, 2004; Zehr, 2002).

First, restorative justice's primary aim is to restore the victims, materially and psychologically, to where they were before the crime occurred. It is in contrast with the conventional justice system that focuses on the offender and considers crime a violation against law and society. Unlike the traditional system where the court determines the appropriate sanction such as incarceration or probation for the offender, restorative justice consists of a three-dimensional approach that includes the victim, offender, and community in dealing with and repairing the crime-caused harms to all the parties.

181

Second, instead of simply punishing offenders, restorative justice is concerned with restoring them to a law-abiding life style by developing their real sense of accountability, and making them understand the harm that they caused to the victim. With a strong disapproval of bad conduct but respect for the person who committed the bad act, restorative justice encourages offenders to experience feelings of shame regarding the offenses, accept responsibility, sincerely apologize, and develop commitment and concrete steps to self-regulatory actions, which, in turn, work against future transgression of the law. Thus it restores the dignity of offenders. The key to this process involves the social connection with family, friends, and community.

Third, restorative justice attempts to repair the offense-produced harms to the community, as well as involve the community in the reintegration of the offender. Restorative justice practice in the community is usually managed by nonprofit groups with the help of some criminal justice personnel. In this situation, community members, together with the victim and offender, develop a consensually supported plan that includes elements for both reparation and crime prevention. In order to achieve these goals, the plan must address the victims' and community's needs and specify offenders' obligations for those needs, as well as identifying their risk areas for the offenses and the corresponding solutions. By doing so, restorative justice has the potential to transform the lives of the victim, the community, and the offender.

Fourth, restorative processes are typically implemented either in addition to or instead of standard judicial proceedings (Van Wormer, 2004; Zehr, 2002). This is because this type of practice needs to be flexibly applied to where it is most effective. For instance, two studies by Gromet and Darley (2006) showed that people view both restorative justice and the conventional retributive justice system as appropriate according to crimes of varying severity. In particular, the seriousness of the crime predicts which procedure people preferred to assign for each crime. They primarily picked the pure restorative procedure for low-seriousness crimes, but increasingly chose the mixed procedure (a combination of the two types of justice) for more serious crimes. In other words, people regard retributive justice and restorative justice as complementing each other.

In short, restorative justice, cooperating with the traditional justice system, emphasizes accountability and healing for the victim, offender and community with a focus on service, social justice, dignity and worth of a person, and value of human relationships.

The Effectiveness of Restorative Justice

Several studies have demonstrated the effectiveness of restorative justice in reducing recidivism (e.g., Bergseth & Bouffard, 2007; de Beus & Rodriguez, 2007; Hurley, 2009; Rodriguez, 2007). For example, Bergseth and Bouffard (2007) found that juveniles referred to RJ programming performed better than those referred to traditional juvenile court processing on four outcome measures: prevalence of reoffense, number of later contacts with police, seriousness of later offense, and the length of interval to re-offense. RJ programs, however, reduce recidivism by interacting with other variables. For example,

Rodriguez (2007) found that gender and prior offenses indirectly influence recidivism in important ways. Girls and offenders with minimal criminal history records exhibit the most success from participating in such programs.

It needs to be emphasized that restorative justice also represents a much less expensive approach to dealing with crime and offenders, because it uses volunteers and available community resources, thus immensely reducing the cost spent in the traditional justice system. It also needs to be noted that reduced recidivism or reoffending is a byproduct of, but not the primary goal of restorative justice. The restorative procedure that addresses the victims' needs, requires offenders to take responsibility, and involves community participation is more important than the narrow goal of reducing recidivism (Zehr, 2002).

A Brief History of Restorative Justice

Many cultures and religions in the ancient world had already proposed some notions similar to the modern concept of restorative justice, including the Jewish notion of "tikkun"—to heal, repair, and change the world—the Christian belief about forgiveness (Van Wormer, 2009), and Confucian principles about the goodness of human nature and a humanistic approach to wrongful deeds (Hui & Geng, 2001). However, as a regular practice of conflict resolution, the root of restorative justice is found in indigenous traditions. For example, the Maori people of New Zealand have a sentencing form that involves the victim, offender, and families, and friends of both in resolving a criminal or delinquent incident. The talking circles of Native Americans for peacemaking can also be seen as a form of restorative justice (Fred, 2005; Van Wormer, 2004).

The modern restorative justice movement in North America started with the victim–offender reconciliation movement in the 1970s in Canada. This form of justice continued to be used in Canada and came to the United States subsequently. Concurrently, the feminism-inspired victims' rights movement played a role in raising consciousness regarding the need for victims to be heard in the criminal justice process. Although most restorative justice programs in the United States mainly deal with juvenile offenders and minor/first-time offenses, restorative justice has also been increasingly practiced with adult felony offenders in correctional settings. Augmented by endorsement from the United Nations, meanwhile, restorative justice programming has increasingly become incorporated into criminal justice processes worldwide, including English-speaking countries such as New Zealand and Australia (where this approach has been closely associated with indigenous populations), the European Union, and many other national governments (Van Wormer, 2004; Zehr, 2002).

Types of Restorative Justice

Four of the most popular forms of restorative approaches include victim–offender mediation/conferencing, family group conferencing, community conferencing, and community reparation boards. Although each of these forms has unique procedures and concentrations, they all share such common features as a community-based sanctioning focus, nonadversarial and informal processes, and decision making by consensus (Bergseth & Bouffard, 2007; Gumz & Grant, 2009; Katz & Bonham, 2009; Van Wormer, 2004, 2009).

Victim–Offender Mediation

Victim–offender mediation (VoM) is the most common type of restorative justice practice used in the United States. VoM is a face-to-face meeting involving a trained mediator, crime victim, and person who committed the crime, with the victim's needs as the center of the process. After the offender shows a remorse for his or her crime and the victim is willing to meet, VoM is initiated for the victim to meet face-to-face with the offender(s) in a safe, structured, trusting environment (sometimes surrounded by family members and key players in the event). During the process, the facilitator engages with the parties to talk about the crime and the impact on the victim. The offender and the victim may speak to each other about what happened, the effects of the crime on their lives, and their feelings about it. They may choose to create a mutually agreeable restitution plan to repair any damages that occurred as a result of the crime. The mediator may be a community-member volunteer, clergy, criminal justice professional, or counselor/social worker.

Although the practice of VoM in the past was most often applied with juvenile offenders who were involved in nonviolent property crimes, it has recently been utilized with youth offenders of serious violent crimes. For the offender, such a mediation process has the advantage of offering diversion from prosecution and provides an opportunity for rehabilitation and healing.

Family Group Conferencing

The **family group conference (FGC)** was adapted from traditional practices of the Maori people. Currently FGC is used in many countries (e.g., New Zealand, Austria, England, Wales, Canada, and the United States) as a preferred sentencing and restorative justice forum for youthful offenders.

This practice is slightly different from VoM in that in addition to the victim and offender, it involves their families, friends, and key supporters of both sides in the process of assessing the nature and the harm of the offense and the decision regarding appropriate sanction. By soliciting the families' support in helping the offender make amends and repair the harm, it empowers the individuals and the family systems.

Community Conferencing

Community conferencing, which is often called *peacemaking circles*, *sentencing circles* or *talking circles*, was derived from Canadian aboriginal and Native American cultural traditions as a community-based way to resolve conflict. Community conferencing can be described as a more inclusive process than victim–offender mediation or family conferencing. Sitting in these circles, community members, victims, offenders, families and friends, and a facilitator (also known as a *circle keeper*) speak out in a nonjudgmental, egalitarian way while passing around a "talking piece." After the healing circle meets, a sentencing circle may be formed (with feedback from family, community, and the justice system) to determine a course of action. Other circles, if necessary, are organized to monitor compliance about restitution or community service in the follow-up process.

The circle keeper, who may be a criminal justice professional, a respected community elder or member, or a social worker, needs to possess a nonjudgmental approach, good listening skills, empathy, respect, patience, and understanding.

Community Reparative Boards

Community reparative boards (CRBs) are known by different names in different communities, such as *restorative boards, accountability boards,* or the "Vermont model" of reparative probation. Although they are similar to other types of restorative justice programs by involving a broader community in the restoring process, this form of restorative conferencing is unique in that it is implemented within existing structures and processes of the criminal justice system. CRB meetings include the offenders, their respective families, the police, the court, correctional staff, and other community partners. The victim's participation has been minimal in the past, although an effort to improve this issue has been made.

During the meeting, the board members evaluate the nature of a specific crime and its harmful impact on the victim and the greater community. They interview the offender and his or her parents (in the case of a juvenile offender), hear the offender's version of the offense (if possible, together with the version of the victim), and ask probing questions about the circumstances of the crime as well as about what is going on in the offender's life.

After consulting the relevant members, the board develops an accountability plan for the offender by mandating some kind of restitution to the victim and/or engaging in community service and receiving counseling.

Community reparative boards are often referred to as the "Vermont model" of reparative probation because they were initially created and implemented in Vermont in the 1990s in response to the public's disappointment with the criminal justice system. During that time, Vermont originated statewide reparative boards to focus on repairing the damage to the victims and community by low-risk nonviolent offenders. These boards made offenders aware of the impact of their conduct and mandated that they make reparations to both the victim(s) and to the community.

In summary, restorative justice procedures usually involve a face-to-face meeting of the victim, the offender, community, and/or family members for both sides. This approach gives individuals, families, and community most directly impacted by wrongdoing the opportunity to participate in the resolution process. This process not only creates emotional healing for the participants, but also produces some agreements that usually involve an apology, monetary compensation, some services that the offender must perform for the victim, community service, and the like.

It should be noted that not all restorative justice programs involve direct encounters between the "matched" victims and offenders (Zehr, 2002). That is, the participating victims may be the victims of other offenders. Even so the process is still restorative-focused: encouraging offenders to understand and take responsibility for what they have done and giving victims an opportunity to tell their stories to the offenders, and together explore a variety of topics and issues, for the benefit of all involved.

Success of Restorative Justice Depends Upon Upholding Six Core Values

Restorative justice practice is viewed as highly compatible with the mission of a set of core values/principles in social work and other mental health professions. These principles include *social justice, service, human dignity and worth, importance of human relationships, integrity,* and *competence* (Katz & Bonham, 2009; Umbreit, & Armour, 2010; Van Wormer, 2009). This author, however, maintains that the compatibility of these principles with restorative justice does not automatically put them into operation, because the participants vary in their knowledge, training, experience, preparation, and background in understanding and applying these principles. The facilitator or counselor must meticulously apply them to the process.

Social Justice

The effectiveness of restorative justice is based on applying the principle of social justice, which comprises both "justice" and "social" components. The concept of *justice* entails both fair outcome and fair procedure. The fair outcome is described as *distributive justice* (the fair ratio between the input and outcome) and the fair process refers to *procedural justice* (Törnblom & Vermunt, 2007). Restorative justice has an advantage over the conventional justice in that it promotes the goal of distributive justice, emphasizing "restoration" (i.e., repairing the harms associated with crime) rather than "retribution" (i.e., "an eye for an eye" philosophy) by addressing the needs of all the parties or stakeholders (Bergseth & Bouffard, 2007). The practice also emphasizes a type of procedural justice by giving both the victim and the offender a chance to be heard with fairness to all parties. As the result, all parties are more satisfied with their outcomes and with the procedures.

In addition, the effectiveness of restorative justice in producing better outcomes for all persons and entities affected by crime is increased by a *social* or collaborative approach to justice, offering communities an opportunity to play a larger role in addressing the problems that cause crime. When the community is involved in restorative justice efforts, people living there feel empowered and experience less fear of crime. This social approach particularly benefits juvenile offenders, who are most likely to respond to early and community-based intervention efforts for change.

Service and Human Dignity and Worth

The efficiency of restorative justice is sustained by providing excellent service and maintains human dignity and worth for the victim and the offender. To implement these values, the counselor must make sure that the process primarily makes victims feel more satisfied with restorative processes than traditional court procedures by meeting the victims' needs. The counselor needs to assess victims' expectations about the process and their emotions about the victimization, and provide ample opportunities in the process for the victims to confront the offender in a controlled and secure environment, seek the answer from the perpetrator, receive an apology, and play a role in determining what the offenders must do to repair the harm. The process should encourage victims to communicate their anger, frustration, and sense of violation directly to the offender. Doing so will give victims a sense of empowerment and closure that is rarely achieved in the traditional juvenile justice system (Katz & Bonham, 2009).

The process also provides a good service to the offenders when it condemns the bad acts but not the persons, developing their accountability while treating them with more respect than in the traditional court system. To reintegrate the offender into the community, the restorative justice process requires the offender take some concrete actions, including making restitution to victims and/or the community for the harm or monetary losses as the result of the crime.

Importance of Human Relationships

Human relationships are important in restorative justice for the following reasons:

1. Dysfunctional human relationships (e.g., associations with delinquent peers, parental criminal behavior, and abusive interpersonal contexts) represent the social contexts that cause and aggravate people's involvements in criminal activities (Elze, Stiffman, & Dore, 1999; Fergusson & Horwood, 1998; Zehr, 2002). Additionally, crime is considered a violation of social relationship from the perspective of restorative justice (Ryals, 2004).

2. Offenders' distorted cognitions of human relationships lead to their illegal or delinquent activities. Dysfunctional human relationships (e.g., interpersonal conflicts, frustrations and trauma, and other dysfunctional social interactions) promote involvement in criminal activities by forming and validating the offender's distorted interaction schemas of interpersonal reality, which are responsible for generating various maladaptive behaviors. The distorted cognitions include misperceptions of the intentions, needs, feelings, thinking, mental validation or invalidation of interpersonal communications and actions of the victims, correctional staff, and others, as well as falsely or inaccurately perceived patterns, criteria and norms for evaluating, interpreting, explaining, and reacting to the self's and others' attributes and actions in social situations. Offenders maintain

their distorted cognition because communication from others or the environment has not invalidated their cognitive distortions.

3. Employing the power of functional and authentic human interactions in the restorative justice process is a key to developing the offender's sense of accountability for the offense by modifying the client's misrepresentations of the self, victims, others and relationships among them.

   Authentic human interactions in restorative justice, which are broader than merely letting the offender learn about the harm he or she has inflicted on the victim and the community, are embodied by honest and constructive interpersonal communications, evaluations, exchanges, and dialogues among the offender, victims, the family and/or community members (e.g., victims' emotional reactions to the offense, the offender's attempt to rationalize or deny the wrongdoing, and the others' rebuttals of the offender's explanations). This type of interpersonal interaction serves to invalidate the offender's false beliefs that sustain the denial of individual responsibility and allow the perceiver to see the discrepancy between his or her perceptions and the interpersonal reality and adjust his or her mismatched cognitive system. In other words, offenders develop a sense of responsibility/accountability for their offenses and new self-regulation mechanisms, change their future behavior, and feel and express remorse for their actions only when authentic human interactions nullify the cognitive distortions that enable their defense mechanisms (e.g., denial or rationalization of wrongdoings).

Integrity and Competence

According to Umbreit and Armour (2010), integrity in restorative justice consists of two aspects of the process: First, it entails that the dialogue process between the involved parties be honest, voluntary, nonmanipulative, noncoercive, and nonadversarial, with the encouragement of open expression of feelings and discussion of the context and history of the offense and the harm. Second, the counselors or social workers facilitating the process must empathize with and show respect and concern for all the participants.

Competence for the professionals refers to developing and maintaining their professional knowledge and ability that enable them to manage diverse situations and issues in the restorative justice process.

Summary

Correctional counselors or community correctional officers may participate in facilitating an emerging program known as restorative justice, which represents a relatively new and alternative approach to administering justice. Restorative justice may vary in form (e.g., victim–offender mediation/conferencing, family group conferencing, community conferencing, and community reparation boards). It operates in concert with or instead of the traditional justice system, with the intention of restoring the victim and the community materially and psychologically, in addition to reintegrating the offender and crime prevention. To guarantee its success, counselors need to imbue the practice with six core values, including social justice, service, human dignity and worth, importance of human relationships, integrity, and competence.

Key Terms

Restorative justice

Distributive justice

Procedural justice

Victim-offender mediation

Family group conferencing

Community conferencing

Community reparative board

Discussion Questions

1. How many differences between restorative justice and traditional justice can you list?

2. Describe some psychological benefits of restorative justice for the victim of crime.

3. Describe the six core values for social workers/mental health professionals.

References

Bergseth, K. J., & Bouffard, J. A. (2007). The long-term impact of restorative justice programming for juvenile offenders. *Journal of Criminal Justice, 35*(4), 433–451. doi:10.1016/j.jcrimjus.2007.05.006

de Beus, K., & Rodriguez, N. (2007). Restorative justice practice: An examination of program completion and recidivism. *Journal of Criminal Justice, 35*(3), 337–347. doi:10.1016/j.jcrimjus.2007.03.009

Elze, D., Stiffman, A. R., & Dore, P. (1999). The association between types of violence exposure and youths' mental health problems. *International Journal of Adolescent Medicine & Health, 11*, 221–255.

Fergusson, D. M., & Horwood, L. J. (1998). Exposure to interparental violence in childhood and psychosocial adjustment in young adulthood. *Child Abuse & Neglect, 22*, 339–357.

Fred, S. (2005, February). Restorative justice: A model of healing philosophy consistent with social work values. *NASW News, 50*(2). Retrieved from http://www.socialworkers.org/pubs/news/2005/02/justice.asp.

Gromet, D. M., & Darley, J. M. (2006). Restoration and retribution: How including retributive components affects the acceptability of restorative justice procedures. *Social Justice Research, 19*, 395–432.

Gumz, E. J., & Grant, C. L. (2009). Restorative justice: A systematic review of the social work literature. *Families in Society, 90*, 119–126.

Hui, E., & Geng, K. (2001). The spirit and practice of restorative justice in Chinese culture. In M. L. Hadley (Ed.), *The spiritual roots of restorative justice* (pp. 99–118). Albany, NY: State University of New York Press.

Hurley, M. (2009). Restorative practices in institutional settings and at release: Victim wrap around programs. *Federal Probation, 73*(1), 16–22.

Katz, J., & Bonham, G. (2009). *Effective alternatives to incarceration: Police collaborations with corrections and communities.* Washington, DC: U.S. Department of Justice, Office of Community Oriented Policing Services (COPS).

Rodriguez, N. (2007). Restorative justice at work: Examining the impact of restorative justice resolutions on juvenile recidivism. *Crime & Delinquency, 53*(3), 355–379. doi:10.1177/0011128705285983

Ryals, J. R. (2004). Restorative justice: New horizons in juvenile offender counseling. *Journal of Addictions & Offender Counseling, 25*(1), 18–25.

Törnblom, K. Y., & Vermunt, R. (2007). Towards an integration of distributive justice, procedural justice, and social resource theories. *Social Justice Research, 20*, 312–335.

Umbreit, M., & Armour, M. (2010). *Restorative justice dialogue: An essential guide for research and practice.* New York, NY: Springer Publishing Co.

Van Wormer, K. (2004). *Confronting oppression, restoring justice from policy analysis to social action.* Alexandria, VA: Council on Social Work Education.

Van Wormer, K. (2009). Restorative justice: What social workers need to know. In T. Maschi, C. Bradley, K. Ward, T. Maschi, C. Bradley, & K. Ward (Eds.), *Forensic social work: Psychosocial and legal issues in diverse practice settings* (pp. 299–310). New York, NY: Springer Publishing Co.

Zehr, H. (2002). *The little book of restorative justice.* Intercourse, PA: Good Books.

Chapter 13

Overcoming Prejudice and Promoting Diversity

Correctional counselors need to understand the issue of prejudice, a counseling issue that appears frequently for correctional clients. Some clients are prejudiced or are prejudice-motivated offenders (Sun, 2006), whereas some are victims of prejudice or discrimination (Banks, 2004). Because the experience of prejudice has impaired the normal functioning of a large number of correctional clients, addressing the issue is part of correctional counseling. In addition, counselors may encounter the issue when interacting with other criminal justice personnel and people in the community.

The Meaning of Prejudice

Although the term *prejudice* may be associated with negative feelings and behavioral tendencies, the essence of prejudice involves distorted cognitions (Bodenhausen, Macrae, & Hugenberg, 2003; Fiske & Taylor, 1991; Myers, 2002).

In general, **social cognition** includes knowledge structures (schemas) about the self, others, and the world. It also includes related cognitive processes (e.g., encoding, recalling, reasoning, perceiving, and decision making) concerning social entities. In particular, prejudice as a type of cognitive schema is based on a distortion of social reality. The indicators include: (1) erroneous generalization and oversimplification (e.g., assuming that a person's behavior represents his or her racial group or social category); (2) the formation of social attitudes before or despite objective evidence (e.g., prejudgment and denial of objective evidence); (3) a lack of appreciation of situational constraints on the actions of people who may be members of a group (e.g., using group membership to explain behavior with no attention to the impact of environment and learning experience on behavior) (Schaller & O'Brien, 1992); and (4) other inaccuracies in categorizing, evaluating, and explaining social entities. The distorted cognitions about social reality in turn rationalize clients' attitudes and behavior that deviate from a normative standard or moral value, such as the principle of fairness, equity, or equality (Sun, 1993a).

In short, prejudice involves viewing invalid cognitions, such as faulty categories or distorted schemas about the self and others, as the universal truth representing the social entities; and employing the distorted cognitions to evaluate, explain, and adjust one's own and others' psychological activities. From the social cognitive perspective, although *motivation* and *cognition* represent two separate psychological activities, they are also intimately related. All motivation (including the motivation behind prejudice-motivated crime) operates on the perceiver's level of awareness of human reality (Sun, 2006).

In order to overcome prejudice and help the victims, counselors working in the criminal justice system need to recognize three types of cognitive errors: (1) stereotypes; (2) blaming the victims of prejudice; and (3) using offenders' group membership to explain their bias and related offenses.

Stereotypes and Their Psychological Causes

According to Hilton and von Hippel (1996), *stereotypes* are defined as beliefs about groups and their members. In this definition, stereotypes operate much like schemas of objects or events, allowing easier and more efficient processing of information about others. However, these stereotypes are selective, focusing on group features that are the most distinctive and that provide the greatest differentiation between groups. These perceptions show the least within-group variation. Stereotypes that are based on relatively enduring characteristics of some social categories (such as race, religion, and gender) have enormous potential for error.

One stereotype involves representation of a group and its members according to a **prototype**—an "averaged" and abstract representation of a category with many attributes, but with no set of defining group attributes. For example, when people think about the prototype for social activists, they may assume that the person is an antiwar protester, a Democrat, and an environmentalist. Other stereotypes may include such assumptions as "all athletes are more brawn than brain" or "all women like to shop." When criminal justice personnel evoke a concept of an offender of domestic violence, they also have certain assumptions about the attributes of the person; some are accurate, some are not. Abstracted representations of a group's typical features, used by perceivers to judge individuals, lead to erroneous evaluations and actions, as demonstrated by numerous illegal racial profiling instances (U.S. Commission on Civil Rights, 2000).

Another stereotype is based on **exemplars**, a model in which perceivers mentally represent groups and their members through particular, concrete examples. The stereotype of African Americans as athletic, for example, is thought to be stored in the form of specific individuals (e.g., star athletes). Upon encountering an individual who can be categorized as a member of a group, perceivers may call to mind exemplars in the category they immediately think of (Fiske & Taylor, 1991; Hilton & von Hippel, 1996).

Two psychological causes of stereotypes involve the cognitive process of categorization and the inability to differentiate between the deductive and inductive processes (to be explained subsequently).

According to the **social categorization** perspective (Gaertner et al., 2000; American Psychological Association [APA], 2003), when people are categorized into groups—**in-groups** and **out-groups**—members of the same group seem to be more similar than they actually are but differences between members of different groups tend to be exaggerated and overgeneralized. For most therapists and psychologists, individuals in racial or ethnic minority groups are in out-groups. People who consciously hold egalitarian beliefs have, in fact, shown unconscious endorsement of negative attitudes and stereotypes about the groups. Research has demonstrated that mere social categorization influences differential thinking, feeling, and behaving toward in-group and out-group members. This social categorization may influence attitudes and prejudice thoughts, which are often automatic, toward individuals who are seen as out-group members. It includes a tendency to exaggerate differences between groups and similarities within one group and favors the in-group over the out-group. Those with the strongest in-group affiliation show the most prejudice. This inclination will create more harm when one group holds much more power than another group or when resources among in-groups are not distributed equitably. According to Fiske (1993), stereotypes lead to hate, exclude and even kill the victims. Stereotypes exert control through prejudice and discrimination. Victims of stereotyping know this and attempt to resist stereotypes for those reasons. They do not want to be stereotyped because it limits their freedom and confines their outcomes, even their lives.

According to Fiske (1993), lack of attention to others contributes to the formation and maintenance of stereotypes. One of the main reasons that people do not pay attention to others can be found in the disparities that occur in social interactions that are based on **power**, a characteristic of individuals who have more control over the outcome of interacting than the other party. Power and stereotyping are mutually reinforcing and mediated by **attention**.

The powerless know more about (and pay more attention to) the powerful in their environment, than vice versa. This is because the powerless need to form more complex, potentially accurate impressions about the powerful in order to enhance prediction and control. In contrast, the powerful pay less attention to the powerless and are more likely to stereotype them because less is at stake, and they do not need to attend to those who have little influence on their lives. Stereotyping and power are mutually reinforcing because stereotyping itself exerts control, maintaining and justifying the status quo (Fiske, 1993). If we apply the principle to correctional settings, we can expect to find that the "powerless" (e.g., inmates) know more about (and pay more attention to) the "powerful" (e.g., correctional officers) in their environment than vice versa.

Another cognitive factor that contributes to perceivers' stereotypes involves the misunderstanding of two separate cognitive processes: (1) the deductive process, and (2) the inductive process. The **deductive process** involves reasoning from a general concept to a particular observation, or applying a category to explain and make sense of observations.

For example, the use of a person's group membership (e.g., race or ethnicity) to explain his or her social actions represent an example of deductive reasoning. In contrast, the **inductive process** involves reasoning from observation to concepts or theories. The source of knowledge comes from observation or the inductive process. However, when people assume that the deductive process (the use of categories or groups) represents the understanding of social reality, with no discernment of the discrepancy between their mental category and reality (e.g., target individuals and their actions), they will have stereotypic mental representations of the individuals (Sun, 2002). The accurate understanding of the two processes involves the discernment that all the concepts or categories we use to describe the world are not features of reality, as we tend to believe, but are creations of the mind; they are parts of the map, not of the territory (Capra, 1999).

Misattributing the Cause of Prejudice to the Victims

Another type of cognitive error focuses the explanation of prejudice on the victims rather than on the offender, using the victims' group memberships or distinctiveness (e.g., race, ethnicity, sexual orientation, or religious beliefs) to explain prejudice. In other words, this type of cognitive distortion involves the assumption that individuals become the victims of prejudice or hate crime because of their group memberships.

This error may result from misunderstanding the legal definition of hate crime. The law defines a *hate crime* as an offense in which the victim is targeted because of his or her actual or perceived race, color, religion, disability, sexual orientation, or national origin (Sullaway, 2004). This definition is based on federal legislation that defines a hate crime as an offense "that manifests evidence of prejudice based on race, religion, disability, sexual orientation, or ethnicity" (Hate Crime Statistics Act, 1990), or more recently, as a crime in which "the defendant intentionally selects a victim . . . because of the actual or perceived race, color, religion, national origin, ethnicity, gender, disability or sexual orientation of any person" (Violent Crime Control and Law Enforcement Act, 1994).

On the basis of the legal definition, most researchers of prejudice and hate crime conceptualize them as motivated by the distinctiveness of the victims, because offenders target only victims with different group memberships. In reality, however, the legal definition specifies the mental state of the offender, including: (1) the required criminal intent and (2) the offender's cognitive distortions, rather than suggesting that the victim's group membership is the cause for prejudice or hate crime.

The legal definition of hate crime is a criminal law definition stating that the defendant is guilty of a crime only when the offender's criminal commission or omission occurred with a simultaneous ***mens rea*** or criminal intent (Scheb & Scheb, 1999).

Hate crimes, like other types of criminal offense, require a specific criminal intent, or the presence of *mens rea* as one of the key elements for establishing the perpetrator's criminal responsibility. The "because" statement in the legal definition of hate crime, regarding the distinctiveness of the victim(s), denotes the offender's *mens rea* and perceptions of difference in group membership.

The criminal intent for hate crime is not a causal description for the offense (nor is it supposed to be), just as the *mens rea* for sex offenders who intentionally and knowingly target certain types of victims (e.g., children or women) does not indicate that the victim is the cause of the crime. In other words, legislation-based definitions are not scientific explanations about the cause-and-effect relationship between two variables.

Furthermore, prejudiced offenders may believe that their offenses or hate are caused by the victims, but their perceptions cannot be used to suggest that the victims' groups cause hate crime. Offenders' reasoning about their offenses tends to misrepresent the reality by blaming their victims, or other factors, rather than seeing themselves as responsible. Research in social cognition has shown that self-serving bias tends to characterize offenders' explanations for their actions (Bodenhausen, Macrae, & Hugenberg, 2003; Fiske & Taylor, 1991). This bias includes rationalizing or justifying their actions, making them desirable and reasonable from the agent's viewpoint (Davidson, 1990).

Misattributing Offenders' Prejudices to Their Group Membership

A common misperception attributes the cause of prejudice and bias-motivated crimes to the offenders' group memberships (e.g., race, ethnicity, or religion), assuming that this group membership is responsible for related prejudice and offenses. This type of attribution is based on the overgeneralization and oversimplification of psychological activities. In fact, most prejudiced acts and related offenses are instigated by the individual's cognitive distortions and are not caused by group membership.

The majority of biased offenses do not satisfy the criteria of group actions. In order for an action to be called a group action, it must satisfy certain sociological and social psychological criteria (Sun, 1993b). In other words, a hate offense can be defined as an instance of intergroup conflict only when it results from the dynamics of the group—a collection of individuals who interact or communicate with one another according to their role or status specified by some implicit or unwritten rules or norms. Their performance is characterized by a high level of cohesion and normative consensus and by shared emotional involvement in evaluation and perception of the meaning and mission of the action.

Although the difference in group membership between the prejudice-motivated offender and the victim is often a necessary condition for instigating hate crime, recognizing the difference is insufficient to understand and overcome ambiguities in identifying the transgression (Nolan, McDevitt, Cronin, & Farrell, 2004). Neither is there evidence suggesting that other people sharing the same group membership with the hate offenders endorse hate crime. For example, far less than 1% of the members of a particular group (e.g., racial or religious) were involved in hate crimes (National Criminal Justice Reference Service, 2011). Because both hate-crime offenders and law-abiding people share the same group memberships, the commonality between criminals and noncriminals is an invalid explanation for an offender's behavior. In addition, using group differences between the hate offender and the victim to explain hate crimes (e.g., ethnic conflict) only focuses on how the victims are distinctive from the offenders. This approach ignores individual and situational characteristics that separate the offender from the members of the group.

In summary, the weakness of using different group memberships to explain hate crimes involves a false suggestion that it is the distinctiveness of the crime victims or their different group membership, rather than the offender's individual and situational characteristics, that is responsible for the hate offenses. This belief takes the responsibility away from the individual offender. In addition, this type of explanation implies that the hatred is innate and permanent, because a group membership (e.g., race, religion, or sexual orientation) involved in hate crime generally represents a stable and ascribed status.

How to Reduce Prejudice and Counsel Victims

Because prejudice manifests as cognitive distortions, counselors who want to reduce individuals' prejudice need to engage in a practice that invalidates distorted cognitions while developing a more accurate understanding of social reality.

Cognitive Distortion and Moral Judgment

Prejudice as a type of cognitive distortion is often conceptualized as a type of immorality or social attitude that deviates from a normative standard or moral value, such as the principle of fairness, equity, equality, or need (what ought to be) shared by society (Sun, 1993a). However, we cannot assume offenders' cognitive distortions can be rectified simply by improving moral judgment or education. Offenders' unjustified attitudes are based on their distorted perception of social reality, so their cognitive distortion rationalizes and justifies their immoral or illegal offenses.

To understand how cognitive distortions cause the prejudice-based acts of some personnel in the criminal justice system, we must understand the distinctions between two types of ethics: (1) external ethical standards for criminal justice personnel; and (2) internal ethical standards (Sun, 2004).

External ethical standards are defined by various codes of ethics in criminal justice agencies. However, *internal ethical standards* and values about right and wrong and ethical decisions in criminal justice are based on individual interpretation of the external ethics based on each person's understanding of social reality.

The impact of all external ethical criteria concerning the fairness and justice of actions are mediated by internal ethics and perceptions of social reality. It is the internal judgments and perceptions of individuals rather than the external ones that support and control their moral thinking, evaluation, and actions. They use their internal ethics to evaluate, explain, encode, accept or deny, adjust, or maintain their attributes and actions, and to react to various situations (Sun, 2004).

Cognitive distortions of interpersonal reality initiate and sustain the mental justification for discrimination and prejudice. This principle can be described as the perception of "what is" determining the perception of "what ought to be." In other words, people view their unethical conduct (e.g., discrimination and racial profiling) as ethical because their limited and distorted cognitions of social reality serve as the basis for their moral judgments and actions.

There are two sources of cognitive distortion: (1) stereotypes produced by social categorization (see previous discussion in this chapter); and (2) the prevalence of distorted information about minorities in this country provided by the media, books, and other sources. Several studies have investigated the second issue, particularly the link between **media** and **prejudice**.

Using data derived primarily from newspaper archives, modern films and documentaries that focus on hate, research monographs of various hate-watch organizations, and secondary documents, Judson and Bertazzoni (2002) showed that the rhetoric of hate in mainstream dialog and the discourse of our political parties, the Internet, the media, and popular movies, has reinforced hate crime, stereotyping, and the atmosphere of intolerance. As cited in this research, only 15% of U.S. drug users are African American, but 50% of network news stories on drugs focus on African Americans. Asians, Asian Americans, and Latino characters are often the victims of racial humor and stereotypes. American films have a long legacy of stereotyping the "other," which is often the basis for hatred.

By examining newsmagazines and network television news shows, Gilens (1996) found that news media distortions coincide with public misperceptions about race and poverty. Both are biased in ways that reflect negatively on the poor in general and on poor African Americans in particular. On the one hand, the media are subject to many of the same biases and misperceptions that afflict American society at large and therefore reproduce those biases in their portrayals of American social conditions. On the other hand, Americans rely heavily on the mass media for information about the society in which they live. The media shape Americans' social perceptions and political attitudes in important ways. Media distortions of social conditions are therefore likely to result in public misperceptions that reinforce existing biases and stereotypes. Similarly, a study by Klein and Naccarato (2003) shows that Blacks and Latinos are portrayed more frequently as criminals in local television news than European Americans, and minority misrepresentation has been shown to be out of proportion to crime statistics. European Americans are also overrepresented as homicide victims compared to crime statistics, whereas blacks and Latinos are underrepresented as victims. The worst part is that most viewers believe that the real world is similar to the television world.

Dixon and Linz (2002) measured the extent of pretrial publicity on Los Angeles television news and examined the relationship of the race of the accused compared with the amount of prejudicial information in the newscast. They found that blacks and Latinos were twice as likely as whites to be associated with prejudicial statements on local television news. Latinos who victimized whites were almost three times as likely as white defendants to be associated with prejudicial information. The pretrial publicity information can be summarized in the following nine statements that led to biased opinions about the target case:

1. Prior convictions of the defendant (could be explicitly stated or implied by reported prison term served)

2. Prior arrests of the defendant

3. Negative statements about the defendant's character or reputation (e.g., the person seemed deranged, chronic troublemaker)

4. Defendant's confession or admission (a direct quotation by the defendant or a report that the defendant had confessed)

5. Defendant's refusal to make a statement

6. Defendant's performance on any examination or test (e.g., lie detector, breathalyzer)

7. Defendant's refusal to submit to an examination or test

8. The possibility of a plea of guilty to the offense charged or a lesser charge (any discussion of potential plea bargains)

9. Opinions of guilt or of a strong case against the defendant (not defendant admission)

Using Superordinate Goals to Reduce Group Boundaries

Counselors can use superordinate goals to lessen offenders' perceived group boundaries produced by social categorization. This method was based on a study by Sherif (1966). His experiment showed that when 22 boys attending summer camp were randomly assigned to two groups and were made aware of the other group's existence, they began to engage in a series of competitive activities that generated overt intergroup conflict and hostility. According to Gaertner et al. (2000), it is the participants' mental categorizations of the in-group and the out-group, independent of (and before) the competition that instigated intergroup biases. Later in the experiment, the researchers introduced a series of super-ordinate goals (goals to be achieved only by the full cooperation of both groups, such as locating a problem with the camp water supply, moving a truck that "broke down" on a camping trip) that transformed the intergroup conflict into a harmonious relation between them, because the goals functioned to develop new awareness of the self and others through three alternating psychological strategies: (1) **de-categorization** (creating the perception that everyone is an individual), (2) **re-categorization** (structuring an inclusive, higher level of category so that all share a superordinate and cross-cutting group membership), and (3) **mutual intergroup differentiation** (dividing the labor in a complementary way so that the members of each group recognize and appreciate the indispensable contribution of the others).

Intergroup Contact for Reducing Prejudice

Another important strategy that has proven effective for reducing prejudice involves the optimal intergroup contact (Allport, 1954; Pettigrew & Tropp, 2008). Allport (1954) presented the first contact hypothesis, claiming that true acquaintance lessens prejudice.

According to Allport, **optimal intergroup contact** contains four essential elements, including equal status, cooperation towards a superordinate goal, institutional support, and contact-produced desirable results for members of the separate groups. A meta-analysis of about 500 studies by Pettigrew & Tropp (2008) shows that intergroup contact diminishes prejudice through three main mediators: (1) enhancing knowledge about the out-group, (2) reducing anxiety about intergroup contact, and (3) increasing empathy and perspective taking.

However, the original contact hypothesis suggests that the face-to-face contact is the only form of optimal contact. This principle has not taken into consideration various types of contact between individuals and groups in today's world (e.g., contact and communication through information technologies and other media, such as the Internet, books, newspapers, TV news, cell phones). Sun's study (2011) indicates that some indirect contact contains the basic components of the direct or face-to-face contact that can also reduce prejudice. The most important element involves reciprocal or bilateral influences by the interacting partners who psychologically validate and invalidate each other's communication. People who communicate with one another through indirect channels and bilateral validating and invalidating processes have actually engaged in authentic contact, which may be termed **information contact**. It needs to be separated from information exposure, which involves a unilateral exposure to information about a country or group, with a varying degree of frequency, quantity, and (in)accuracy. Although information exposure may help people learn something about others, it does not have the basic ingredient of learning how and why the self's communication to others is evaluated and interpreted in their mind in the interaction.

Separating Prejudiced Offenders from Others in the Same Group

Counselors help the victims of prejudice or discrimination to see how social learning environments, economic conditions, and other social variables influence biased offenders' cognitions and motivation, rather than focusing on differences between group memberships. This process occurs through developing, validating, and sustaining the offenders' distorted cognitions of themselves and others, and of interpersonal and/or intergroup realities. In other words, counseling processes that help individuals to understand their experience of prejudice and to heal, need to examine the characteristics of biased offenders that separate them from others who share the same group membership. These characteristics may include such psychological variables as the offenders' childhood traumas and harsh treatment, rigid thinking, categorization, deindividuation, dehumanization, and sense of self-vulnerability (e.g., Berkowitz, 2005; Staub, 2005).

Reattribution of the Victimization Experience

Mental health professionals increase the effect of counseling for victims of prejudice by helping them understand the cognitive distortions of perpetrators. In addition to psychological distress, fear, anger, and feeling insecure and unworthy, and the perception that the world is disorderly (Willis, 2004), one of the main mental symptoms of hate-crime survivors is self-blame (Herek, Gillis, & Cogan, 1999). The study by Herek et al. showed that the victims demonstrated significantly more symptoms of depression, anger, anxiety, and posttraumatic stress, and more attributions of their victimization experiences to themselves than the nonbias crime victims. Weiss (2005) suggested that therapists working with victims of hate crimes should take into consideration such factors as intergroup relations, fear, anger, racial/ethnic group histories, current concerns and family contexts of the victims, legal issues, and mediation between the victim and the offender. However, these clinical approaches, which are apparently based on the assumption that hate crime manifests intergroup conflict, have difficulty addressing the issue of self-blame and the victims' misperception that their group membership is the source of their own victimization.

Clinical interventions need to include teaching the survivors of prejudice-motivated crime to attribute their victimization to the cognitive distortions of the offenders rather than to the distinctiveness of the victims. Research in social cognition has produced evidence that the attribution method can alter negative self-concepts and self-blame. For example, attribution retraining has shown some effectiveness. It involves techniques of teaching child victims of sexual abuse to attribute responsibility for the abuse to the perpetrators rather than to themselves (Celano, Hazzard, Campbell, & Long, 2002).

Finally, research in social psychology has provided other approaches to reduce prejudice. Interpersonal outcome dependency can motivate people to form more individuated or accurate impressions rather than category-based ones (see Fiske, 1987). When people fear that their judgment may be invalid, they are more inclined to form accurate perceptions and less likely to base their judgments on preexisting cognitive structures (Kruglanski, 1988). Their prejudice will be reduced when they have more accurate mental representations of a target person that categorize the individual as having multiple group memberships (e.g., male, black, over 30 years of age, college graduate, salesman) rather than being a member of a single group (Hamilton, 1981). Intergroup prejudice can be minimized by the cognition that there is an exchange relationship between groups (Homans, 1974). In brief, counselors help correctional clients and others to gain new and more accurate knowledge structures, cognitive capacity (see Schaller & O'Brien, 1992), or motivation (Fiske, 1987; Kruglanski, 1988). With these tools they are able to categorize, evaluate, and explain social stimuli according to the standards of social reality.

Understanding Diversity

Worldwide social changes are currently prompting researchers (psychologists, demographers, sociologists, anthropologists, and other social scientists) to rethink issues of culture and cultural diversity both within and across national boundaries. Global connectivity is shrinking cultural uniqueness and has led to increased awareness of differences and similarities in cultures that used to be insular. Scholars need to search for new models of culture because the traditional definition of culture appears to be insufficient to incorporate the new developments (Cooper & Denner, 1998; Bandura, 2006).

The following changes, in particular, are stimulating people to rethink culture:

1. Trans-national economic interdependencies and global market forces are not only restructuring national economies but also shaping the political and social life of societies.

2. Advanced telecommunications technologies (e.g., the cyber world, communication satellites) that transcend time zones, distance, place, and national borders are disseminating ideas, values, and styles of behavior internationally at an unprecedented rate. This technology is altering national cultures, producing intercultural commonalities and fostering a more extensive globalization of culture through the growing role of electronic acculturation.

3. Mass migrations of people and the global mobility of employees of multinational corporations, entertainers, athletes, journalists, and academics are changing cultural panoramas. The intermixing and growing ethnic diversity within societies create the need for individuals to live with various cultural forms by blending elements from several cultures (Bandura, 2006).

4. The changes in U.S. racial diversity can be shown by demographic statistics. In 2000, about 67% of the population identified as white, either alone or with another race. Of the remaining 33%, approximately 13% indicated they were African American, 1.5% American Indian or Alaskan Native, 4.5% Asian/Pacific Islander, 13% Hispanic, and about 7% some other race (APA, 2003).

Understanding multiculturalism or diversity in correctional settings is one of the most important areas of correctional counseling. Indeed, correctional counselors and other mental health professionals need to use multicultural perspectives to evaluate, explain, and interact with offenders and correctional staff from diverse backgrounds. Counselors need to learn and implement psychological and counseling knowledge from multicultural sources.

The following sections will examine the issue of diversity and related assessment and interventions.

Definition of Culture

Culture is defined as a collection of belief systems, value orientation, knowledge, history, customs, norms, practices, social and economic institutions, and language shared by individuals in some definable population that are distinct from those shared in other populations. These social and economic establishments, beliefs, cognitions, and behaviors provide resources for realizing individual and collective goals. Moreover, each culture has the means to transmit beliefs, knowledge, and behaviors to new members of the cultural population, so that the culture may continue over very long periods of time (APA, 2003; Lehman, Chiu, & Schaller, 2004).

Inherent in this definition is the acknowledgment that culture is *learned*. Individuals become cultural beings only through learned and transmitted beliefs, values, historical, economic, ecological, political forces and practices, including religious and spiritual traditions (APA, 2003; Sun, 2002). From a psychological perspective, cultures exist in the form of mental structures (schemas) used to perceive, process, store, and retrieve information, and to make inferences about such structures (DiMaggio, 1997). Other psychological perspectives explain cultural variations in behavior as a function of psychological processes, particularly perceptions of opportunity and efficacy (Cooper & Denner, 1998).

Race and Ethnicity

Diversity and multiculturalism are often seen as interchangeable with race and ethnicity, although the notions have distinct meanings. According to the American Psychological Association (2003), the biological basis of race has at times been the source of heated debate in psychology. Research has shown that *race* has no consensual definition and that, in fact, biological racial categories and phenotypic characteristics have more within-group than between-group variation (i.e., the biological variation within a race is greater than the variation between two races). The APA (2003) considers race to be socially constructed rather than biologically determined. This position is supported by recent advances in human genome research. The studies have shown that all human beings, who share 99.9% of the same genetic information, originated in Africa some 150,000 to 200,000 years ago, although people differ superficially in their physical appearances as the result of adaptation to extremely varied terrains, habitats, climates, and other challenges. People migrated from Africa to what is now the Middle East, Europe, and Asia between roughly 30,000 and 50,000 years ago, and there have been constant gene flows among people throughout human history (Jackson, 2011).

APA (2003) defines *ethnicity* as the acceptance of the group mores and practices of the culture of origin and the associated sense of belonging. In addition, individuals may have multiple ethnic identities that are more or less relevant at different times. Sun (1995a) argued that examining race and ethnicity should not only go beyond genetically based differences but also pay attention to the complex relations among the terms *race, ethnicity*, and *culture* when they are used in social-psychological research and social contexts. For example, anyone attempting to define *race* scientifically is obliged to examine how the meaning of race in the social world is distinct from and related to the biological world. This is necessary because the concept of race is used in both domains. The obsession with racial problems remains a critical social issue, and is eliciting the attention of more psychologists than the debate about genetically based differences (see Katz & Taylor, 1988).

On the one hand, a racial category in the social world refers to people who possess not only similar biological characteristics but also identical social experience, such as being the victims of collective discrimination or prejudice (McKee, 1993). The social meaning of race has been investigated in many ways: (1) social-psychological studies of the effects of social categorization (including the phenotype-based racial classification); (2) studies on cognitive distortions, such as misconstruing information about the self and others in the deduction process (e.g., out-group homogeneity bias); (3) studies on in-group favoritism and stereotypes (see Fiske & Taylor, 1991); and (4) through the induction process (e.g., linking an individual's action to the whole racial category of the person, even though the majority of the people in the group are not cognitively, emotionally, and evaluatively involved in the action; see Tajfel, 1978).

In addition, designating any variable (including race) in research requires specifying not only the *conceptual* definition but also the *operational* one, which consists of defining the observable and measurable aspects of the variable. Ethnic groups in the United States are generally considered the same categories of people as the "races," with the exception that they are euphemized as epitomizing black, white, Hispanic, and Asian cultures. The fact that people have not minimized their "racial awareness" after their transition from racial to ethnic categories (see McKee, 1993) may be partially due to the lack of a different operational definition for "ethnicity."

On the other hand, memberships in the social categories of race are defined, not according to individuals' alterable or learned attributes—such as their cognitions, actions, or achievements—but according to their inherited and unchangeable biological characteristics. When racial categories are used to explain intergroup behavior or perceptions (e.g., racial conflicts, prejudice), the social meanings of the racial categorization refer only to whatever social experiences or perceptions are dependent on or strongly correlated with the phenotypes designated by the folk taxonomy of "race." They do not imply various social influences that are independent of the individuals' genetic characteristics and that may have fomented intergroup actions and perceptions. These may include historical factors, such as the period of European exploration, the rise of capitalism and English ethnocentrism, and the misuse of sciences (Smedley, 1993).

Multiple Meanings of Cultural Diversity

The term *diversity* has both a narrow and a broad definition: (1) the narrow definition refers to racial diversity or territorial (regional) cultural differences; (2) the broad definition covers cultural differences stemming from race, ethnicity, language, sexual orientation, gender, age, disability, class status, education, religious and spiritual orientation, and other cultural dimensions (APA, 2003; Mannix & Neale, 2005; Markus & Lin, 1999). Understanding the perceived differences between the dimensions is necessary because they shape the perceiver's worldview by organizing social information, placing people in categories, and explaining the behavior of others. This normal process leads to associating various traits and behaviors with particular groups, even though the perceptions are often stereotypical and inaccurate (APA, 2003).

The Narrow Definition of Cultural Diversity

Most current research on cross-cultural psychology focuses on the differences between two types of cultures: (1) collectivist, and (2) individualistic (Oyserman, Coon, & Kemmelmeier, 2002).

The core element of **collectivist culture** is the assumption that groups bind and mutu-ally obligate individuals through communal societies characterized by diffuse and mutual obligations and expectations. In these societies, the commonalities—common fate, com-mon goals, and common values—are shared by all people. However, collectivism is also a diverse construct, referring to a broader range of values, attitudes, and behaviors than individualism.

The impact of collectivism-based cognitions on psychology processes, such as self-concept, well-being, and attribution style, has been observed (Oyserman, Coon, & Kemmelmeier, 2002; Smith, Spillane, & Annus, 2006). The following characteristics per-tain to collectivism:

1. With regard to the self, collectivism implies that group membership is a central aspect of identity. Valued personal traits involve sacrifice for the common good and maintaining harmonious relationships with close others.

2. With regard to well-being and emotional expression, collectivism implies that life satisfaction derives from successfully carrying out social roles and obligations and avoiding failure in these domains. As a result, people exercise restraint in emotional expression, avoiding open and direct expression of personal feelings.

3. In contrast to the Western preference for an analytic and linear way of thinking and locating the responsibility for behavior primarily in the individual, people of East Asia emphasize a holistic understanding of phenomena and the whole context of behavior. Therefore, East Asians are more likely to see an individual's actions as caused by situations rather than determined by the individual's disposition, compared with people in an individualistic society. This tendency may be called *situationism* or *contextualism*. Whereas Westerners focus on the individual, Easterners focus on the social situation.

Psychological research on comparing cultural differences among the four main cultural groups in the United States (European Americans, African Americans, Asian Americans, and Mexican Americans) is limited. A notable study by Markus and Lin (1999), however, revealed that people in the four cultural groups appear to view causes, meanings and prac-tices of conflict very differently. The differences between the European Americans and Asian Americans are related to their different conceptions of self and other.

In European American cultural contexts, individuals are seen as being independent, concerned about achieving success, and in control of personal goals through choices and opportunities. They are expected to express their own beliefs and pursue their own goals. Conflict occurs because the activities of two persons interfere with one another. People in the Western cultural context tend to confront others directly while propagating the position and actions taken or not taken with the intention of ending the conflict quickly (Markus & Lin, 1999).

In contrast, individuals with cultural origins in East Asia are seen as being interdepen-dent with others. They prefer orientation toward harmony with others and conformity with social norms, and they are more likely to subordinate their personal goals and objectives to the standard of the collective to which they belong. The Asian concept of relationships (e.g., families, communities, and nations) and philosophical traditions (e.g., Buddhism, Confucian perspective) influence the meanings attached to conflict. Resolution is intended to reduce animosity and save face through mediation and bargaining while avoiding direct confrontation (Markus & Lin, 1999).

In Mexican American cultural contexts, conflict is defined as a loss of harmony between individuals. The goal to handle conflict involves the mutual coordination of feelings rather than a resolution of the issue. Respecting elders and accepting their opinions serve as a way to handle conflict.

In African American cultural contexts, the meaning of conflict is simultaneously individual and relational, rather than just relational. People tend to confront others about points of disagreement in an attempt to settle the problem that initially caused the disagreement. The method of resolution involves a compelling presentation of arguments (Markus & Lin, 1999).

Some attempts have been made to create a general guideline for counseling with the main cultural groups, including African Americans, Hispanics, Native Americans, Asian Americans, and multiracial individuals, but almost all these groups are very heterogeneous (Nugent & Jones, 2005). Guidelines are therefore problematic.

Criticisms of the Narrow Definition of Diversity

Bandura (2006) argues that the previously examined diversity may be called *territorial culturalism*. For example, residents of an East Asian country are categorized as collectivists and those in the United States are conceptualized as individualists. This approach appears to see culture as fixed rather than dynamic and containing internally diverse systems. This view overlooks the substantial diversity among societies placed in the same category. For instance, collectivistic systems based on Confucianism, Buddhism, and Marxism may share a communal idea, but they define and practice collectivism and its related values and customs very differently.

Neither are the alleged **individualistic cultures** identical. Americans, Italians, Germans, French, British and other Western European cultures all have different interpretations of their brand of individualism. Diversity across regions within the same country can also be found. In the United States, for example, residents in the Northeast, the Midwest, the Western regions, and the Deep South do not share the same version and practice of individualism. Given this diversity, the bicultural contrasts and comparisons tend to produce misleading generalizations.

Smith et al. (2006) contended that research in cross-cultural psychology has demonstrated that human behavior represents a complex interplay among three processes: (1) universal mechanisms (e.g., social, psychological and physical mechanisms shared by all people); (2) culturally specific variables; and (3) individual differences. Ignoring one of them will generate faulty conclusions. Smith et al. argue that although we need to understand cultural *differences*, in fact we need to pay more attention to cultural *commonalities* in psychological processes. The apparently different cultural characteristics of Western and Eastern cultures actually serve similar social purposes. There are at least four cross-cultural, **universal psychological processes**:

1. There is a universal need to be a "good self." Although Western (individualistic) cultures may emphasize individuals' personal achievements and Eastern (collectivistic) cultures may focus on understanding their interdependence with others, in each case, the successful, valued person has secured status and opportunities for survival and development within the cultural context. A lack of social skill undermines the ability to belong and to be a "good self" across cultures. Differences in social ability are associated with variations in well-being regardless of where the person lives.

2. Individuals from both individualistic and collectivistic cultures (e.g., South Korea, Russia, Turkey, China, and the United States) endorse *autonomy*, which means willingly choosing behaviors and endorsing actions and values. The only difference is that people in individualistic cultural contexts tend to show more autonomy for individualistic behaviors than for collectivistic behaviors, and persons from collectivistic cultures are inclined to practice more autonomy for collectivistic behaviors than for individualistic behaviors.

3. Another universal need is the desire to belong and to have good *relationships*. Lack of belonging appears to have a negative effect on health and to undermine subjective well-being and adjustment; when people are in good relationships, their subjective well-being increases.

4. People from all cultures manifest the universal need for *cognitive competence*—the need to understand and make sense of the world. Humans everywhere seek to develop an accurate understanding of their social context (i.e., group norms and group symbols, the ways information is transmitted socially, and other social systems). Cultures vary only in how this need is met. Independent cultures emphasize individual control, whereas interdependent cultures prefer group control. This need is universal because greater competence appears to be associated with greater well-being in all cultures, even though the challenges to be faced are distinct in different circumstances.

In short, psychological universals exist because humans everywhere face common physical and social challenges. In fact, the ability to operate in physical and social milieus depends on the capacity to engage in swift learning that is both cultural and universal.

In addition, the narrow view of diversity implies that individuals' thinking and actions are shaped only from within their own cultural perspective, but this overlooks the fact that cross-cultural information and knowledge exchange, contacts, and influences, though moderate in the past, have transformed all cultures, including the field of psychology. For example, Taoist psychology, which is derived from Chinese philosophy, has influenced Western psychotherapy (Ehrlich, 1986), social psychology (Sun, 1995b), Jungian psychology (Coward, 1996; Rosen, 1996), transpersonal psychology (Gross & Shapiro, 1997), and humanistic psychology (Chang & Page, 1991; Jenni, 1999; Lee, 2003; Rahilly, 1993; Rosen & Crouse, 2000).

A Broad Definition of Diversity

Mannix and Neale's (2005) examination of the workplace shows increasing diversity. However, there has been tension between the promise and the reality of diversity in team process and performance. The sanguine view holds that diversity will produce an increase in the variety of perspectives and approaches to deal with problems by creating opportunities for knowledge sharing. The result should be greater creativity and higher quality of team performance. However, a more pessimistic view sees diversity creating social divisions, which in turn creates negative performance outcomes for the group. Mannix and Neale (2005) suggest that the problem may result from the definition of diversity. Clarifying the mixed effects of diversity in work groups will only occur by broadening the views of all to include other types of diversity such as knowledge, skills, experiences, emotions, and networks, and by focusing more carefully on mediating mechanisms such as context.

The word *diversity* originally referred to many types of difference among people across various dimensions. Physical appearance may be used to define race or gender. The size of the group indicates whether it is a minority or majority. These categorization methods are expedient, but they tend to focus on only one type of diversity and thereby overestimate its relevance. Mannix and Neale (2005) recommended using a broad definition of diversity that includes the following:

1. **Social-category differences:** race, ethnicity, gender, age, religion, sexual orientation, and physical abilities

2. **Differences in knowledge and skills:** differences in education, functional knowledge, information or expertise, training, experience, and ability

3. **Differences in values or beliefs:** cultural background, or ideological beliefs

4. **Personality differences:** cognitive style (e.g., enmeshed in thinking or acting on intuition), affective disposition (e.g., ranging from highly emotional to unemotional), motivational factors (intrinsically versus extrinsically motivated)

5. **Status differences:** organizational or community status differences, length of service, and/or title

6. **Differences based on personal connection:** work-related connections and friendship ties

Although the broad definition of diversity is more related to organizational environments (e.g., the workplaces of prisons and community correctional offices) than to correctional counseling processes, this issue certainly influences the operation of correctional counseling and treatment. Mannix and Neale (2005) concluded that if diversity in the workplace involves integrating just the surface-level social category differences (such as those of race/ethnicity, gender, or age), it tends to have negative effects on the ability of groups to function effectively. However, when diversity involves all of these dimensions (such as differences in functional background, education, cognitive style, and/or personality) coupled with carefully administered group processes, it has a positive effect.

Embracing new types of diversity facilitates creativity or group problem solving because these diversities serve as potential mediators (social integration, communication, and conflict resolution) (Mannix & Neale, 2005).

Culturally Sensitive Assessment

The APA (2003) has defined *culturally sensitive assessment* of clients as the correct match between the therapist, the therapeutic methods, and the client. Therefore, this type of assessment in correctional settings involves evaluating the issues of the client, the therapist or counselor, and the therapeutic modes from the diversity perspective.

When evaluating clients, counselors, therapists, and psychologists need not only to perform standard assessments but also to evaluate clients' learning experiences and how they are socialized. For example, clients might have socialization experiences, physical and mental health issues, and workplace concerns associated with discrimination and oppression. Therefore, the treatment staff is encouraged to acquire an understanding of the ways in which these experiences relate to current concerns for counseling. This may include how the client's worldview and cultural background interact with individual, family, or group concerns (APA, 2003).

These culturally and sociopolitically relevant factors in a client's history may include: (1) relevant generational history; (2) level of education; (3) fluency in standard English and other languages or dialects; (4) availability of community resources; (5) current social status and the change of social status; (6) work history; and (7) level of stress related to adjustment to different environments (APA, 2003).

The treatment staff and counselors are encouraged to recognize that, as cultural beings, they also may hold attitudes and distorted beliefs that can detrimentally influence their perception of and interaction with individuals who are from culturally different backgrounds. This is because counselors and treatment personnel socialize and obtain their attitudes and knowledge in an environment that emphasizes certain racial identity or socioeconomic experiences that predispose professionals to certain biases and assumptions about themselves and others (APA, 2003). The worst mistake therapists can make when interacting with clients is to impose their own stereotypes on the client.

This faulty **cultural sensitivity** consists of two errors: (1) assuming that the client's appearance represents a stereotypic culture (e.g., a person who looks Asian does not necessarily come from an Asian country and may in fact be a fifth-generation Asian American);

or (2) being unaware that one's own knowledge about a culture is distorted or purely false, and even imposing one's ignorance on the client (Sun, 2002).

According to the APA (2003), the traditional Eurocentric therapeutic intervention models may not always be effective in working with other populations and may do harm by mislabeling or misdiagnosing problems and treatments. To deal with the issue, helping professionals need to develop new knowledge, skills, and theories that are culturally sensitive.

Culture-centered practitioners need to be aware that the use of standardized assessment instruments, diagnostic methods, and instruments may have limitations. Clients may interpret them negatively if the administering procedures are not fully explained.

Culturally Sensitive Intervention

Culturally sensitive intervention allows practitioners to develop skills and practices that are attuned to the cultural background of each client. This broadly defined cultural background includes knowledge of history, literature, arts (visual arts and music), philosophy, traditions, medicine, and other symbol-transferred information in the culture. In other words, ignorance about the cultural background of clients (not in terms of category, but in terms of cultural literacy) will hamper counselors' efforts to conduct effective interventions.

Helping practices used in non-Western cultures in and outside the North American and Northern European context may often be appropriate for interventions with clients who have a culturally based healing system. To learn more about culturally based knowledge and healing methods, helping professionals should seek opportunities to participate in diverse culture-specific activities to enrich their own repertoire.

In short, to conduct culture-centered assessments and interventions, counselors must bear in mind that culture represents a person's learning experiences. Successful culture-based evaluations and treatments are thus those assessments and interventions that match clients' learning experiences. In contrast, stereotype-based counseling involves using a social category or the appearance of clients rather than the clients' learning experiences.

Summary

Overcoming prejudice and promoting diversity are two important issues in correctional counseling. The term *prejudice* may be associated with negative feelings and behavioral tendencies, but in essence it involves distorted cognitions. Three types of cognitive errors are related to prejudice: (1) stereotypes, (2) blaming the victims of prejudice, and (3) using offenders' group membership to explain their bias and related offenses.

Culture is defined as a collection of belief systems, value orientations, knowledge, history, customs, norms, practices, social and economic institutions, and language shared by individuals in a society. Inherent in this definition is the acknowledgment that individuals become cultural beings only through learned and transmitted beliefs, values, and historical, economic, ecological, political forces and practices, as well as religious and spiritual traditions.

The term *multiculturalism* or *diversity* has a narrow definition and a broad definition. The narrow definition refers to racial diversity or territorial (regional) cultural differences, whereas the broad definition covers cultural differences stemming from race, ethnicity, language, sexual orientation, gender, age, disability, class status, education, religious/spiritual orientation, and other cultural dimensions.

Research in cross-cultural psychology has demonstrated that human behavior represents a complex interplay among three processes: (1) universal mechanisms (e.g., social, psychological, and physical mechanisms shared by all people), (2) culturally specific variables, and (3) individual differences. Ignoring any one of them will generate faulty conclusions.

Diversity-based assessments involve evaluating the issues of both the client and the therapist. When evaluating clients, therapists need not only to perform standard assessments but also to discern clients' learning experiences and how they have been socialized. In addition, correctional counselors must recognize that they may hold attitudes and distorted beliefs that can detrimentally influence their perceptions of and interactions with clients who are from culturally different backgrounds. In short, counselors must conduct culture-based assessments and interventions that match the clients' learning experiences. In addition, therapists must learn to avoid stereotype-based counseling that imposes their own ignorance on clients.

Key Terms

Collectivist culture

Culturally sensitive assessment and intervention

Culture

Decategorization

Deductive process

Diversity

Ethnicity

Faulty cultural sensitivity

Hate crime

Individualistic culture

Inductive process

In-group and out-group

Media and prejudice

Mens rea

Mutual intergroup differentiation

Optimal intergroup contact and its four elements

Power and attention

Prejudice

Prototype

Recategorization

Social categorization

Stereotypes

Universal mechanisms

Discussion Questions

1. What are the differences between culturally sensitive assessment and stereotype-based assessment?

2. Describe how distorted cognitions facilitate rationalization of prejudice and discrimination.

References

Allport, G. W. (1954). *The nature of prejudice*. Reading, MA: Addison Wesley.

American Psychological Association. (2003). Guidelines on multicultural education, training, research, practice, and organizational change for psychologists. *American Psychologist, 58*, 377–402.

Bandura, A. (2006). Toward a psychology of human agency. *Perspectives on Psychological Science, 1*, 164–180.

Banks, C. (2004). *Criminal justice ethics: Theory and practice*. Thousand Oaks, CA: Sage.

Berkowitz, L. (2005). On hate and its determinants: Some affective and cognitive influences. In R. J. Sternberg (Ed.), *The psychology of hate* (pp. 155–183). Washington, DC: American Psychological Association.

Bodenhausen, G. V., Macrae, C. N., & Hugenberg, K. (2003). Social cognition. In T. Millon & M. J. Lerner (Eds.), *Handbook of psychology* (Vol. 5, pp. 257–282). Hoboken, NJ: Wiley.

Capra, F. (1999). *The Tao of physics* (4th ed.). Boston, MA: Shambhala.

Celano, M., Hazzard, A., Campbell, S. K., & Long, C. B. (2002). Attribution retraining with sexually abused children: Review of techniques. Child Maltreatment: *Journal of the American Professional Society on the Abuse of Children, 7*, 65–76.

Chang, R., & Page, R. C. (1991). Characteristics of the self-actualized person: Visions from the East and West. *Counseling and Values, 36*, 2–10.

Cooper, C. R., & Denner, J. (1998). Theories linking culture and psychology: Universal and community-specific processes. *Annual Review of Psychology, 49*, 559–584.

Coward, H. (1996). Taoism and Jung: Synchronicity and the self. *Philosophy East and West, 46*, 477–496.

Davidson, D. (1990). Paradoxes of irrationality. In P. K. Moser (Ed.), *Rationality in action: Contemporary approaches* (pp. 449–464). New York, NY: Cambridge University Press.

DiMaggio, P. (1997). Culture and cognition. *Annual Review of Sociology, 23,* 263–287.

Dixon, T. L., & Linz, D. (2002). Television news, prejudicial pretrial publicity, and the depiction of race. *Journal of Broadcasting and Electronic Media, 46,* 112–136.

Ehrlich, M. P. (1986). Taoism and psychotherapy. *Journal of Contemporary Psychotherapy, 16,* 23–38.

Fiske, S. T. (1987). On the road: Comment on the cognitive stereotyping literature in Pettigrew and Martin. *Journal of Social Issues, 43,* 113–118.

Fiske, S. T. (1993). Controlling other people: The impact of power on stereotyping. *American Psychologist, 48,* 621–628.

Fiske, S. T., & Taylor, S. (1991). *Social cognition* (2nd ed.). New York, NY: McGraw-Hill.

Gaertner, S. L., Dovidio, J. F., Banker, B. S., Houlette, M., Johnson, K. M., & McGlynn, E. A. (2000). Reducing intergroup conflicts: From superordinate goals to decategorization, recategorization, and mutual differentiation. *Group Dynamics: Theory, Research, and Practice, 4,* 98–114.

Gilens, M. (1996). Race and poverty in America: Public misperceptions and the American news media. *Public Opinion Quarterly, 60,* 515–541.

Gross, P. L., & Shapiro, S. I. (1997). Characteristics of the Taoist sage in the Chuang-Tzu and the creative photographer. *Journal of Transpersonal Psychology, 28,* 175–192.

Hamilton, D. L. (1981). Some thoughts on the cognitive approach. In D. L. Hamilton (Ed.), *Cognitive processes in stereotyping and intergroup behavior* (pp. 333–353). Hillsdale, NJ: Erlbaum.

Hate Crime Statistics Act of 1990, 28 U.S.C. 534 (1990).

Herek, G. M., Gillis, J. R., & Cogan, J. C. (1999). Psychological sequelae of hate-crime victimization among lesbian, gay, and bisexual adults. *Journal of Consulting and Clinical Psychology, 67,* 945–951.

Hilton, J. L., & von Hippel, W. (1996). Stereotypes. *Annual Review of Psychology, 47,* 237–271.

Homans, G. C. (1974). *Social behavior: Its elementary forms.* New York, NY: Harcourt Brace Jovanovich.

Jackson, L. M. (2011). *The psychology of prejudice: From attitudes to social action.* Washington, DC: American Psychological Association. doi:10.1037/12317-000

Jenni, C. B. (1999). Psychologists in China: National transformation and humanistic psychology. *Journal of Humanistic Psychology, 39,* 26–47.

Judson, J. L., & Bertazzoni, D. M. (2002). *Law, media, and culture: The landscape of hate.* New York, NY: Peter Lang.

Katz, P. A., & Taylor, D. A. (1988). Introduction. In P. A. Katz & D. A. Taylor (Eds.), *Eliminating racism: Profile in controversy* (pp. 1–16). New York, NY: Plenum Press.

Klein, R. D., & Naccarato, S. (2003). Broadcast news portrayal of minorities: Accuracy in reporting. *American Behavioral Scientist, 46,* 1611–1616. doi:10.1177/0002764203254617

Kruglanski, A. W. (1988). Knowledge as a social psychological construct. In D. Bar-Tal & A. W. Kruglanski (Eds.), *The social psychology of knowledge* (pp. 109–141). New York, NY: Cambridge University Press.

Lee, Y. (2003). Daoistic humanism in ancient China: Broadening personality and counseling theories in the 21st century. *Journal of Humanistic Psychology, 43,* 64–85.

Lehman, D. R., Chiu, C., & Schaller, M. (2004). Psychology and culture. *Annual Review of Psychology, 55,* 689–714.

Mannix, E., & Neale, M. A. (2005). What differences make a difference? The promise and reality of diverse teams in organizations. *Psychological Science in the Public Interest, 6,* 31–55.

Markus, H. R., & Lin, L. R. (1999). Conflictways: Cultural diversity in the meanings and practices of conflict. In D. A. Prentice & D. T. Miller (Eds.), *Cultural divides: Understanding and overcoming group conflict* (pp. 302–333). New York, NY: Russell Sage Foundation.

McKee, J. B. (1993). *Sociology and the race problem: The failure of a perspective.* Urbana, IL: University of Illinois Press.

Myers, D. G. (2002). *Social psychology* (7th ed.). Boston, MA: McGraw-Hill.

National Criminal Justice Reference Service. (2011). *Hate crime statistics in 2009.* Retrieved from https://www.ncjrs.gov/spotlight/hate_crimes/facts.html.

Nolan, J. J. III, McDevitt, J, Cronin, S., & Farrell, A. (2004). Learning to see hate crime: A framework for understanding and clarifying ambiguities in bias crime classification. *Criminal Justice Studies: A Critical Journal of Crime, Law and Society, 17,* 91–106.

Nugent, F. A., & Jones, K. D. (2005). *Introduction to the profession of counseling* (4th ed.). Upper Saddle River, NJ: Pearson/Merrill Prentice Hall.

Oyserman, D., Coon, H. M., & Kemmelmeier, M. (2002). Rethinking individualism and collectivism: Evaluation of theoretical assumptions and meta-analyses. *Psychological Bulletin, 128,* 3–72.

Pettigrew, T. F., & Tropp, L. R. (2008). How does intergroup contact reduce prejudice? Meta-analytic tests of three mediators. *European Journal of Social Psychology, 38,* 922–934. doi:10.1002/ejsp.504

Rahilly, D. A. (1993). A phenomenological analysis of authentic experience. *Journal of Humanistic Psychology, 33,* 49–71.

Rosen, D. (1996). *The Tao of Jung: The way of integrity.* New York, NY: Viking Arkana.

Rosen, D. H., & Crouse, E. M. (2000). The Tao of wisdom: Integration of Taoism and the psychologies of Jung, Erik, and Maslow. In P. Young-Eisendrath & M. E. Miller (Eds.), *The psychology of mature spirituality, integrity, wisdom, transcendence* (pp. 120–129). New York, NY: Brunner-Routledge.

Schaller, M., & O'Brien, M. (1992). Intuitive analysis of covariance and group stereotype formation. *Personality and Social Psychology Bulletin, 18,* 776–785.

Scheb, J. M., & Scheb, J. M. III (1999). *Criminal law and procedure.* Belmont, CA: Wadsworth.

Sherif, M. (1966). *In common predicament.* Boston, MA: Houghton Mifflin.

Smedley, A. (1993). *Race in North America: Origin and evolution of a worldview.* Boulder, CO: Westview Press.

Smith, G., Spillane, N., & Annus, A. M. (2006). Implications of an emerging integration of universal and culturally specific psychologies. *Perspective on Psychological Science, 1,* 211–233.

Staub, E. (2005). The origins and evolution of hate, with notes on prevention. In R. J. Sternberg (Ed.), *The psychology of hate* (pp. 51–66). Washington, DC: American Psychological Association.

Sullaway, M. (2004). Psychological perspective on hate crime laws. *Psychology, Public Policy, and Law, 10,* 250–292.

Sun, K. (1993a). Two types of prejudice and their causes. *American Psychologist, 48,* 1152–1153.

Sun, K (1993b). The implications of social psychological theories of group dynamics for gang research. *Journal of Gang Research: An Interdisciplinary Research Quarterly, 1,* 39–44.

Sun, K. (1995a). The definition of race. *American Psychologist, 50,* 43–44.

Sun, K. (1995b). How to overcome without fighting: An introduction to the Taoist approach to conflict resolution. *Journal of Theoretical and Philosophical Psychology, 15,* 161–171.

Sun, K. (2002, March). *The meanings of cultural diversity and similarity and the implications for criminal justice.* Paper presented at the annual meeting of the Academy of Criminal Justice Sciences, Anaheim, CA.

Sun, K. (2004, March). *The impact of cognitive distortions of interpersonal reality on unethical behavior.* Paper presented at the annual meeting of the Academy of Criminal Justice, Las Vegas, NV.

Sun, K. (2006). The legal definition of hate crime and the hate offender's distorted cognition. *Issues in Mental Health Nursing, 27,* 597–604.

Sun, K. (2011, June). *Information contact, its characteristics and importance for prejudice reduction.* Poster presented at the Annual Convention of the Canadian Psychological Association, Toronto, Canada.

Tajfel, H. (1978). Interindividual behavior and intergroup behavior. In H. Tajfel (Ed.), *Differentiation between social groups* (pp. 27–60). London, UK: Academic Press.

U.S. Commission on Civil Rights (2000, November). *Revisiting who is guarding the guardians?: A report on police practices and civil rights in America.* Retrieved from http://www.usccr.gov/pubs/guard/main.htm.

Violent Crime Control and Law Enforcement Act of 1994, Public. Law No. 103-322, H.R. 3355.

Weiss, J. C. (2005). Working with victims of hate crimes. In G. L. Greif & P. H. Ephross (Eds.), *Group work with populations at risk* (2nd ed., pp. 197–221). New York, NY: Oxford University Press.

Willis, D. G. (2004). Hate crimes against gay males: An overview. *Issues in Mental Health Nursing, 25,* 115–132.

Appendix

American Correctional Association Code of Ethics

1. Members shall respect and protect the civil and legal rights of all individuals.

2. Members shall treat every professional situation with concern for the welfare of the individuals involved and with no intent to personal gain.

3. Members shall maintain relationships with colleagues to promote mutual respect within the profession and improve the quality of service.

4. Members shall make public criticism of their colleagues or their agencies only when warranted, verifiable, and constructive.

5. Members shall respect the importance of all disciplines within the criminal justice system and work to improve cooperation with each segment.

6. Members shall honor the public's right to information and share information with the public to the extent permitted by law subject to individuals' right to privacy.

7. Members shall respect and protect the right of the public to be safeguarded from criminal activity.

8. Members shall refrain from using their positions to secure personal privileges or advantages.

9. Members shall refrain from allowing personal interest to impair objectivity in the performance of duty while acting in an official capacity.

Source: Adopted by the Board of Governors and Delegate Assembly in August 1994. Reprinted with permission.

10. Members shall refrain from entering into any formal or informal activity or agreement which presents a conflict of interest or is inconsistent with the conscientious performance of duties.

11. Members shall refrain from accepting any gifts, services, or favors that is or appears to be improper or implies an obligation inconsistent with the free and objective exercise of professional duties.

12. Members shall clearly differentiate between personal views/statements and views/statements/positions made on behalf of the agency or association.

13. Members shall report to appropriate authorities any corrupt or unethical behaviors in which there is sufficient evidence to justify review.

14. Members shall refrain from discriminating against any individual because of race, gender, creed, national origin, religious affiliation, age, disability, or any other type of prohibited discrimination.

15. Members shall preserve the integrity of private information; they shall refrain from seeking information on individuals beyond that which is necessary to implement responsibilities and perform their duties; members shall refrain from revealing nonpublic information unless expressly authorized to do so.

16. Members shall make all appointments, promotions, and dismissals in accordance with established civil service rules, applicable contract agreements, and individual merit, rather than furtherance of personal interests.

17. Members shall respect, promote, and contribute to a workplace that is safe, healthy, and free of harassment in any form.

A BRIEF GLOSSARY

addiction   a compulsive pattern of drug-seeking and drug-taking behavior that takes place at the expense of most other activities.

anger   a negative, tumultuous emotion, subjectively experienced as an arousal state of hostility toward someone or something perceived to be the source of an aversive event.

art therapy   a therapeutic approach that uses visual art media (two- and three-dimensional materials, such as drawings, paintings, sculptures, and images) and the creative process as an assessment and intervention tool to understand and overcome mental and interpersonal conflicts.

assessment in corrections   the procedure of gathering information about offenders by using standardized inventories, interviews, tests, mental health and medical examinations, and/or legal records.

behavioral therapy   a therapeutic model that uses two types of learning mechanisms (classical conditioning, operant conditioning) as the basis for understanding and modifying harmful and dysfunctional behaviors.

classification in prison   the procedure of placing prisoners in one of several custody levels (e.g., maximum, close, medium, and minimum) to match offender risk and needs with correctional resources (e.g., the type of facility to which they will be assigned and the level of supervision they will receive once they are there).

cognitive distortions   (distorted cognitions)   inaccurate mental representations of social entities (e.g., others, situations); more specifically, cognitive distortions consist of two dimensions: (1) an objective discrepancy between the perception and the reality, and (2) the perceiver's unawareness of the discrepancy.

cognitive processes   the application of cognitive structures or schemas to make sense of social experience and the living environment by administering such mental processes as encoding, evaluating, attributing, reasoning, and decision making.

cognitive structures (schemas) the organized mental representations of social entities (self and others, events, situations), their interactions and perceived patterns that govern mental and interpersonal experiences.

cognitive therapy a therapeutic model that views cognition or thinking as largely determining feelings and behavior. Cognitive therapy in corrections is typically used to revise a person's negative self-concept, to develop offenders' social and problem-solving skills, and to help offenders discern how their deviant thinking leads to their criminal acts.

counseling process the counseling procedure, which typically consists of three phases: assessment, intervention, and termination/follow up.

culture a collection of belief systems, value orientation, knowledge, history, customs, norms, practices, social and economic institutions, and language shared by individuals in some definable population that is distinct from those shared in other populations.

deindividuation a perception that a person's illegal or deviant behavior cannot be identified in a situation either because others are doing the same thing or because the setting generates anonymity.

deinstitutionalization a policy that guided the release of thousands of mentally ill people from psychiatric facilities to the community, with the intention to reduce reliance on state and county mental hospitals and to develop a treatment network of services in the community for individuals with mental disorders.

drug courts the courts designed to integrate the judicial processes (e.g., involving the judge, prosecution, defense, and offenders) with substance abuse treatment programs for drug-involved participants.

DSM-IV-TR the fourth edition (with text revision) of the *Diagnostic and Statistical Manual of Mental Disorders (DSM-IV-TR)* published by the American Psychiatric Association; it is a major manual for assessing offenders' psychological conditions and mental disorders in correctional settings.

dual status of mentally disordered offenders the overlap between the status of both the offender and the mentally disordered patient.

dynamic risk factors attributes or conditions related to the offender that can be changed by programs, treatment, counseling, and other interventions; examples include marital distress, skill deficits, substance abuse, pro-crime attitudes, companions, mental conflicts, low educational attainment, and antisocial supports and peer association. Because these factors are associated with recidivism and criminal behavior, they are also referred to as criminogenic needs.

eclecticism the process of selecting concepts and strategies from various theories (e.g., cognitive-behavioral therapy, social learning model, self-efficacy, art therapy, and other social science approaches) for use in one treatment. It also refers to flexibility in applying a variety of methods (e.g., individual counseling, group modality) and the extensive use of combinations of verbal, visual, and kinesthetic media during the process of counseling.

ethical dilemmas in corrections   dilemmas generated by the two roles mental health professionals perform (the helping professional and the enforcer of the correctional policies of the government) and by two codes of ethics that overlap but are distinct from each other.

false positive, **false negative**   two errors in correctional assessment. The false positive refers to cases when offenders have a low risk of reoffending but their assessment scores put them in the high-risk category. In contrast, the false negative designates the opposite situation: offenders have a low score on the measurement when they are actually high-risk offenders.

family therapy   a variety of family-based therapeutic approaches that view family members (particularly parents and children) as consisting of an interdependent system. Family therapy focuses on helping family members identify and analyze both dysfunctional and functional aspects of the family system, and then engaging them in reducing or eliminating the dysfunctional factors and in developing a healthy and positive family environment.

group cohesion   a group environment in which members feel comfortable and are able to trust the therapist and one another with the shared feeling that group members are valued and unconditionally accepted and supported by one another.

involuntary clients   clients who are mandated to receive treatment. Convicted offenders with a resistance attitude toward treatment represent involuntary clients.

Level of Service Inventory-Revised (LSI-R)   a theoretically based offender risk-needs assessment tool that focuses on assessing the offender's criminal history, education/employment, finances, family/marital conditions, accommodation, leisure and recreation, companions, alcohol/drug problems, emotional/personal issues, and attitude/orientation.

mental health courts   designated courts with the special responsibility and expertise to handle defendants with mental disorders and other impairment. Mental health providers are involved in the judicial process. Court decisions are based on considering needs and risks of mentally ill people, emphasizing mental health treatment, problem solving, diversion, community-based supervision and service, voluntary participation, safety to self and others, and monitoring compliance for court-imposed conditions.

mentally disordered offenders   offenders with mental disorders in the criminal justice system. They may include four categories of individuals: (1) not guilty by reason of insanity (NGRI), (2) incompetent to stand trial (IST), (3) mentally disordered sex-offenders, and (4) mentally disordered inmates.

motivational interviewing (MI)   an intervention technique that helps clients see the discrepancy between their current conditions and their goals/values. It emphasizes and honors client autonomy and his or her ability to choose whether, when, and how to change.

overcontrolled offenders   a subgroup of violent offenders who have one of two characteristics: (1) a low level of experiencing angry thoughts, feelings, and hostility because of anger suppression, or (2) a strong control or self-regulation of an internal anger reaction, with ruminating about provocations and being preoccupied with violent fantasy after being assaulted or bullied.

positive psychology   a psychological approach that suggests looking beyond human weakness and damage by understanding and facilitation of human strength and virtue. It conceptually overlaps with the strengths perspective.

prisoner reentry   the returning of convicted offenders back to the community after they have served time in federal or state prisons or local jails. Reentry offenders face many challenges, including issues of obtaining housing, education, employment, family acceptance, health care, and treatment for substance abuse or dependence

Psychopathy Checklist-Revised (PCL-R)   an instrument for assessing offenders' psychopathy or antisocial personality disorder. Items in the PCL-R are divided into three categories: (1) interpersonal or affective defects (e.g., glibness or superficial charm, grandiose feelings of self-worth, conning or manipulative behavior, lack of remorse or guilt, shallow affect, callousness or lack of empathy, cruel disregard for the rights of others); (2) social deviance (irresponsibility, parasitic lifestyle, impulsivity or disinhibition, a propensity for predatory behavior and violence); and (3) additional items (e.g., unstable relationships, criminal versatility).

restorative justice   an alternative approach to administering justice to adult and juvenile offenders, with a focus on serving victims whose needs are often overlooked in a retribution-oriented system and bringing together all parties affected by the harm or wrongdoing (e.g., offenders and their families, victims and their families, other members of the community, and professionals). It is also intended to solve the conflict and heal the wounds of the parties affected by the offense.

routine activity theory   a theory that explains a criminal act as facilitated by three situational elements: (1) a potential criminal, (2) a suitable target, and (3) the absence of a capable guardian against crime.

self-efficacy   individuals' confidence in their ability to organize and execute a given course of action to solve a problem or accomplish a task by mobilizing motivational and cognitive resources.

setting principle   a principle that suggests that services to offenders are more effective in a community than in prison.

social control theory   a criminological theory that focuses on what keeps people from committing crimes rather than concentrating on the factors or conditions that produce crime. It maintains that law-abiding people do not commit crimes because they are influenced by four strong social bonds: attachment, commitment, involvement, and belief.

social disorganization theory   a criminological theory that suggests that criminal acts are learned beliefs that view crime as an appropriate response to social conditions. Criminals are individuals who are behaving in accordance with the values of their particular group, neighborhood, or community.

social learning theory   a psychological model that maintains that direct and observational learning, as well as internal reward or punishment, determines how people acquire and execute antisocial responses, just as they acquire and implement other forms of social behavior.

static risk factors   attributes or conditions related to an offender that happened in the past or are not responsive to correctional interventions. Examples of static risk factors include the perpetrator's age, number of past offenses committed, intellectual disabilities, favored choice of victim, age at first conviction, gender, race, social class of origin, criminal history, antisocial childhood modeling, and childhood trauma. Some static factors cannot be changed by correctional efforts, but they can change naturally, such as age.

strengths perspective   a perspective in counseling and social work practice arguing that individuals, however unfortunate, can discover strengths or potential in themselves. Counselors' and social workers' primary responsibility is to promote the well-being of clients by tapping into possibilities rather than focusing on their current negative conditions.

stress inoculation   a cognitive approach to anger management that uses restructuring and reappraising of anger and the learning of arousal reduction and behavioral coping skills to deal with the emotion.

subculture   a segment of society that holds norms, values, and beliefs contradictory to or deviant from those of the dominant culture.

therapeutic community (TC)   a highly specialized type of residential treatment program in which members are involved in their own treatment and supporting one another in an around-the-clock learning and living environment. Treatment is intended to address all aspects of the person (e.g., trauma, emotional injuries, education, interpersonal communications, relationships, negative patterns of thinking, feeling, and behaving).

therapeutic relationship (therapeutic alliance)   a trusting and collaborative relationship between a therapist and client characterized by three primary components: (1) agreement between the counselor and the client on the goals of intervention;

(2) a joint effort in developing and completing goals; and (3) therapeutic values (e.g., trust, respect, acceptance, empathy, and support).

Victim–offender Mediation (VoM)   the most common type of restorative justice practice. VoM is a face-to-face meeting involving a trained mediator, crime victim, and person who committed the crime, with the victim's needs at the center of the process.

withholding judgment   a therapeutic value that emphasizes helping offenders to become better persons by assisting them to take responsibility for shifting their maladaptive thinking and behavior in the right direction, regardless of their crimes and other dysfunctions.

Name Index

Subject Index

A

A-B-C theory of personality, 65
accountability expectation, 147, 182, 188
action self-efficacy, 76–77, 175
addiction, defined, 168. *See also* substance abuse and treatment
adolescence-limited juvenile offenders, 49
African American cultural context, 205
aggression, human
  anger's regulation of, 141–142
  and cognitive distortions in offenders, 105
  defined, 52
  displaced, 53
  and social learning theory, 74
aggression replacement training, 124
aggressive cues as crime triggers, 53
anger, defined, 141
anger management, 141–148
antisocial personality disorder, 31
art therapy, 82–84
ASAM Criteria, 171
assessment
  and art therapy, 83–84
  of cognitive capacity, 117–118
  COMPAS software, 30
  counseling process role of, 113, 114, 115–117
  culturally sensitive, 208–209
  good lives model on, 81
  group counseling phase, 137
  juvenile offenders, 32–33, 122–123
  Lifestyle Criminality Screening Form, 32
  LSI-R, 26–30, 50
  mentally disordered offenders, 31, 33–34, 152, 158, 172
  PCL-R, 31
  responsibility of counselors for, 11
  RNR model, 25–30

  self-assessment inaccuracies, 70–71
  sex offenders, 29–30, 31
  Static-99, 31
  strain theory effects on, 52
  substance abuse, 31, 34, 171
  summary, 34–35
  WRNA, 30–31
attachment in social control theory, 50
attention and stereotyping, 193
attribution retraining, 200
attribution theories, 43, 95
autonomy, value of, 126–127, 206
aversive therapy, 59

B

behavioral therapies, 4, 57–63, 124, 142–144, 175–176
belief, in social control theory, 50
beliefs vs experiences as source of emotions and behavior, 65
beneficence in counseling ethics, 126
biochemical effects of psychoactive drugs, 169
biomedical vs social cognitive explanations, 160–162
biopsychosocial model for substance abuse, 168–169
blaming of the victim by offenders, 94, 194–195

C

callous-unemotional (CU) traits, 124
case management, 28, 32, 40, 122
CBT (cognitive-behavioral therapy), 4, 57, 124, 142–144, 175–176
chemical dependency assessment, 31. *See also* substance abuse and treatment
child molesters, cognitive distortions of, 94, 104
childhood trauma, cognitive distortions from, 95–96, 107

civil commitment of mentally ill persons, 153, 154–155
civil rights movement era, handling of mentally disordered offenders in, 153–154
class, socioeconomic, and prison population demographics, 157
classical conditioning theory, 57–60
classification of offenders, 23, 24–26, 28
clinical expertise in EBP, 41
clinical utility of intervention, 41
CMT (cognitive mediation training) program, 105
Code of Ethics, 14–15, 215–216
coercive power and ethical issues in corrections, 15
cognition. *See also* social cognition
  as basis for behavior, 63
  distortions in, 94–95, 102–105, 192, 196–198
  processes defined, 64
  structures defined, 64
cognitive capacity, assessing, 117–118
cognitive competence as universal psychological value, 206
cognitive mediation training (CMT) program, 105
cognitive therapies, 63–73, 175–176
cognitive-behavioral therapy (CBT), 4, 57, 124, 142–144, 175–176
cognitive-scripts model, 105
cohesion, group, 135–136
collectivist vs individualist culture as basis of diversity, 203–206
commitment in social control theory, 50
community
  reentry issues, 7–8, 12
  reintegration issues, 8, 12, 182, 187
  resources for clients in, 13